CAPITAL GAINS

CAPITAL GAINS

How the National Lottery
transformed England's arts

Prue Skene

FP

First published in 2017 by
Franchise Press
19a Eccleston Street, London SW1W 9LX

A CIP record for this book is available from
the British Library

ISBN 978-0-9955896-0-5

Edited and designed by Jane Havell Associates
Printed and bound in the UK by Imprint Digital

'The National Lottery has provided us with probably
the most important means of cultural regeneration that
this country has ever seen . . . Gave us the opportunity
to dream.'

Stephen Daldry (in Omnibus)

'If you look at the history of what's been achieved,
both during the early years and subsequently, anyone
with half an ounce of common sense would see an
absolutely extraordinary transformation.'

Sir Hayden Phillips GCB

'If you wanted to demonstrate a genuine
transformation of the quality of experience in
participation and simple attendance at cultural
activity in this country, there was a massive change
in the number of opportunities and in the quality
of opportunities that existed as a result of this
investment . . . I am very proud to be part of
something, with others, that really did deliver
something quite extraordinary.'

Peter Hewitt CBE

'What the lottery did was fantastic, extraordinary. You
know, all those nice sound-bite things like 60 per cent
of our money went to foyers, public spaces, which
really helped. When you are in America you realise
how little public space there is within arts buildings
and how lucky we are.'

Moss Cooper

CONTENTS

ACKNOWLEDGEMENTS

This book is written very much from a personal perspective: I was a member of the Arts Council of Great Britain and then of England from 1992 to 2000 and chaired its Lottery (subsequently Capital) Panel from 1996 to 2000. It is based on paperwork from that time, together with a diary which I kept intermittently; flesh has been added to these bones by a series of interviews. These have been with people who were involved with the lottery programme during that period, either through direct connection with the Arts Council or through being the champions for some of the projects it funded. I would like to express my profound gratitude to all of the following who have generously given of their time and of their memories, and have given permission for the direct quotations contained within the text:

Ian Albery, Mary Allen, the late Bryan Avery, Baroness Bottomley of Nettlestone PC, Lord Chadlington, Rory Coonan, Moss Cooper, Alan Davey CBE, Marcus Davey OBE, Beverley Dawson, Graham Devlin CBE, Professor Anthony Everitt, Mark Fisher, Sir Christopher Frayling, Felicity Goodey CBE, Lord Gowrie PC, Alan Grieve CBE, Jeremy Grint, David Hall, Simon Harper, Peter Hewitt CBE, Vikki Heywood CBE, Graham Hitchen, Lady (Patty) Hopkins, Sue Hoyle OBE, Tess Jaray, Peter Jenkinson OBE, Carolyn Lambert, Richard Lee, Melanie Leech CBE, Peter Longman, Graham Marchant OBE, Braham Murray OBE, John Newbigin OBE,

Jeremy Newton, Lord Palumbo, Judith Strong, Nicole Penn-Symons, Sir Hayden Phillips GCB, David Pratley, the late Linda Pratley (Fredericks), Lord Puttnam of Queensgate CBE, Andrew Ramsay CB, Sue Robertson, Sir Gerry Robinson, Lord Sainsbury of Preston Candover, Nadia Stern, Lord Smith of Finsbury PC and Sir Richard Stilgoe.

Thanks are also due to Crispin Raymond, Julian Evans and John Nicoll who read and helpfully commented on drafts of the book; to David Burnie who supplied facts about The Place, Derek Hicks for unravelling the mysteries of HEFCE funding, and to Deborah Bull CBE and Nick Ratcliffe of King's College London, Cate Caniffe of ACE, Guy Eades of Healing Arts, Sir Richard Eyre CH CBE, Thelma Holt CBE, Liliane Lijn, Nicolas Kent, Lord Rogers of Riverside CH and Rosemary Squire OBE for their kind permissions to use quotations. I am grateful to all the interviewees who supplied photographs and to the following who helped to source them: Julie Brown at The New Art Gallery Walsall, Veronica Castro and Jane Pritchard at the V&A, Simon Davison at Caruso St John, Anna-Maria Frastali and her successor Sorcha Hunter at The Place, Florence Hawkins at Children & the Arts, Suzy Hicks, PA to Sir Gerry Robinson, Amy Lawton at The Lowry, Clair Montier of the Jerwood Foundation, Anneka Morley and Stella Lowe at the Royal Exchange Theatre, Manchester, Caroline Pedley, PA to Sir Richard Stilgoe, and Christopher Williams at the Royal Court Theatre. Credit and thanks go to Arts Council England, and in particular Mags Patten, Dan Smith and Mist Kinsman there, for permission to quote from Arts Council minutes and to use photographs from annual reports. It was a great pleasure to work with Jane Havell who edited this book and guided it through to production: I give her my warmest thanks. And my gratitude to Michael Pennington is immense, not only for being an excellent colleague in English Shakespeare Company days but also for subsequently becoming so very much else. Memory is elusive and subjective: I have done my best to check facts but any errors in these pages are entirely my responsibility.

In its early days, arts lottery money could go only to capital projects – which mainly meant buildings but also public art, equipment, etc. One of the most extraordinary features of the capital programme was the way in which arts managers and others who had never previously had direct experience of dealing with a major building project took up the challenge and, through passion, forbearance and often sheer bloody-mindedness, delivered successful enterprises. This book is dedicated to them as it is to all the Lottery Panel members who wonderfully supported me during my years as chair. The hours of their time they gave voluntarily, both at meetings and in reading through the forests of papers which preceded them, and the wisdom, knowledge and intuition they contributed, enabled the successes that the programme brought. The reasons for its challenges will, I hope, become apparent.

LIST OF ILLUSTRATIONS
AND PHOTOGRAPHIC CREDITS

Between pages 64 and 65

Every effort has been made to obtain permission for the reproduction of photographs; any errors or omissions are inadvertent and will be corrected in future editions upon notification to the publisher.

LIST OF ACRONYMS

As with any sector, the arts world has a lot of acronyms. The following are those found regularly throughout this book:

A4E   Arts for Everyone programme
ACE   Arts Council of England up to 2002, when it became
        Arts Council England
ACGB   Arts Council of Great Britain (abolished 1994)
ANF   Advance Notice Form (for submitting lottery applications)
BFI   British Film Institute
CP1   First capital programme
CP2   Second capital programme
CSCB   Coin Street Community Builders
DCMS   Department for Culture, Media & Sport (created 1997)
DEE   Department for Education and Employment
DNH   Department for National Heritage (1992-1997)
ENB   English National Ballet
ENO   English National Opera
ERDF   European Regional Development Fund
ESC   English Stage Company
HLF   Heritage Lottery Fund
LSO   London Symphony Orchestra

NAO   National Audit Office
NESTA   National Endowment for Science, Technology and the Arts
NOF   New Opportunities Fund
NPO   National Portfolio Organisation
RAB   Regional Arts Board
RADA   Royal Academy of Dramatic Art
RALP   Regional Arts Lottery Programme
RFO   Regularly Funded Organisation
RSC   Royal Shakespeare Company
SBC   South Bank Centre
TMA   Theatrical Management Association

TIMELINE OF EVENTS

March	A White Paper on *A National Lottery Raising Money for Good Causes*
April	Department for National Heritage created
May	PS [Prue Skene] appointed ACGB Council member
September	David Mellor resigns as Secretary of State for National Heritage; replaced by Peter Brooke
December	National Lottery Bill presented to House of Commons; PriceWaterhouse review of ACGB commissioned

1993

January	*A Creative Future* published by ACGB
May	Artistic review of ACGB clients
June	PriceWaterhouse review presented to Council
October	Royal Assent for the National Lottery Bill
November	ACGB Council agrees to set up a lottery department
December	The Hoffmann report on London orchestras presented to Council

1994

April	ACGB becomes Arts Council of England; Peter Palumbo succeeded by Lord (Grey) Gowrie as chair; Mary Allen appointed secretary-general
May	Jeremy Newton appointed lottery director; Lottery Panel established with Peter Gummer as chair
November	First National Lottery draw
December	First lottery packs distributed

1995

January	First lottery applications received; lyric theatre review presented to Council
March	First ACE lottery grants awarded
July	Virginia Bottomley appointed Secretary of State for National Heritage; first lottery grant to the ROH announced
September	Moss Cooper appointed lottery operations director
October	First lottery grant to Sadler's Wells announced

1996

April	PS succeeds Peter Gummer as chair of Lottery Panel; Nicole Penn-Symons appointed lottery projects director; all RAB chairs appointed to Council; new lottery directions announced
August	ACE lottery logo approved
September	New revenue lottery programmes agreed; delivery of RAB priority lists
November	Pilot A4E programme launched

1997

January	First stabilisation grants awarded
March	Second tranche of ROH grant agreed; first round of A4E Express grants awarded
April	Graham Devlin replaces Sue Hoyle as deputy secretary-general; revisions to capital programme launched

May	'New' Labour wins general election; Chris Smith appointed Secretary of State for National Heritage; Mary Allen appointed chief executive of the ROH and resigns from ACE; Edward Walker-Arnott commissioned to undertake review of ACE/ROH relationship; Graham Devlin appointed acting secretary-general
June	Second round of A4E Express grants awarded
July	Department of National Heritage becomes Department for Culture, Media & Sport; first indications of a substantial drop in ACE lottery income
August	First A4E grants awarded; White Paper on revisions to the National Lottery
September	Walker-Arnott report delivered; revised RAB priority lists received
October	Lord Gowrie announces his retirement; Richard Eyre report on the ROH/ENO commissioned
November	Culture, Media & Sport select committee report on the ROH published; Council strategy group meets for first time; changes to the capital programme agreed
December	The drama panel rebels; Council discusses the SBC bid

1998

January	Gerry Robinson appointed chair designate; RABs submit their £50 million tranches
February	Strategy group disbanded
March	Peter Hewitt joins ACE as secretary-general, title changed to chief executive; SBC bid rejected; Jeremy Newton announced as new chief executive of NESTA
April	Gerry Robinson succeeds Lord Gowrie as chair; preliminary priority list agreed and then ignored; Hayden Phillips succeeded by Robin Young at the DCMS
May	Existing Council stands down; Orpheus Centre opens
June	PS invited to join the new Council; Richard Eyre's report published

July	First formal meeting of the new Council; new Lottery Act published
September	Creation of CP2 (second capital programme) agreed
October	Sadler's Wells re-opens

1999

April	Lottery Panel re-named Capital Advisory Panel
May	Priority list for ending of CP1 (first capital programme) drawn up and circulated to RABs and artform departments; NAO report on 15 major projects published
June	Peter Hewitt appears before Public Affairs Committee
July	Final list for CP1 agreed; lottery grants of less than £100K devolved to RABs
September	Theatre review commissioned
December	ROH re-opens; consultation paper on CP2 circulated

2000

February	Consultation responses on CP2 received
March	Royal Court Theatre re-opens
April	Film Council established
May	Tate Modern and The Lowry open
June	PS's last Council meeting
July	CP2 launched
November	RADA re-opens

2001

June	List of CP2 entrants announced
September	The Place re-opens

1

SETTING THE SCENE

*Introduction to the need – introduction to a Polished Corner –
introduction to the Arts Council – first impressions*

The National Lottery is now very much a feature of British life but I think it's true to say that very few people understand how it works. It's been administered since its inception in 1994 by a company called Camelot which set up the machines that deliver the tickets, decide which games are to be played, organise the draws and look after the winners. They also take a share of the profits, as do the Treasury, the prize winners and what are called the good causes; the last account for around 28 per cent of the income and give an aura of respectability to the proceedings. The whole process is overseen on the government's behalf by the Department of Culture, Media & Sport. Not being of a gambling nature, I would have known little of all this had I not got involved in the 1990s with one of the good causes, the Arts Council of England (ACE),[1] and been part of a revolution that substantially changed the landscape of the arts in England.

1. For the purposes of this book, both the Arts Council of England and its successor Arts Council England will be known as ACE.

And change was much needed. In 1992 Gateshead was a desolate area desperately in need of regeneration as it faced its livelier sister Newcastle from an empty south bank of the river Tyne. An attempt by Walsall Council to refurbish its museum and art gallery, which housed the important Garman Ryan Collection (365 works of art left to Walsall by Jacob Epstein's widow Kathleen Garman and her friend Sally Ryan) in appalling conditions, had been defeated when council budgets were slashed as a result of the poll tax. Amid the wasteland that was Salford Quays, Salford City Council had launched an architectural competition to design an arts centre of international standing but was unable to meet the substantial costs of building it. Members of the Royal Ballet company, having warmed up at their headquarters in west London, had to take a longish tube journey to performances at the Royal Opera House, where the Crush Bar was aptly named and stage managers fell through holes backstage. At another of London's lyric theatres, Sadler's Wells, wing space was so limited that a dancer being lifted off the relatively tiny stage into the wings was likely to crash into a brick wall. Buckets were put out to hold the rain-water coming through the roof at the National Theatre on the south bank of the Thames where it had been in residence since 1976. And there were pockets of rural England without any arts facilities at all.

If you were in any way disabled, access to artistic events was pretty well denied you – unless, if you were a wheelchair user, you were prepared to make a call to the manager of your local theatre, cinema or gallery in advance to arrange an embarrassingly public lift by staff up the steps. Other disabilities were barely catered for at all. As far as working in the arts was concerned, backstage and administrative areas were firmly for the able-bodied since offices were often perched at the top of many flights of stairs and the only lifts were the cumbersome ones for transporting scenery. Many theatres on the touring circuit were only slowly emerging from decades of ownership by theatrical 'empires' or local authorities to become independent trusts which mostly lacked the capital reserves to do much refurbishment, front or back of house. Auditoria were often threadbare and lacking in modern facilities such as air-conditioning or the cabling for broadcasting that new technology was beginning to offer. As the manager of a touring dance company, I had on occasion to threaten cancellation of performances when stage temperatures dropped so low that dancers' bodies were endangered. Dressing-room showers to wash off the sweat of performance or body make-up were a rare luxury. At least there were no longer holes in the actual stages, which featured in early films of Ballet Rambert's history, but overall the conditions for performing, participating in and viewing art in all its forms were primitive.

The Arts Council of Great Britain (ACGB) was formed in 1946, arising out of the Council for the Encouragement of Music and the Arts which had been established during the Second World War. Its main purpose initially was to support performing arts companies but its first chairman, John Maynard Keynes, managed to negotiate a small refurbishment loan (later converted into a grant) for the Bristol Old Vic. He appeared on stage on the opening night with a warning that the Council would never be able to afford to contribute to capital needs on a regular basis. None the less ACGB did start a Housing the Arts scheme in 1965 with a budget of about £250,000, which acted as 'encouragement' funding. Peter Longman, its first administrator, and his successor Judith Strong also provided advice and support to the projects to which it contributed, which included the building and refurbishment of many regional theatres. The budget grew to approximately £1.5m a year until, in 1984, the programme was questioned in ACGB's *Glory of the Garden* report, which considered the revenue – as opposed to the capital – claims of clients paramount. After that the scheme was slowly run down as its projects were completed; it finally closed in 1985.

In 1992/93 the ACGB received an annual grant of £221.2m from the Treasury via the Office of Arts and Libraries (part of the Department of Education and Science); by a wondrous device then known as the Goschen formula, this was allocated as £185.8m to England, £22.69m to Scotland and £12.708m to Wales. The amount had dwindled under the Thatcher government and the revenue needs of the Council's Regularly Funded Organisations (RFOs) were coming under strain. While the more enlightened local authorities did what they could to maintain the buildings under their control, there was no immediate way of getting at the necessary funds to address urgent capital needs.

*

As a young girl I always wanted to act. It's a common ambition, but not for the faint-hearted – only those who know they have such power of feeling that they can do nothing else should pursue it. Inherent timidity prevented me from even voicing the desire, although I did discover that there was a preliminary school to the Royal Academy of Dramatic Art (usually known by its acronym RADA) called PRADA (not to be confused with a certain handbag company) and I furtively applied for a brochure. There was no obvious hereditary reason for my thespian ambition: I came from a fairly conventional middle-class family with a father who ran the educational advisory agency Gabbitas & Thring and a mother who, in spite of having been an Oxford undergraduate, never worked professionally but brought her four children up with great love. She also instilled in us an interest in literature and reading. The theatrical spark perhaps was a visit to the musical *Salad Days* when I was ten: I can still remember the thrill that this produced, together with the names of the cast and most of the lyrics, and I became stage-struck. Further fuel was added to the theatrical fire by regular visits with my mother to Stratford-upon-Avon during Peter Hall's early years there, which took me into a world of magic of which I longed to be a part.

Although I attended a supposedly top London private girls' school ('That our daughters may be as the polished corners of the temple') and was bright enough to hover around the top of the exam lists, there was no pressure on me to go to university. I left school at sixteen and did a London coming-out 'season'. This no longer involved a trip to Buckingham Palace – curtseys were instead reserved for a huge cake that was wheeled into a ballroom by a flock of white-dressed seventeen-year-olds who were then let fly into a summer of cocktail parties and dances. Our family was by no means of the aristocracy nor with the wealth for which such frolics were intended: my mother said that the reason she inflicted the charade on her three daughters was that she had been brought up by a Christian Science mother who had forbidden entertaining, and she wanted us to feel more socially confident – a result that was not forthcoming in my case. The horror of being a shrinking violet over, I did a secretarial course and was about to start a career in the Foreign Office when I saw an advertisement for a secretary at the National Theatre and successfully applied.

This was early 1963 and the National was in its infancy.

There was a board of directors, of which my boss Kenneth Rae was the secretary, and Laurence Olivier and Stephen Arlen had been appointed artistic and administrative directors. They had not yet taken up their positions full time and were only occasional visitors to the small office in Goodwin's Court, off St Martin's Lane in London's West End. Within a short time we had moved to a collection of Nissen huts on a bombsite in Duchy Street, a few hundred yards from the Old Vic Theatre. Over the next few months, a company of actors, technicians and administrative staff was assembled and rehearsals began in a large room at one end of the long corridor. Actors and staff alike were fortified on a Friday by the spaghetti bolognese miraculously cooked in the tiny kitchen by the Italian lady who ran the small canteen; I can still smell the aroma of the sauce as it wound its way along to my office at the other end of the building. Laurence Olivier – 'Sir' to most of us – had the air of a bank manager when glimpsed in his office, and it was occasionally my privilege to drive him about London in my Mini when a taxi was unforthcoming. I wish I could remember our conversations but fear that the journeys would mostly have been conducted in respectful silence as he meditated on his plans for the future of the National. The local inhabitants around Duchy Street were awe-inspiring in a different way: in the early 1960s it was something of a novelty to hear an urchin telling my elegant boss to 'Fuck off, you smelly old bugger!'

The Old Vic was refurbished, and soon huge sacks of mail arrived for the first booking period which the secretaries of the organisation were recruited to help with. On 22 October 1963 the National Theatre officially opened with Peter O'Toole in *Hamlet*. If I wasn't on the stage, I was at least a tiny part of what lay behind it.

I stayed at the National for two years and thus saw all its early productions. Particular memories include the plays that were transferred from early seasons at the Chichester Festival Theatre, the opening of which provided Olivier with a space to mount shows such as *Uncle Vanya*, *Saint Joan* and *The Royal Hunt of the Sun* – the thrill at the choreography of the Spaniards simulating the impossible stage direction of 'Climbing the

Andes' and a red carpet spilling over the stage at the end of the first act representing the blood of the massacred Indians is with me still. Later these shows went on to the Old Vic. The National Theatre publication, *Stage by State: The Early Years 1963–1975*,[2] lists a 78-strong company for its first year of operation, 1963–64. Amongst those already famous such as Maggie Smith, Peter O'Toole, Robert Stephens and Joan Plowright, I would regularly pass in the corridor many who were yet to become household names: Derek Jacobi, Frank Finlay, Michael Gambon and Sheila Reid. The most exotic person off-stage was the National's literary manager, Kenneth Tynan, dressed in bright coloured suits with a cigarette permanently held between his second and third fingers.

It was an exhilarating organisation to be part of and Kenneth Rae and his assistant Yolande Bird were both special people to work for – Kenneth with his aristocratic sangfroid and ready wit, always finding time in a day's work to do the *Times* crossword, and Yolande, stressed and buzzing, doing most of the administrative work of the International Theatre Institute which was also part of our trio's brief. Kenneth was secretary of the board and I began to get an idea of the politics as I banged out the minutes on my manual typewriter. He also convened the building committee: the Old Vic was only a stop-gap prior to a new theatre being built on the South Bank, and older luminaries such as the sculptor Henry Moore and the director Michel St Denis regularly passed my office door. They appointed the architect Denys Lasdun towards the end of 1963, before handing over to a younger and more immediately involved team headed by Olivier himself. It was the beginning of a long stretch of decision-making, rows, strikes and further delays before the present National Theatre building was opened under the regime of Olivier's successor Peter Hall in 1976.

My exit from the National, after two years of great pleasure and interest, was prompted by my engagement to marry an up-and-coming satirist, Noel Picarda. He had agreed to set up a light entertainment department in an actors' agency run by Willie Donaldson, an early producer of *Beyond the*

2. https://www.nationaltheatre.org.uk/sites/default/files/stagebystage-pt2_early-years.pdf.

Fringe who sold out just before that show hit the jackpot and who subsequently wrote the hilarious *Henry Root Letters*. Neither of us knew what was involved and the agency itself wasn't thriving. Tired of regular visits from the bailiffs and no longer a fiancée, I went on to work for a West End producer, John Gale, and then for journalist and soon-to-be MP Clement Freud before I embarked on an overland trip to India and on to Australia where my secretarial days ended. I was appointed by the Australian Elizabethan Theatre Trust to be tour manager, first to a French theatre company, Le Tréteau de Paris, and then to the English Opera Group. Exploring Australia in the company of European artists was about as good as it got, but it was a long way from home and I didn't feel ready to emigrate. Two years later and back in London, I became deputy administrator at the Roundhouse. This former railway shed in Camden Town had been set up as Centre 42, an arts centre for the people, by the playwright Arnold Wesker; in its first few years it hosted artists from Peter Brook and Nicol Williamson to Pink Floyd and Jimi Hendrix. But by 1970 funding was becoming hard to get and Wesker resigned. When I joined in 1973 the building was still an arts centre but one in search of a *raison d'être*. My job was to help with programming and give some general order to a fairly shambolic regime. This entry to the world of rock'n'roll (one of my duties was to ensure that the lavatories were cleaned of drug evidence after the Sunday concerts) was balanced by an introduction to theatrical events such as Jerome Savary's *Le Grand Magic Circus*, Stomu Yamashta's Red Buddha Theatre and British companies and performers such as Hull Truck, Prospect and Steven Berkoff. In the spirit of the times a Californian company, Beat 72, presented *120 Days of Sodom* but I don't remember that it raised any censorial interest, unlike the visit by a Brazilian dance company, Les Capoieres de Bahia, whose live goat had to be confined to the car park and replaced by a stuffed replica on stage.

Dance also played a part at the Roundhouse. I had my first exposure to contemporary dance with the wonderful Twyla Tharp group but my life was changed as a result of a short season by Ballet Rambert, Britain's oldest dance company (now just known as Rambert). I immediately liked the people involved but was surprised when Tim Mason, its administrator (as the job of chief executive was ungrandly known in those days), said that he was leaving and suggested that I apply for the job. I felt I didn't know anything about dance but, as he pointed out, there was already an artistic director and what was needed was a good manager. I remember going for an interview at the light, plant-filled offices of the company in Chiswick and thinking how good it would be to have a change from the dusty hippiedom of the Roundhouse.

I got the job and spent eleven years with the company, touring the UK and indeed much of the world with a varied repertoire of contemporary work and making many friends among the dancers, choreographers and staff. It was 1975 when I joined and I would know the redoubtable Marie Rambert until her death at ninety-four in 1982; I found her truly inspirational, with not only a remarkable gift for spotting talent in both dancers and choreographers but also the ability to quote long tracts of Shakespeare, Dante and Goethe in their original languages. She encouraged continual cultural self-improvement in all whom she befriended and I wish that I had followed her instruction to learn a Shakespeare sonnet a week. What struck me most about her was the fact that she had been in her late seventies when her then artistic director, Norman Morrice, had suggested that the classical ballet company she had formed and run for so many years should be disbanded and re-formed with 22 dancers, using the modern choreographic techniques from America led by such pioneers as Martha Graham. I feel that most people in her position and at her age would have had difficulty adapting to the new, and perhaps opt for a shadowy presidential role. Not Madame Rambert: she was a regular attender at rehearsals and performances, taking it all in with an eagle eye and giving pertinent notes and encouragement.

Marriage and a move to Bath provided the impetus for change. My husband was Brian Wray, marketing director of Imperial Tobacco, whom I had met when his company sponsored Rambert: in those days, tobacco money was still eagerly accepted by the arts. However, the tide was turning against smoking and he left the company shortly after we wed. He then worked freelance, one of his favourite clients being Courage brewers who owned Guinness. They were supporters of the Wexford Festival and for several years we had the great pleasure of annual visits to that most enjoyable of operatic events.

I became executive producer of the English Shakespeare Company, a rollicking venture led by the director Michael Bogdanov and the actor Michael Pennington. In their first year they had presented *Henry IV Parts 1 and 2* and *Henry V*; now they wanted to add *Richard II*, *Henry VI* edited from three to two parts and *Richard III*, with 25 actors taking and understudying over 500 roles. The brief was to tour the large-scale circuit of British theatres, something no other full-time company was doing, with international dates providing both variety and income. The full story is told in the Michaels' book, *The Wars of the Roses*. Not wanting to tour any more, I oversaw its progress from a London office on a supposedly part-time basis. The first board meeting I attended saw the departure of three board members who thought such an enterprise carried too much risk, so it was good to be able to deliver a small surplus at the end of the two-year adventure.

It was at this stage that my non-executive experience began. I was appointed a trustee of the Dancers' Resettlement Fund and Trust, an excellent organisation that provided (and now, as Dancers' Career Development, still does) training support for dancers when they had to retire for reasons of age or injury. Sitting around a committee table seemed to suit me and various appointments within the Theatrical Management Association (TMA) followed, with my ending up as its first female president in 1991. This was usually a position held for three or four years but at the end of the first year I received a telephone call from Lord (Peter) Palumbo, asking me to join ACGB as chair of its dance panel. I was sad that Rupert Rhymes, the TMA's chief executive whom I had first met as house manager at the National Theatre, seemed to regard a move to ACGB as little short of treasonable, but it seemed a great opportunity to be at the top table in terms of contributing to dance and the arts in general. Most of the organisations I had worked for to date had received public funding and I had imbibed and experienced all the arguments for its necessity: I passionately believed, as I still do, that any nation that considered itself civilised should invest in artistic work that can't, for reasons of size, experiment or risk, exist commercially. In what seem to me now to be golden days of arts management, mission statements and business plans didn't exist and executive directors had more time to work near the creative base without the need to concentrate on lengthy funding applications and key performance indicators (KPIs). I certainly wasn't of the mindset to think about the strategic importance of the role and do a personal risk assessment, as I might be encouraged to do nowadays. All the major opportunities of my life have been presented to me rather than planned and this was a good example of not thinking twice. It was flattering to be invited and it would be interesting to have a say in how ACGB funding was directed.

*

I had first walked through ACGB's doors when I took up my post at Rambert. The dance department had only recently been promoted from a subsidiary position in the music department to stand in its own right and was led by the supportive Jane Nicholas; the other department with whom I had considerable dealings was that of touring. Its director was the legendary Jack Phipps, the sort of maverick unwelcome in today's climate of conformity, who was responsible for many changes to the touring scene such as the formation of Opera North, the Royal Shakespeare Company's annual seasons in Newcastle and a system called 'spheres of influence' whereby touring opera and ballet companies had their own regular dates. He had also encouraged the creation of the English Shakespeare Company, the formation of which had been overseen by Jodi Myers and Fleur Selby in his department. In the late 1970s it was Jack's ambition to push contemporary dance into the larger theatres, a policy which excitingly stretched the scope of Rambert and its sister, London Contemporary Dance Theatre. Jack was always ebullient, even describing Hull as 'a nice little fishing town' when I queried whether the delights of contemporary dance would be appreciated there (at the time the city had few of the cultural amenities that would see it appointed City of Culture for 2017). It was only when I subsequently joined his touring panel that I experienced the frustration of reading in the papers about the finalisation of some deal involving a touring theatre that our panel thought was still for future discussion.

ACGB itself was set up to operate (as its successor still supposedly does) on an 'arm's length' principle from government – it distributed public funding for the arts on an independent basis without political involvement. This not only meant that its decisions were taken on the basis of informed, often peer, advice but also that politicians had protection from decisions and could be shielded from irate artists refused a grant. However, as we shall see throughout this book, often the arm withered to a stump, particularly where large amounts of money and/or organisations were concerned. The politicians also loved to tinker with its structure and by 1992 the result was pretty dysfunctional.

The central organisation, based in Great Peter Street in London's Westminster, consisted mainly of specialist artform departments advised by panels on which artists and other practitioners of high distinction voluntarily sat, with each panel chair having a seat at the Council table. Then there were the ten Regional Arts Boards (RABs) whose setting up, to replace the previous twelve Regional Arts Associations, had first been proposed by Richard Luce as Minister for the Arts in 1990; they finally came into being under Luce's successor Peter Brooke during 1991, with five of their chairs being appointed to the main ACGB Council through a system of rotation. These were independent bodies which received the majority of their funding from ACGB and the desire of ministers was to devolve many of the Council's clients and responsibilities to the more local level. This desire was not shared by the central artform departments – nor, it has to be said, by many of their clients – and the extent of such devolution remained a source of tension between the central office and the RABs for many years.

A particular focus of the squabble in the early 1990s was Projects and Schemes – in reality, development money. The RABs were of the strong opinion that this was needed at a grass-roots level, whereas the artform departments felt that its distribution was of nationally strategic importance. While political pressure was constantly applied to devolve, the centralists held firm: in the summer of 1994 an integrated working group (of which I was a member) recommended that devolution should happen but only under the strategic control of the national office. This was upheld, but neither side could claim victory and it was some time before anything actually happened. At an executive level a series of COGs, SMOGs and JOGs (chief executive/senior management/joint officer groups) negotiated their territories, but 'them and us' tensions remained during my whole time on the Council. In 2002 the then chair/chief executive combination of Gerry

Robinson and Peter Hewitt suddenly announced the merging of what had become the Arts Council of England and the RABs into one single body, Arts Council England, the pay-off being that the remaining clients were delegated while the national office retained a strategic – but somewhat nebulous – role. Since then the regions have shrunk to nine and then to the current five: London, North, Midlands, South East and South West. This seems to be a sensible compromise and certainly makes for a tighter structure. I do feel it a loss to artistic confidence, however, that although national directors for each artform remain (under an overall executive director of arts) they seem to have relatively little strategic say or status. Their presence on the ACE website remains almost invisible.

*

My first Council meeting was on 13 May 1992. My appointment had been delayed for a short while by the 'purdah' created three weeks before the May 1992 election, which meant that all government business, including ACGB appointments, was put on hold. But finally a confirmatory letter arrived from Hayden Phillips, the first permanent secretary at the newly established Department for National Heritage (DNH) which had replaced the Office of Arts and Libraries, followed by a press announcement by David Mellor, himself just appointed as the department's first Secretary of State. I was now the latest ACGB member. Like any newcomer I found it all somewhat daunting. The meeting took place in a semi-basement at Great Peter Street (a room from which many pairs of legs passing in the street outside would be viewed over the coming years), and consisted of a considerable number of eminent people sitting around a large table under the genial chairmanship of Peter Palumbo. The Council numbered 15, most of whom chaired either artform panels/committees or RABs and, in the case of William Brown and Mathew Prichard, the Scottish Arts Council and the Arts Council of Wales respectively. There was one 'independent', Peter Gummer, brother of MP John Gummer who was soon to become the Secretary of State for the Environment.[3] Anthony Everitt as

3. For a full list of Council members please see Appendix I.

secretary-general radiated calculated bonhomie. With other staff, an observer from the DNH and four advisors joining for specific items, the total attendance was 29. Paperwork for the meeting weighed 5lb: Brian Rix, chair of the drama panel (who in a drastic career change had gone from being a famous farceur to secretary-general and then chair of Mencap, for which he received a peerage), had put it on his bathroom scales that morning. It had been circulated only four days before – the ability to speed-read should have been listed as an essential skill for Council membership. The English Shakespeare Company featured on the agenda as it was seeking confirmation of its status as franchise-funded (a mid-stage on the pilgrimage from project- to regularly funded): I had to declare an interest and leave the room when that item came up for discussion.

The only familiar face among my fellow councillors was the vice-chair Denys Hodson, an urbane local authority man who had breathed life into Swindon's arts and recreation department over a number of years and whom I had met when touring to the Wyvern Theatre. He was to remain a good friend, and such was his appetite for Council meetings that when his term of office ended he persuaded Palumbo's successor to let him continue to attend as an observer for a further two years. Others who made an immediate impression were the cultural historian Christopher Frayling, who chaired the visual arts panel, and two of the RAB chairs, that great figure of inspiration Ernest Hall, a businessman-cum-concert pianist who had created the wonderful Dean Clough in Halifax where commercial enterprises supported artists' studios and venues, and Clive Priestley, the civil servant whom Margaret Thatcher had appointed to investigate the affairs of the Royal Opera House and who had gone gloriously native by suggesting it was under-funded. Ernest chaired the Yorkshire & Humberside Arts Board and Clive that of London.

The agenda for my first Council meeting was long (and the English Shakespeare Company application was rejected, an immediate recognition that being an ACGB member brought no special favours). Its central feature was a discussion on a national arts and media strategy, which had originally been requested by Arts Minister Richard Luce in 1989. Anthony Everitt remembers feeling that what the Office of Arts and Libraries really wanted was a strategy showing how the Arts Council could cope with a much smaller grant in aid, which he was obviously reluctant to deliver. None the less a massive consultation was undertaken: by 1992 this was moving towards a conclusion and the 'rather tedious document' (in Everitt's words) was eventually published as A *Creative Future* in early 1993. A two-day artistic review was held by the Council in May of that year, supposedly to realign the funding portfolio with its findings, but in reality no substantial changes were made – after which it seems to have sunk without trace. But the minutes of the May 1992 Council discussion do contain a pertinent reference:

> . . . the final document should be clear about the nature and pattern of current investment and on priorities for the future, taking into account the proposed National Lottery.

The final version of A *Creative Future* urged the need for the arts funding system to work with local authorities to provide a national arts infrastructure and to ensure that all arts buildings were as physically accessible as possible. It identified the National Lottery as a potential major source of funding for capital needs but felt that the role of ACGB would be more 'as facilitator, advisor and partner, rather than as major contributor'. So much for foresight: it was as the most major of all contributors that the Arts Council was to feature for the first few years following the birth of the lottery.

2

ENTER THE NATIONAL LOTTERY

Birth of the lottery – starting to get to grips – ACGB is reviewed –
London orchestras – the cast list changes – setting up the Lottery Panel
and processes – lyric theatre review – all set to go

National lotteries have been used as additional sources of public income right back to Elizabethan times. The first one was run in 1567 and an advertisement for it can be seen in the British Library. Its purpose was to raise money for the development of ports and the building of ships to support England's growing export market; the first prize was £5,000 although of this only £3,000 was paid in cash, the rest being in plate and textiles. Anyone buying a ticket was promised freedom from arrest for all crimes other than murder, felonies, piracy and treason.

Over the following centuries state lotteries remained a part of British public life, particularly in the eighteenth century when one funded the building of Westminster Bridge and another contributed towards both the Duke of Marlborough's campaign expenses and the defence of the American colonies. The practice was stopped, however, in the 1820s after it was brought into disrepute by a secondary betting industry which had developed around the results and was deemed to tarnish the real thing.

By the latter part of the twentieth century it was becoming obvious that there were many areas of cultural, heritage and leisure activity which could benefit from extra money, unlikely to be forthcoming from Treasury sources. A Royal Commission on Gambling chaired by Lord Rothschild in 1978 recommended the setting up of a lottery whose proceeds would go to the arts, sport and other deserving causes. Any attempt to pursue the subject was stifled when Margaret Thatcher came to power in 1979 – that daughter of a Methodist did not believe in making money in any way but hard graft. Peter Palumbo remembers her banging her fist on the table at its very mention and declaring it sinful; Lord (Grey) Gowrie, a former Minister of the Arts who was himself to become Chairman of the Arts Council in 1994, saw his own efforts to set one up rejected more softly with a 'No gambling, dear.' Her successor, John Major, had other ideas. As Prime Minister he was persuaded that arts, sport and heritage all had investment and infrastructure needs that would never be fulfilled if they had to compete for additional public expenditure within the ordinary Budget. In the manifesto that won him the 1992 election he included the setting up of a Department for National Heritage (DNH), one of whose major tasks would be the introduction of a National Lottery, 'which would help provide funds for a number of good causes in the artistic, sporting, heritage and charitable fields'; the establishment of a fund to celebrate the forthcoming millennium was also mentioned. Permanent Secretary Hayden Phillips feels that Major has never received the credit due to him for his overall vision, a view shared by Virginia Bottomley who became Secretary of State in July 1995. When she visited projects funded by the lottery she remembers feeling irritated at people's 'meanness of spirit' in refusing to acknowledge John Major's role. She singles out Nicholas Serota as a notable exception: at the opening of Tate Modern he paid full tribute to Major. It is also probably fair to say that some of the impetus came from Major's colleague David Mellor who had particular interests in those areas to be supported by the lottery, such as sport and the arts.

The tale of the National Lottery's setting up, the appointment of Peter Davis as regulator and its management from the beginning by the commercial company Camelot, including the skirmishes which that body had with its would-be rival Richard Branson, is well told in Raymond Snoddy and

Jon Ashworth's book *It Could Be You*. As far as the good causes were concerned, the great fight, as Hayden Phillips recalls, was to keep lottery income out of the hands of the Treasury: he is proud that he did so, apart from a 12p tax on every £1 ticket sale. Perhaps the fact that he had been a major figure in the Treasury before his DNH appointment helped, as there is nothing like inside knowledge when facing up to your opponent. Andrew Ramsay, then head of arts, sport and lottery at the department, considers it a great achievement that the basic concept of what the lottery was set up for has continued and that it has never been swallowed up by the Treasury and used for something else – which, he says, is what has happened in other countries. The other department which had to be faced down was the Home Office, which had always had responsibility for all gambling matters. Alan Davey (the chief civil servant at the DNH responsible for drafting the Lottery Bill who was himself to become ACE's chief executive in 2007) remembers that they

> wanted to completely hobble it so that there'd be limits on it all the way along; limits on the jackpots and that kind of stuff. We argued against that . . . at one point there were four people doing the lottery bill at DNH and 25 people briefing against us at the Home Office . . . if we'd allowed it to be regulated by the Home Office it would never have happened in the way it did.

He describes the setting up of the lottery department within the DNH as a kind of 'guerilla exercise' with four people in one small room sharing one telephone:

> We couldn't afford to go abroad so we used to telephone a lot of people in New Zealand because the New Zealand lottery had many similarities with the positioning of the lottery that we'd established was the best, a kind of soft retail product that people spend a marginal amount of money on. The marginal pound as it were.

Hayden Phillips feels that there were two absolutely crucial actions taken by his department at the beginning. First, they insisted that the good cause distributors should use lottery income for capital not revenue – thereby ensuring that Treasury grants in respect of the latter were not prejudiced. Secondly, it had to be used in addition to and not as a substitute for any public expenditure: the lottery was not taxpayers' money and a new word, 'additionality', entered the dictionary of funding. He also ensured that the financial directions governing the lottery were drawn up in close consultation with the National Audit Office so that that body could not afterwards claim that it wouldn't have agreed.

A White Paper on *A National Lottery Raising Money for Good Causes* had been published in March 1992. This proposed five good cause distributors which were to benefit in equal shares from 25 per cent of every lottery pound spent – i.e. each distributor would receive 5p of every £1 ticket bought. Hayden Phillips confirms that the Arts and the Sports Councils were the obvious choices to distribute the arts and sports money as they were already set up to disburse government grants. Heritage was more problematic because both English Heritage and the National Heritage Memorial Fund were contenders: the latter finally won and founded the Heritage Lottery Fund (HLF). A Millennium Commission was included because, Hayden Phillips asserts, the Treasury was never going to be persuaded to fund the necessary celebrations for such an event; he ensured that this would be chaired by the Secretary of State for National Heritage

> as a way of trying to make sure that there wasn't a row between the government and the Millennium Commission about how we celebrated the millennium.

Hayden believes that it was right to have a Charities Fund for more general needs because it was what people expected and it made good political sense. The Charities Fund was initially the only distributor that could give to revenue, as it wasn't practical to insist they provided only capital.

The first question we asked as a Council was how much money we might reasonably plan for. But to this there was no easy answer, as the whole question of forecasting lottery income has been tricky from the start. It was unknown territory. The White Paper of March 1992 was imprecise about the amount of money that might be raised for good causes, mentioning that 'the general experience in other countries seems to indicate that as much as one third of total turnover would be available once the lottery has been running for a few years' (it currently stands at 28 per cent). Research carried out for the Rothschild Royal Commission in 1978 estimated that by the fifth year of operation annual good cause income would be about £1.5 billion; in his launch of the National Lottery in 1994 John Major referred to Camelot's projection of a total of £9 billion being raised for good causes by 2001. (The actual figure, shown in the National Lottery Commission's annual report for 2000–1,[4] was £9.758 billion: ACE's share of this was £1.527 billion – less than originally planned because of the changes to the distribution that had taken place by 2001, but still an impressive sum.) Hayden Phillips remembers that in spite of his taking advice from professional experts, total income for the first year exceeded estimates by three times. It is my recollection that initially ACGB was being given intimations of annual proceeds of around £150 million, which Grey Gowrie says he always knew was far too low. As a former non-executive director of Ladbrokes he was well aware of the British appetite for gambling.

In December 1992 the National Lottery Bill was presented to the House of Commons. This indicated that ACGB would be responsible for distributing 97.2 per cent of lottery proceeds allocated to the arts, films and crafts in Great Britain, the remaining 2.8 per cent being handled by the Arts Council of Northern Ireland. Royal Assent for the Bill was finally granted on 21 October 1993.

It was exciting to feel that it was now official and we were going to be given a huge extra responsibility even if most of the detailed planning was being done by the DNH. Hayden Phillips remembers regular meetings with the chief executives of the five distributing bodies, which gave them the opportunity to talk to each other and to outline their problems and what the government might do to solve them:

> We were getting things going . . . the people who were obviously paid to think most about it most of the time were obviously my staff and me. So we built up quite a bit of expertise in the area, and on the whole people like the Arts Council and the Sports Council were grateful for the dialogue and the advice that came across. After all, we were all happy bunnies in

4. http://www.natlotcomm.gov.uk/assets-uploaded/documents/Annual%20Report% 202000-2001.pdf (retrieved April 2014).

those days because a cornucopia was about to open . . . normally you're arguing about where the next pound is coming from, now you're wondering how to spend the next pound.

It was during this time that the policy directions were drawn up by the DNH. As far as ACGB was concerned, there were ten of these which covered such areas as the inability to solicit applications; the need to consider applications covering the complete range of activities over which it had power to distribute money, including film and craft; the need for funded projects to promote the public good (including the widening of public access); the ongoing viability of projects; the need for a significant element of partnership funding, and the necessity of giving only capital grants.

The direction which ultimately most affected the Arts Council – and which, in hindsight, could arguably be considered a great folly – concerned the non-solicitation of applications. This meant that no strategy could be set and any application which met agreed criteria had to be awarded a grant. For the first two years or so there would be enough income to allow this to happen but the situation would become unsustainable when income dropped or other programmes were introduced – or both. The intention behind it was to ensure that the system was genuinely open to anyone who wished to apply (was there a suspicion at the DNH that ACGB might otherwise concentrate entirely on its existing clients?). At the time this seemed an honourable course, and one which Grey Gowrie feels was right in view of the 'wattage' of money coming in – the more substantial the funds, the less the need to prioritise – but it is now highly debatable. It may not have led to the best use of money and there may have been missed opportunities. A 'five-year vision' paper which was shown to the Council in February 1994 listed various needs to be addressed: a national dance house, the Royal Opera House (ROH), the South Bank Centre (SBC), English National Opera (ENO), a national network of concert halls including one in the north-east, a refurbishment of all major regional theatres and the rehousing of the Institute of Contemporary Arts. Someone quickly spotted that this contravened the 'no strategy' direction, and by the following meeting a revised objectives paper had adjusted this;

such priorities were never referred to again. Most of the list has been accomplished, although the south-west still lacks a good concert hall and the ICA hasn't been rehoused.

Peter Gummer, the first chair of the Council's Lottery Panel, says that he lobbied hard at the time against the 'no strategy' ruling. He wanted the Council to get money into parts of the country that had an undeveloped arts infrastructure and to be able to instigate projects, his own pet one being the idea of building a new opera house on London's south bank while letting the existing ROH become a dance house. He felt that a purpose-built opera house with sufficient capacity and commercial infrastructure around it could have become independent of Arts Council funding within five years (although the shops and restaurants that now surround the SBC haven't diminished that organisation's need for subsidy). Those running the ROH at the time refused to contemplate the idea and it was never taken forward, which at least managed to avoid a row with the dance world as sightlines remain poorer in the existing building for dance than for opera. Peter's other initiative – to set up a television satellite channel on which work from all lottery-funded projects, big and small, could be shown – also never came off, apparently because it lacked government support.

It was, however, a visionary thought at that time when live screening was unheard of and it at least led to an attempt to ensure that those developing new lottery-funded buildings provided cabling for broadcast use. Peter was also concerned that the open application system meant that the Council was open to judicial review if it turned down projects. In fact this only happened on one occasion: in 1997 the Women's Playhouse Trust appealed against a decision to deny them a grant to turn Wapping Power Station into an arts space on, I think, the grounds of financial instability. The Council won its case.

One smaller-scale project with which Peter remained involved was the tiny Chipping Norton Theatre which received an early lottery grant of £678,520 for a total refurbishment. Later he was one of a group of volunteers who raised money to keep it open in response to the withdrawal of its ACE revenue grant in 2008 (along with several others in rural areas). He feels that the capital investment provided a strong operational base, as public funding for running costs can blunt the motivation of local benefactors, a sentiment more convincing in the Cotswold heartlands than in a less lucky equivalent in the north of England.

Although there weren't many mentions at the Council table of the substantial extra responsibility that was about to come to us, some initiatives started to happen. The *Creative Future* consultations had raised the pressing capital needs of the arts sector and the necessity of auditing them even if we were denied the development of a strategy for meeting them. In the summer of 1992 over 5,000 arts organisations, venues and artists were mailed with questionnaires for an audit of capital needs in Great Britain and Northern Ireland, the Council seeing this as a necessary first step to tackling the backlog of work on the arts infrastructure, whether or not a National Lottery was established. As a result, a substantial document was compiled which seems to have been handed directly to the DNH for consideration in relation to the lottery and not referred to nor seen at the Arts Council again – a great pity as it would have been an immensely helpful checklist in the years to come. Its whereabouts today remain a mystery.

Peter Palumbo, as a patron of architecture, began working with Rory Coonan, director of the architecture unit within ACGB's visual arts department, to ensure that the opportunity offered by the lottery could be used by all the good cause distributors to raise standards of architecture and design. A working group was set up, chaired by architect Colin St John Wilson, himself a Council member. It included representatives from the Scottish Arts Council, the Royal Fine Art Commission, the Royal Institute of British Architects, the Sports Council, the National Heritage Memorial Fund and English Heritage. With a good historical sense, Rory Coonan arranged to hold its first meeting at the British Museum, which itself had been established by a National Lottery in 1753. (This had been held because neither King George II nor Parliament was prepared to put up the requested £20,000 for the magnificent collection of Sir Hans Sloane on which the Museum was founded.) The group's recommendations per-suaded Peter Brooke, who had recently re-entered the arts world as Secretary of State at the DNH (after David Mellor's sudden departure from the post on 24 September 1992 due to a sex scandal), publicly to request good cause distributors to aim for the highest architectural quality and building design standards in their funded projects. His statement was reflected in a document, NATIONAL LOTTERY: Architecture & construction advice for capital projects, published by the working group in 1994. This listed eight points of good practice: in addition to being well-designed and constructed, buildings should be environmentally friendly, energy-efficient, accessible for disabled people and good value for money.

As far as we Council members were concerned, lottery activity otherwise seems to have been minimal except for some squabbling about set-up costs. The most contentious reference appears in the April 1993 Council minutes which state that there had been a meeting between the Prime Minister and key prospective donors to the development scheme planned by the ROH who wanted confirmation that their money would be matched by funds from the lottery. Lord (John) Sainsbury (former chair of the ROH and president of its development appeal) confirms that he and Vivien Duffield (who led the appeal) were clearly told by John Major that the giving of individual lottery grants would not be a decision for the government and that an application would have to be made to ACGB. In spite of this rebuttal, we felt that the ROH was going behind our back and trying to strong-arm us into an early decision – the ROH and the lottery had already begun to be uneasy bedfellows.

If ACGB itself was taking its time preparing for a tsunami of extra income, others also seemed unaware of what was about to come. In December 1992 Peter Brooke commissioned the consultancy firm PriceWaterhouse to undertake a review of ACGB and briefed that this should take account of the implications of the new National Lottery on its work. The review proposed a restructuring of the organisation and a reduction of administration costs by 10 per cent. When this was presented to the Council in June 1993 there was outrage that many of the facts in the review had not been checked and were inaccurate. I was one of an angry deputation of Council members that sought a meeting with Peter Brooke, who as a result agreed to allow a figure of 8 per cent. As far as lottery matters were concerned, PriceWaterhouse saw fit only to recommend that a sub-committee of the Council be appointed to deal with these, stating that although 'a separate unit would not be necessary and would impose extra costs', the employment of a project manager paid for by the government was desirable. This idea was challenged by the Council as we were now beginning to see the lottery as a substantial new responsibility; we looked forward to receiving more ideas from PriceWaterhouse and the DNH.

What is interesting in all this today is Brooke's public statement that he hoped that the PriceWaterhouse work would 'mark the end of the long series of reviews by government into the structure and staffing of the arts funding system'. Wishful thinking: politically driven reviews of ACE have continued at regular intervals, with one of the most severe ever in 2012/13 when a 50 per cent cut to its overheads was demanded by the then Secretary of State Jeremy Hunt. As I write in the spring of 2017 another one has just been issued, this time a 'tailored' one commissioned by the DNH's successor, the Department for Culture, Media & Sport. The actual savings made are not always clear but the human toll caused by all the uncertainties of re-structuring are immense, to say nothing of the constant reinvention of the wheel and the loss of any kind of folk memory about what has or hasn't worked in the past. For some time now it's been a government mantra that fat can be cut from any organisation even as more bureaucratic demands are insisted upon. Its own vast wastages never seem to be called likewise to public account. While I agree that ACE should regularly consider a good pruning, I'm sad that so much arts expertise seems to get lost in the process, to be replaced by rhetoric about 'investment' and 'resilience' – political concerns that do little to ignite passion or, to use another buzzword of our time, creativity. And the occasional (senior) staff member who publicly states how much they hate the arts seems to survive better than other Council officers who strive to distribute diminishing funds as fairly and intelligently as they can.

Back in July 1993 we were at last taking things a little more seriously. The minutes for that month's Council meeting acknowledge that a lot of complex work would have to be done to set up systems to cope with what in some cases would be applications for major building developments. The set-up costs of a lottery unit in 1993/4 were allocated £75,000 with an agreement that a lottery director should be appointed during that year. By November – only a year before ticket sales were due to start – it was realised that this amount was obviously quite inadequate to cover administration costs. It was then agreed to establish a lottery department with £500,000 (to be recovered from future income), and to recruit a lottery director to join the senior management team at once.

*

Before that happened my first big ACGB row developed on the matter of the London orchestras. One of the few concrete decisions coming out of the May 1993 artistic review was that only two of the existing four should continue to be funded: the London Symphony Orchestra (LSO) and another to be selected by a small group led by a judge, Sir Leonard (later Lord) Hoffmann. Why such outsiders were more qualified for the job than ACGB's own music panel and department was not clear. In their report that December they stated that their brief was muddled and recommended that while there might not be a very strong case for continuing to support the Royal Philharmonic, there was really nothing to choose between the Philharmonia and the London Philharmonic in terms of cutting or supporting. This embarrassing outcome led to a furore: the Council complained that it had been under-informed, the Royal Philharmonic lobbied hard on the basis that its touring made it much more than a London orchestra, and the BBC became involved because it was in the middle of an unrelated review of orchestral provision with ACGB. In the end all four orchestras continued to be funded – as indeed they still are more than twenty years later – but the public image of the Council's decision-making was badly shaken. The music director Ken Baird and the philosopher Bryan Magee, who had briefly chaired the music panel, both resigned. The whole debacle showed me how hard it was always going to be to cut clients and how important it was that the Council should take difficult decisions through its own expert conviction rather than *ad hoc* advice.

*

Perhaps it was to punish such shenanigans that the government announced a cut of £3.2 million in its annual grant for 1993/4. So angry was Peter Palumbo that he stormed out of Peter Brooke's office at the DNH during a meeting held to discuss this, only to find himself facing a series of endless corridors and security-locked doors which prevented him from leaving the building. A saviour in the form of a kindly civil servant prevented him from having to return meekly to the room he had just left. This was to be his final grand gesture: his term of office ended in March 1994 and he was replaced by Grey Gowrie. At the same time, the secretary-general Anthony Everitt handed over to his deputy Mary Allen. Mary had been an actress and then involved with arts sponsorship; she had run Watermans Arts Centre in Brentford and had been appointed to ACGB at about the same time as me in 1992. And, in a radical change (discovered by us Council members in a press release), on 1 April 1994 the Arts Council of Great Britain became the Arts Council of England (ACE). Scotland and Wales gained autonomy for their own organisations and their respective chairs left the table at Great Peter Street, taking their just proportions of Treasury and lottery funding with them.

New energy had already been brought to the Council in December 1993 when producer Thelma Holt was appointed chair of the drama panel. Thelma had co-founded an early fringe theatre, the Open Space, and subsequently, after my time there, reinvigorated the Roundhouse; she has since been responsible for bringing many of the world's major theatre companies and individual artists to Britain. Her exuberance and her instinct for which bureaucratic rules could be circumvented in the cause of promoting drama made her an inspiring, if sometimes frustrating, colleague. The April 1994 re-launch resulted in other new appointments: architect Sir Richard Rogers became vice-chair; musician and arts administrator Gavin Henderson took the chair of the music panel, broadcaster Stephen Phillips the touring panel and public servant Usha Prashar that of combined arts. The former director of the RSC, Trevor Nunn, acted as a minister without portfolio. Biographer Michael Holroyd had joined the Council in August 1992 as chair of the literature panel, and critic Richard Cork would shortly be appointed to that of the visual arts panel: the artistic line-up on Council was exceptional and as several of them were old friends life was interesting and enjoyable. As for the five RAB representatives, Ernest Hall and Clive Priestley had been joined by Bob Southgate, Maggie Guillebaud and Stella Robinson who chaired the West Midlands, South West and Northern Arts Boards respectively. Stella in particular was an inspiration: though visually impaired she somehow coped with the massive amount of Council paper-work and had a sweetness that completely belied the toughness she must have needed in a lifetime's work as Labour councillor and activist in Durham and the north-east.

This promising line-up was the Council that oversaw the first year of lottery applications, and I think everyone felt invigorated by what lay ahead. Then, in the autumn of 1995, Grey Gowrie proposed that, in view of the increased responsibilities given to the arts funding system by the lottery, all ten RAB chairs should sit on the Council. This was obviously fair but it did mean that, from April 1996, the number of Council members rose to 21, a hugely unwieldy number.

*

An early task on the Gowrie/Allen to-do list was establishing the structure for distributing funds from the National Lottery, now only months away from putting its tickets on sale. Peter Gummer had wanted the ACE chair-manship but it was apparently felt that having a brother who was a cabinet minister made the arrangement too cosy; perhaps as a consolation prize he was invited by Grey Gowrie to chair what Peter, in an attempt to make it as independent as possible, determined to call the National Lottery advisory board (by October 1995, however, the Council minutes start referring to it as the Lottery Advisory Panel and for ease of reference it will be referred to as the Panel from now on). He energetically set about recruiting a varied group of distinguished people who would play a considerable role in ACE's distribution of lottery funds in its first few years. Having decided who the top people were in the areas which the lottery would involve such as film, architecture and live performance, Peter just rang them up – and he remembers that without exception the first choices all said yes.

These initial members were Jon Foulds (chief executive, Halifax Building Society), Patty Hopkins (architect), Cleo Laine (singer), Ruth Mackenzie (executive director, Nottingham Playhouse), Paddy Masefield (theatre director and a leading figure in the disability arts movement), Tony Pender (chartered surveyor with thirty years' professional experience of economic regeneration in the north-east), Nima Poovaya-Smith (senior keeper of international arts at Bradford Art Galleries and Museums), and

David Puttnam (film producer) who says

> Being a member of the inaugural National Lottery Arts Panel was one of
> the happiest and most instructive periods of my life. Not only were we able
> to breathe new life into Britain's long-neglected cultural infrastructure, but
> I discovered more about the socially regenerative power of the arts than I'd
> ever believed possible.

Jeremy Newton, then director of the Eastern Arts Board, was appointed as
lottery director in May and immediately starting setting up some structures.
By the end of the month he was reporting on the operational timetable,
arrangements for consultative seminars and relationships with other
distributors. He was aided in all of this by his deputy Andrew Milne, and
together they travelled throughout the country, talking, listening, holding
seminars and gathering the architectural and construction advice that
would be needed to assess applications for building work. Jeremy remembers that a benefit of all this was that it was entirely new territory from the
point of view of structure and the needs of capital rather than revenue projects; they had to get it right but had 'room to breathe: we had a lot of
freedom – it was exhilarating'. Mary Allen compares Newton at this time
to

> a speedboat scudding along the top, almost bouncing from wave to wave
> and that was an extraordinarily useful set of skills to have at that point of
> building up the lottery department and putting together the assessment
> processes and the people who would manage it.

Jeremy remembers regular meetings with the chief executives of the other
distributors: he describes it as an attempt to 'share the pain'. How much
was shared depended on the whim of the particular chief executive – he
says that of the Sports Council was the least willing to join in, often
sending his deputy to joint meetings and disregarding attempts to ensure
good design as a basic tenet for lottery-funded buildings (although Geraint
John, chief architect of the Sports Council, did sit on the Coonan working
group). In stark contrast to the consultancy mania that has subsequently
engulfed all public policy areas, there were no exploratory papers asking
for comment; gradually, and with the assistance of regular monthly Panel
meetings, criteria were drawn up, processes settled and application forms

devised. Jeremy pays tribute to the Panel and to Peter Gummer as its chair: they were 'an extraordinarily dedicated group', all of whom attended almost all of the monthly meetings which were 'heavy and full-on right from the start'. There was much agonising over policy and criteria, but a strong sense of independence; several meetings took place before a full presentation was made to the Council for its final approval in September.

*

For those of us not directly involved, that presentation was the first real sniff of what being a good cause distributor meant. The Panel's recommendations were complete enough for us more or less to rubber-stamp them, although such was the vociferous nature of the new Council that everyone had to have their say before that was done. No applications for less than £5,000 would be accepted; partnership funding would have to make up 25 per cent of any total cost, 10 per cent for projects under £100,000; there would be no retrospective funding. Although it is not noted in the minutes and I don't have that memory of the discussion, Jeremy remembers that we made one significant change by removing the proposed £25 million cap on any one application. There were two reasons for this: the forecast for lottery sales had already been tripled by Camelot, and one or two potential applicants – the ROH and the SBC among them – would need significantly more than that amount. These organisations were lobbying hard, but although the Panel had considered their representations it had decided that it would be better to keep the cap – hence their recommendation that the Council rejected. In view of the amount of money coming in the Council was certainly right not to impose any limits at this stage: of the projects that received more than £25 million, possibly only the ROH would have been successful in raising the money from elsewhere. A once-in-a-lifetime opportunity to create or refurbish some substantial buildings would have vanished.

What seems extraordinary now is how little time all the preparatory work took. Eight thousand applications packs had been published and distributed by December, with an opening date of 4 January 1995 for applications to be received. Jeremy Newton is particularly proud of these packs – 'my finest achievement' – and in fact they immediately attracted the

Crystal Mark from the Plain English Campaign, a seal of approval for the clarity of a document. The design was based on the *Jackdaw* series of history learning aids for children, a set of enclosures within a general cover, the most pertinent of which were:

- Outline guidance text on the lottery, good causes, eligibility, assessment criteria, application process and membership of Lottery Panel;
- ACE's own *Guidance Notes on Access for Disabled People to Arts Venues* commissioned by ACE from Chris Davies;
- The *NATIONAL LOTTERY: Architecture & construction advice for capital projects*, mentioned above;
- *Dance Spaces* by architect Mark Foley which ACE happened to be publishing at that time;
- An advance notice form (ANF) which had to precede the submission of each application, the idea being that this would allow future demand to be gauged to some extent;
- The application form itself, the questions in each sector of which clearly related to each of the eight criteria on which lottery decisions could be taken.

The policy directions helped to form some of the criteria, others reflected the priorities of ACE. As they remained the benchmark against which bids were assessed as long as the main capital programme lasted, it's worth setting them out in full, with the reasoning behind each:

Benefit to the public: this allowed for the support of organisations outside ACE's usual constituency, including amateur and commercial enterprises, on the condition that they offered public benefit. Also judged under this criterion was the question of access: full disability access within all projects had been heavily lobbied for by Panel member Paddy Masefield as well as by disability organisations and the architectural working group. Early projects that did not provide for this in their initial applications were awarded additional sums to allow them to deliver it;

Long-term financial stability: obviously a vital criterion and in the long term the one that caused more problems than any other: Jeremy Newton acknowledges it was the issue 'which came back to haunt us'. As well as being at the heart of all realisable visions, it also represented a warning not to create new revenue clients for ACE nor to allow increased demands from existing ones;

Partnership funding: this aimed at demonstrating public support and avoiding 'kite-flying' applications. Each application had to show that other parties – public or private sector, trusts or individuals – were prepared to commit financial (or in some cases 'in kind') support;

Quality of design and construction: the influence of the Coonan working group has already been referred to;

Quality of artistic activities planned: this obviously lay at the heart of ACE's and the RABs' work;

Local/regional/national development plans: this was as near to influencing strategy as ACE could come. It gave a role in decision-making to the RABs, some of whom were unhappy about not having money to distribute directly themselves. However, their independence did put them in a position to advise applicants and indeed to solicit bids in a way that ACE as a lottery distributor was unable to do;

Contribution of artists, craftspeople and film and video makers: the idea of 1 per cent for art in capital projects had been raised in *A Creative Future* and was obviously an important way of ensuring that artists were involved. So that this could not be seen as a charter for visual artists only, the brief was widened to include such things as the commissioning of performances for openings. Projects were encouraged to include artists in the whole design process from the start although it must be said that on the relatively few occasions it happened, artists often felt very excluded within building teams;

Quality of plans for education and marketing: increased access and audience development were expected to be key features of all capital projects.

*

Aware that several of the large theatres presenting opera and ballet in London were lining up lottery bids, in the autumn of 1994 the Council invited the banker Dennis Stevenson to chair a lyric theatre review, helped by Genista (Jenny) McIntosh, then executive director of the National Theatre, Council member Stephen Phillips and consultant Graham Devlin, whose 1989 report for the dance panel, *Stepping Forward,* had led to the creation of national dance agencies. The objectives were:

- To survey the current and potential audience for lyric theatre in London;
- To assess the ways in which that audience's longterm needs might be met;
- To consider the various options available to the two major opera companies who were facing closure periods.

Discussions on this review took up far more Council time in the months before and after its submission than did the lottery itself. The review group reported in January 1995. Its main recommendations were:

- Sadler's Wells was the best placed theatre to lead a dance house network (consultant Crispin Raymond had recently investigated the desire for a national dance house on behalf of Dance UK and had concluded that the country would benefit from a national network of dance houses);
- The ROH had to close for redevelopment and the costs of relocating the Royal Ballet and Opera companies during closure should be covered by lottery funds;
- English National Opera (ENO) should delay its redevelopment plans until the ROH had re-opened; also, its home, the London Coliseum, should become available for a longer period in the year for large-scale dance.

When the time came to discuss the bids from the ROH and Sadler's Wells this obviously provided a helpful background, even if it did not ease our relations with ENO who did not appreciate being asked to delay its plans nor to programme more dance. Graham Devlin remembers an article by Melvyn Bragg in *The Times* which attacked the review team and which he feels was probably written at the behest of ENO. I think this could well be likely given the hostile attitude shown by the ENO management whenever we had a meeting to push the case for dance.

*

By the end of 1994, lottery tickets (which had gone on sale with the first draw on 19 November) were selling like the proverbial hot cakes. Once the first ANFs were received, the lottery department, Panel and indeed the Council awaited the arrival of the first applications on 4 January 1995. We were certainly cheered on by the news that ACE's Treasury grant settlement for 1995/96 had not only been unaffected by this new income source but was much better than had been expected, being just over £5 million more than for the current year, so now coming in at an acceptable £191.1 million.

3

THE FIRST YEAR

Early applications – the Royal Opera House – Sadler's Wells – the lottery department at work – transformation of the cultural landscape begins

Ian Albery, chief executive of Sadler's Wells Theatre, saw his lyric venue both as the people's theatre that all could afford and as a David to the ROH's Goliath. The ROH had taken over the popular Sadler's Wells ballet companies and turned them Royal; Ian was spurred to enter a lottery bid by the feeling that such a predator should not be the first to benefit from arts lottery funding. There had been five theatres built on the Wells' Islington site since the 'Musick House' of 1683 and the latest, opened in 1931, no longer provided the facilities that audiences and companies needed. It was cramped and dingy with poor sightlines in the auditorium and prehistoric conditions backstage. Sadler's Wells was the only London receiving theatre of size where touring companies such as Rambert could hold annual seasons but going there was always a dismal experience.

The ROH had announced to the press that they would be submitting the first National Lottery application to ACE but Ian was determined to submit his application for a complete rebuild ahead of them and informed a few trustworthy journalists accordingly. On 4 January, after an all-night working session to complete the final touches, he and a fifty-strong crowd of Sadler's Wells staff, dancers and supporters (many dressed in 'motley' to emulate the legendary Grimaldi who frequently 'did the double', running between acts from Sadler's Wells to Drury Lane Theatre) set off early from Islington to process on foot the three miles to ACE's headquarters in Great Peter Street, the huge bundle of paperwork following in a taxi. So unexpected were they, and so early, that there was no one there initially to greet them. This, ACE's first National Lottery application, was then accepted, as Ian says, 'with some surprise and with good humour'. This barnstorming performance was followed shortly afterwards by the ROH, by which time Grey Gowrie was waiting on the doorstep together with assorted press to receive them. The public relations department of the ROH had also arranged a terrific show, with their flamboyant general director, Jeremy Isaacs, leading a team which included Royal Ballet principal Darcey Bussell, Royal Opera singers Thomas Allen and Simon Keenlyside, and two students from the Royal Ballet School. The SBC was also there with a £50+ million bid as well as a handful of others. In view of the magnitude of the lottery income and the opportunities it opened up, it is perhaps surprising that there was not a longer queue although I heard the phrase 'It's a marathon, not a sprint' being widely bandied about to discourage people from rushing to submit bids on the grounds that the pile of gold would remain. I remember thinking then that that was stupid advice: no politician nor funding body was going to allow that amount of money to remain uninterferred with for long. The whole idea of such bounty took time for some organisations to grasp. Sue Robertson, chief executive of Southern Arts Board 1994–97 and then that of London, tells a nice story: when it was suggested to the principal of a training organisation in need of a new building that they should try the lottery his response was 'Oh no, do you know it's a 150 to 1 chance that we'll win?' as if his only option was to buy a ticket and hope for a lucky draw. And things did accelerate: by March we were concerned about how a significantly increased number of applications might be processed in future.

Just as the setting up of due processes had been done at considerable speed, so were the early applications addressed. On 29 March 1995 the Council looked at recommendations from the Panel and awarded the first grants. Because of many concerns surrounding the SBC's bid, the Panel recommended a development grant of £980,000, which was agreed, as was a similar grant of £100,000 to the Ikon Gallery in Birmingham. There were seven other successful applicants, four for less than £50,000 each (to buy a touring van and PA system, a grand piano, and two lots of brass band instruments). The Unicorn Theatre, a children's theatre based in London's West End, got £97,999 to upgrade safety and disabled access, and the York-shire Dance Centre in Leeds was awarded £603,483 for the final phase of converting a disused factory into a dance centre. Another dance organisa-tion, The Place, was awarded a feasibility grant of £19,000 to investigate the possible refurbishment of the Grade II listed former drill hall in London's Kings Cross acquired in 1969 by Robin Howard. This amazing man had lost his legs in the Second World War but had been inspired by the visit of the Martha Graham Dance Company to London in 1954; he devoted the rest of his life and his family's wealth to London Contemporary Dance Company and its sister school, both of which he founded. By 1995 The Place was badly in need of a complete overhaul of facilities as well as more studios: the complex now housed The Place theatre, the Richard Alston Dance Company, the London School of Contemporary Dance and an active education department. Graham Marchant, then general manager, remembers that the application form at that time was relatively easy to fill in, but he acknowledges that as a former employee of ACGB he 'knew enough to get us to the top of the queue'; he submitted architectural sketches, outline costings and an indication of where partnership funding might come from. That was enough for a feasibility grant.

At this stage, with money pouring in, the application process probably did favour those with ACE credentials who knew their way around the system. It lacked the rigour which was insisted on with later applications: as long as projects met the eight criteria they were awarded a grant, and it has to be said that 'met' was a term quite loosely interpreted. In the vain hope that capital funding could help to ease revenue pressures and generate earned income, financial viability often got high scores even when business plans showed hugely optimistic attendances. The reality was that good entrepreneurial ideas as to how more income could be accomplished were few; and the increased cost of running new and enlarged buildings was to put considerable strain on ACE budgets long into the future.

There was early talk of setting up a £5 million endowment fund from which to contribute towards the ongoing running costs of lottery-funded projects. Had this been done, it would have made life considerably easier both for ACE and for many of the projects themselves as they struggled to cope with increased maintenance and operational expenses. But in spite of regular discussions endowments were shied away from. Peter Hewitt, then chief executive of Northern Arts Board, soon sensed that the money would not last forever and says he was passionate about the need to think in the longer term. He persuaded Jeremy Newton to let him go to the United States to research endowments but nothing came of his journey. He blames a lack of will, particularly from the politicians, to tie up the money for the future. A few larger organisations angled to be given endowments but this was seen as stacking away too much money for the benefit of a single client.

If the first year's assessment process was more generous to applicants than might have advised in hindsight, there were two mitigating factors: intense political pressure to get the money out to demonstrate the success of the lottery and, at first, more money pouring into the lottery coffers than there were eligible applications to receive it. By the end of the financial year in March 1995 (when tickets had only been on sale for just over four months), ACE had received lottery income of £48.9 million, and by July of that year only about £40 million had been awarded.

*

The general feeling of good cheer received a setback in April 1995 when the HLF approved a grant of £12 million for the purchase for the nation of Winston Churchill's papers. An outcry developed about why 'the people's money' had benefited the millionaire Churchill family. This created some nervousness at ACE as we assessed the ROH's application: we saw that the public perception of such an award would need careful handling even though there was more than enough money in the bank to cover its needs.

A Council meeting was convened in July to discuss the ROH bid. The application was for £78.5 million which would contribute 37 per cent towards the total £213.8 million cost of a complete refurbishment, as well as rebuilding the Floral Hall alongside and providing sufficient studios for the Royal Ballet so that they could give up their rehearsal base in Baron's Court in west London.

ACE's relationship with the ROH had been uncomfortable for some time. There had been critical appraisals of both the Royal Opera and the Royal Ballet companies in 1991/92 and as a result an ACE/ROH monitoring committee had been formed in November 1992. I was a member and had then taken over the chair in May 1994 from Peter Gummer. It wasn't the pleasantest of positions, as the atmosphere at meetings tended to be edgy with a number of ROH board panjandrums led by a blustering Jeremy Isaacs facing ACE officers and members determined not to be intimidated. The intention was to create a better understanding between the two organisations but this had barely succeeded since both sides felt growing frustration. The ROH were irritated by what they saw as ACE's interfering bureaucratic demands; the ACE team was increasingly fed up with the lack of information, particularly budgetary – a surprise, we felt at the time, in view of the number of bankers who attended on behalf the ROH board. The only person who broke rank and joined the ACE representatives in their demand to see figures was ROH board member Vivien Duffield, perhaps for the reason that much of the donated money that was going to be used for the redevelopment came from her own Clore Duffield Foundation.

The Council discussion on the ROH bid accepted that the development plans were visionary and there was praise for the architectural proposals of Jeremy Dixon and Edward Jones; on the downside there were substantial concerns about financial stability. The ROH's projected deficit for 1994/95 was £1 million – its accumulated deficit by the end of March 1996 would be £3.294 million. (It was not, however, the highest: at the same time the RSC had an accumulated deficit of £5.568 million and ENO £3.961 million. A list of 23 ACE clients in serious difficulty at March 1996 showed a total accumulated deficit of £23.414 million. Most of the major lyric companies and several leading repertory theatres were included.)

As a result of the debate, the Council agreed to award the ROH £55 million with some stringent conditions about the management of the project including increased access and an integrated monthly cash flow; a further £23.5 million would be dependent on ACE being satisfied that three further conditions had been met. One of these was a clearer vision of the purpose and use of a second auditorium. No one at the ROH could clearly demonstrate what this was needed for and how its programming was to be funded; ACE's dance and music departments wanted to see it used for experimental work by both the ballet and opera companies. In an attempt to woo the local community, some of whom were vocal against the development, promises had been made about its availability for community use, but only twelve days a year seemed to be scheduled for this. The two other conditions related to the technical viability of purpose-made stage equipment estimated to cost £20.5 million, and satisfactory arrangements for the closure period for which there were no coherent plans on the table.

The media reaction to the award was similar to that given to the Churchill papers: this was another 'elitist' award, which used money taken from the poorer section of the public who bought lottery tickets for the pleasures of the rich. The public relations were not helped by reports of the press announcement at the ROH being fuelled by champagne and comments that the award was 'no more than we deserve'. In his book *Never Mind the Moon* the champagne is disputed by Jeremy Isaacs; he also gives a vivid account of the bid seen from his perspective. What went unreported at the time was that there was more than enough lottery money to cover the amount, and that conditions were attached to the grant to ensure more public access and accountability.

*

Things were escalating: by September 1995 ANFs had been received for £1.9 billion worth of projects of which ACE through the lottery was being asked to fund 50 per cent of the total cost. Rather than meekly following the recommendations of the Lottery Panel as we had usually done during the first few months, the Council now requested more time to consider applications and suggested that some of the major projects should be supported by applicant presentations in person. We were feeling frustrated: after a long assessment, the Panel had been reluctant to recommend the application from Sadler's Wells because of concerns about its ability to raise partnership funding and its ongoing financial viability. This hesitation was compensated for by strong support from us artform chairs, led by myself as chair of the dance panel. I had received a presentation about the need for change from Ian Albery, the blast effect of which Gavin Henderson described as 'going through the car wash with the windows open'; I needed little further persuasion. Sadler's Wells' role as a London dance house had long been mooted: in a radio interview Grey Gowrie had expressed his personal desire to create such a London house while he was at ACE and this had inspired Ian to put in the bid. The lyric theatre review had also highlighted the importance of Sadler's Wells' role in a dance theatre network.

But those who had looked at the bid weren't happy. David Hall worked at ABSA (the Association for Business Sponsorship of the Arts). He was invited by Jeremy Newton to assess the Sadler's Wells fundraising and business plans and advised that there was one convincing argument for proceeding. If ACE wanted a dance house in London then Sadler's Wells was realistically the only site for it, but 'if you didn't want it to be the national dance house then you shouldn't really touch it with a bargepole'. He found a lack of realism about the revenue predictions and, in hindsight, was shocked at the technical assessors' inability to see that the project was seriously under-costed. At the Council table, however, after fervent discussion and with reassurances about the professionalism of the construction costings and the capability of the fundraising department (both of which were in fact to prove decidedly shaky), the Council overturned the Panel's suggested caution and agreed a grant of up to £30 million, subject to conditions. Ian Albery says that he had originally bid for £21 million but, encouraged by Grey Gowrie and others to be bolder about such things as the foyer design (marble was mentioned but, thankfully, rejected) this rose to £30 million. Ian admits that in those days Sadler's Wells was effectively bankrupt and that at many board meetings there was an initial formal agenda item to discuss if they could legally continue trading – as Sadler's Wells was not at that time a Regularly Funded Organisation (RFO), no ACE officers were present to know about this. Obtaining partnership funding for a virtually bankrupt theatre was a nightmare. Ian and his general manager, Nadia Stern, had to use every theatrical trick in the book, as she describes:

> Things apparently 'in kind' were my salary, and then we thought, well, I need an office and then we worked out that if I was in an office with a high ceiling it was actually better to measure it cubically!

On one point ACE was pressing for – what Ian refers to as 'the zero option' – he refused to budge. This was his maintaining of the lease on the Peacock Theatre off London's Kingsway which was considered by ACE to add considerably to his risk. Graham Devlin (who had been part of the lyric theatre review team) acknowledges now that continuing to programme the Peacock was an 'absolutely brilliant idea – everyone thought risk, risk, risk while Ian thought opportunity, opportunity, opportunity'; it meant that Ian kept his team, his audience and his visiting companies warm throughout the rebuilding period. It also brought in a surplus which helped his cash position considerably.

This initial grant was only the start of a long process of further negotiations during which the Panel's hesitations – and that of its assessor, David Hall – came to seem fully justified.

*

Apart from these lottery decisions the rest of the Council's work chugged along in an uncontentious way: from my point of view 1995 was the calmest of my years as a Council member. There was the ongoing sour relationship between ACE and the RABs and the work of the integrated steering group to deal with; policies for drama, new music and jazz, cross-border touring to be formed; appraisals of ACE's RFOs, which were done every five years and inevitably (and vainly) recommended more grant; and towards the end of the year the allocation of the 1996/97 grant-in-aid gave us a chance to have an overview of clients. The dance department was a pleasure to work with, being in the capable hands of its director Sue Hoyle and then, when she moved on to become Mary Allen's deputy, of Hilary Carty. Gently we argued our way to a larger share of the overall grant, building up an infrastructure of independent dance companies, national dance agencies and audiences. Peter Gummer's desire to keep lottery work as independent as possible from the rest of ACE meant that it never synchronised with the artform departments, and at dance panel meetings there was little recognition of the work of our elephantine lottery neighbour apart from pleasure when a dance application won a capital award or when we felt particularly concerned about a bid such as that of Sadler's Wells.

In the lottery department Moss Cooper, an Australian-born venue manager who had been running the Wolsey Theatre in Ipswich, became operations director in September 1995, replacing Andrew Milne who had died suddenly the previous May. Further pressure arrived in December: Jeremy Newton suffered a serious fall at home and made only a gradual return to work over the following weeks. The department itself was rapidly increasing: as more staff were taken on to cope with the increasing load of applications it soon outgrew its space at Great Peter Street and moved to Portland House near Victoria station, about half a mile away.

David Pratley was a consultant who had been called in to assist the lottery department at the time of Jeremy's accident:

> What a factory it was! I remember that by that point we were operating two shifts and there was a day shift and a night shift; we were hot-desking in this vast open-plan office and one team went home at 5 p.m. and the next team arrived at 5 p.m. and worked through until late in the evening. We were processing 150 applications a month, and when people sort of sneeringly ask, 'Well, didn't an awful lot go wrong?' it was an absolute miracle to me that about 98 per cent of what we funded didn't go that wrong. By any commercial project management standard, let alone government procurement, it was a kind of wondrous story. And in a sense it was being done by, can I say, amateurs in the best sense – there was no particular training within the Arts Council about how to do it, it was all invented and we had the money to bring in wise advisors but it was so long since the Arts Council had had even a Housing the Arts programme, it was new to everyone. And I remember the pressure to get the money out of the door which was absolutely compelling – from ministerial level, from Council level, get it out! And particularly when the Royal Opera House got its money, get it out to everyone else so we've got something to balance it against.

The operations division of the lottery department received and assessed applications, but it was becoming clear that there was a need for a monitoring division to oversee how the money handed out to successful applicants was being spent. Under the financial directions ACE had to demonstrate that lottery grants were used for the purposes intended, that the projects supported represented value for money and that they delivered the benefits identified in the application. Recruitment for a lottery projects director who would head such a department was started.

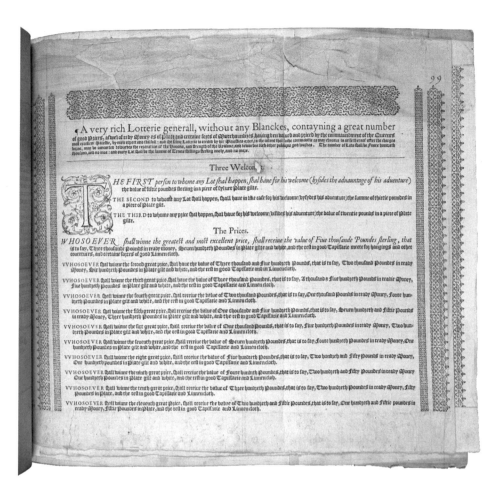

First page of the advertisement for England's first
National Lottery issued by Queen Elizabeth I in 1567.

Top left: Sir Hayden Phillips. Top right: Lord Palumbo.
Below: Mary Allen and Lord Gowrie.

Top: ArtSway in June 2017, showing the poster for Linda Fredericks's exhibition of her life, *Making an Exhibition of Myself.*

Below left: Linda Fredericks (Pratley). Below right: Jeremy Newton.

Opposite, top: Stephen Daldry and Vikki Heywood with the model showing Steve Tompkins's refurbishment of the Royal Court Theatre, London.

Opposite, below: Braham Murray in the bomb damage at the Royal Exchange Theatre, Manchester.

Above right: The New Art Gallery Walsall.

Right: Peter Jenkinson.

Top: The Jerwood Space laid out for Michael Pennington's
70th birthday party in 2013.
Above left: Alan Grieve.
Above right: Prue Skene in front of the tapestry of R. B. Kitaj's
If Not, Not for the British Library, which she cut from the loom at
Dovecot Studios, Edinburgh.

Top: *The Koan* by Liliane Lijn at St Mary's Hospital, Newport, Isle of Wight.
Above: one of Thomas Heatherwick's *Twin Cones*, familiarly known as
'Madonna's tits', at the Goresbrook Interchange on the A13.

Top: press launch to announce the new art gallery at the top of the Baltic Flour Mill, Gateshead, June 1997 (Prue Skene wearing a beige mac).

Left: Statue of Raoul Wallenberg by Philip Jackson, Great Cumberland Place, London W1.

*

By the end of 1995, the imbalance of awards between London and the regions and the lack of projects in areas of cultural diversity were beginning to emerge as issues. The inability to solicit applications and thus have a strategy prevented ACE from addressing them early on. Had it been able to do so, it is possible that neither issue would have grown into two of the major problems that still face ACE today, over twenty years later.

None the less, capital funding through lottery grants had started to transform ACE's reach. The need for policies on radio stations, village halls and commercial theatre began to find its way to the Council table during that autumn. There was even a debate about whether morris dancing could be counted as an artistic activity: Christopher Frayling was particularly exercised about these harmless celebrants, describing them as 'rural fascists'. Referring to the encouragement given to brass bands to commission contemporary compositions alongside their grants for new musical instruments, he felt that even if Harrison Birtwistle had done the accordion music they should not have been considered to come under the umbrella of 'art'. Magic was also questioned, which resulted in an angry letter from John MacGregor MP, a leading cabinet minister in the Thatcher government, who was a member of the Magic Circle (and possibly the only magician to have performed successively in 10 Downing Street and the Speaker's Chambers in the House of Commons). He wanted to know why magic was not considered an art, when circus was. As a result ACE backtracked and a letter from Grey Gowrie agreed that magic should be considered 'an important element in cultural diversity in the arts'. Had the world of magic been more on the ball this could have opened the floodgates to applications for two-way mirrors and saws to cut ladies in half; as it was, the Magic Circle was awarded £475,053 for the acquisition and refurbishing of a theatre.

Other early recipients of grants were the Kirkby Lonsdale Handbell Ringers, who got new handbells; Joanne's Community Entertainers, who were able to purchase a van; and the Champagne Barbershop Chorus from Cornwall, who equipped themselves with stage risers and a transporter. The Czuplak Ukrainian Folk-Dance Company and Musicians, based in the East Midlands, successfully applied for a new sound-mixing console and

PA system. In the religious field, the Hindu Temple Cultural and Community Centre, also in the East Midlands, and the Liverpool Jewish Youth and Community Centre got technical equipment and new buildings. Newmarket Operatic, Musical & Dramatic Society was one of several amateur companies who were able to improve their buildings, as was Yaa Asannewaa Arts and Community Centre (representing carnival arts), while Zippo's Academy (circus art) got a new tent. Merseyside TU Community and Unemployed Resource Centre received £98,450 for equipment and furnishing.

Disability was being addressed: in spite of cynical comments questioning the need for wheelchair access to fly-towers, it was good to have the money and thus be able to insist on 100 per cent disabled access in all bids. Projects specifically benefiting the disabled included the splendid Richard Attenborough Centre at the University of Leicester, where a grant of £730,000 provided an arts centre that welcomed students and community participants with a wide range of aptitude and skills. The Royal School for Deaf Children in Margate converted a building into an art and technology centre; many branches of Shape, the disability-led arts organisation, refurbished properties and bought equipment.

Then there were the brass and silver bands which applied in droves for new instruments, touring vehicles and even bandrooms. Some impatience arose with the amount of grants going to these groups and it was suggested in the summer of 1996 that a moratorium be placed on them – a proposal that was rejected although rumblings remained. In 1998 the journalist Richard Morrison wrote that ACE was 'barmy' to have awarded £11million of lottery money to 281 brass bands across the country, claiming that they were extremely well-sponsored ensembles. This may sometimes have been the case, but the investment was in line with the policy directions to widen access and it certainly saved some colliery bands which had lost their support through the closing of the mines – a situation graphically illustrated by the film *Brassed Off* (made at about this time but ironically not financed by ACE's lottery funds). Furthermore, youth bands provided the only musical training for young people in some areas of the country and, as noted, bands receiving lottery funds were encouraged to commission new work by contemporary composers. A seemingly win–win situation, you might say, but not if you were a journalist needing to have a go. (Brass bands still seek ACE support: the March 2014 edition of Arts Industry magazine reported that a clutch of MPs were lobbying ACE to press for more recognition for the work of an artform that is 'key to Britain's industrial and cultural heritage'.[5])

One area that ACE didn't really get to grips with was craft. Christopher Frayling regrets the lack of applications from this sector, which he thinks was due to craft organisations 'so used to thinking small that they just couldn't get the hang of getting into the rather larger league of the lottery'. Apart from an early £235,000 to Contemporary Applied Arts in London for relocation to new premises, most of the craft distribution formed part of larger bids from arts centres such as Cornerhouse in Manchester and FACT in Liverpool where there were small craft galleries. Subsequently an allocation was reserved for a new headquarters for the Crafts Council, but nothing came of this.

But in many other areas lottery money was making big changes, not only in the cultural sector but also through the other good cause distributors. In sport, stadia and sports grounds were being built and the long investment would soon begin in athletes that would lead to the triumphant British medal count at the London and Rio Olympic Games; in the heritage sector, historic buildings, museums, places of worship, parks and countryside were all being polished up. The Charities Board, set up originally as the Charities Fund to help the needs of those at greatest disadvantage in society and also to improve the quality of life in the community, got off to a slow start as they had to begin their processes from scratch; they too had to suffer journalistic abuse for worthy grants to the likes of refugees or gay people but then achieved the best record in getting money into poorer regions. Meanwhile the time-limited Millennium Commission seemed to concentrate on *grands projets*, the grandest of which was about to become the most contentious of all lottery projects, the Dome.

5. http://www.artsindustry.co.uk/features/embracing-brass/320 (retrieved April 2014).

ARTSWAY, SWAY, NEW FOREST

A good example of the way the lottery was beginning to bring people's dreams to life was an early application made by a former head of art at a comprehensive school in the New Forest. Linda Fredericks had long regretted that there was no dedicated resource for contemporary visual art in an area better known for ponies, landscape and sailing ships; on taking early retirement in 1991 she had found a derelict Victorian coachhouse attached to the local pub in the village of Sway and turned it into a studio. It was good timing: the New Forest District Council (NFDC) had recently commissioned a report which had lamented the lack of visual arts in the area. As a result, Linda obtained a £500 grant from the Sway Parish Council and persuaded the pub owners, Whitbreads, to offer the space at an annual peppercorn rent. Architect Tony Fretton agreed to provide free concept drawings for a new art gallery; his subsequent commission in the face of the Victorianesque designs suggested by NFDC's architect was a triumph for Linda and her steering group. In spite of this snub, the NFDC pledged £60,000 and a further £80,000 was granted by the Foundation for Sport and the Arts, the body set up by Littlewoods and other football pools companies as a protective measure when the introduction of the National Lottery threatened their livelihoods (it was to prove a useful source of partnership funding for several lottery projects). Planning permission was granted for the Fretton designs and then the National Lottery arrived. Linda's bid for ArtSway was one of the first submitted from the Southern region and she wished that she hadn't listened to the advice of Southern Arts who, she felt, were very sceptical about the rural location and the historical lack of contemporary visual arts in the locale. They recommended her to keep the bid low. With £140,000 already in the bag, she could have applied for as much as £560,000 but the first application to ACE was for only £206,000, which was granted in September 1995. This proved insufficient and she had to go through the whole application process again for a second bid for £190,000. Linda did the initial bid herself, with help on programming and the business plan, the latter from a partner from Business and the Arts whose advice was

> Keep it simple, I want the story of what you're going to do in year 1, the story of what you're going to do in year 2 and the story of what you're going to do in year 3. I just want it in one paragraph at the top, key points and a budget, that's all I want. And that is a business plan, A4 one sheet.

This was revolutionary: most bids were accompanied by massive documentation. David Hall recalls having panic attacks when he received three suitcases of paperwork for the Sadler's Wells business planning assessment – with more to come and only four days allotted for the work (although he does say that on no other project assessment did he have to wade through so much repetitive information).

As for actually delivering the project, Linda (who received no salary until 1996) was on the site herself all the time to oversee the contractors and often to spot errors that the architects had missed. In spite of feeling that ACE could have provided much more expertise and advice (which wasn't actually available within the system in the early days), she found the building process

> absolutely fascinating and tremendously rewarding . . . it was the building I wanted with all the things in it that I wanted – how often does one get to do that?

Lack of programming money was a problem but Linda spoke warmly of the generosity of Deanna Petherbridge, professor of drawing at the Royal College of Art, who opened her address book to provide all the contacts for the opening exhibition of drawings by contemporary artists that Linda had set her heart on. Linda also found funds for a resident video artist to set up a very early website for work with the local community, and a digital studio – also one of the first – was incorporated into the building. It was sad therefore for Linda when she got bad food poisoning and had to rise from a hospital bed to attend the opening night in January 1997: this contributed to the exhaustion and burn-out which would lead to her standing down as director in 1998. Before she left she put in successfully for an A4E grant (more about these later) for £299,000 which ensured a three-year programme. It was a success story and for many years the gallery provided exactly the kind of artistic presence in the New Forest which had been its *raison d'être* and about which Southern Arts had been so sceptical.

In later years the programming became more esoteric and there was little attempt to raise money from sources other than the public sector. In 2012 Southern Arts withdrew its grant and the gallery had to close its exhibitions programme for a time, but through a series of local partnerships it has now re-opened in a modest way and with its excellent education work offers an interesting visual arts programme in an area otherwise bereft of such a thing. Nicole Penn-Symons, who was to become ACE lottery projects director, comments that

ArtSway was 'a really lovely resource'. For Linda herself the project represented huge highs and lows. The highs were the fascination and reward of realising the concept, the collaboration with the highest quality of professionals and the rich variety of the local community who gave an immense amount of voluntary time. The lows were her stress and illness, and the fact that her board accepted her resulting resignation without any attempt to persuade her to stay, which left her with a sense of isolation from the project she had created.

4

I TAKE OVER

*What I faced – my first meeting – RADA – starting to monitor – The Public –
new directions – English Stage Company – problems of acknowledgement –
a lot of lobbying – South Bank Centre*

The Council agreed at its January 1996 meeting that the ROH had satisfied, or made satisfactory progress towards, the conditions set for its £55 million grant. This money could therefore start to be released, subject to the receipt of an integrated monthly cash flow model. This was finally produced but became the subject of much acrimony between ACE and the ROH, who seemed to think it outrageous that such a thing should be requested: it even led to one of the ROH board members storming out of a meeting at ACE, kicking and denting a lift door as he went.

The queasy relationship between the ROH and ACE was to take another turn in March when it was announced that Peter Gummer would be leaving the Council to become the chair of the ROH. Before the official announcement was made, he rang me to say that Grey Gowrie was considering asking me to take over the chairing of the Panel. I had in fact heard a rumour about this both from Mary Allen and from Hilary Carty, but had dismissed it as unlikely given my comparative lack of involvement with the capital programme so far; my position as an artform chair barely intersected with the harsher world inhabited by capital projects. I suppose I also didn't see myself as the 'big hitter' that the position seemed to demand. But the call from Grey did indeed come and I was flattered into accepting – I also felt that this was too interesting an opportunity to turn down. A letter followed, dated (perhaps ominously) 1 April, from Virginia Bottomley, now Secretary of State at the DNH, appointing me as a Council member for a further three years 'during which I should like [you] to take special responsibility for the Arts Council's activities as a National Lottery distributor'.

The April Council meeting confirmed my appointment (Deborah MacMillan, artist and widow of the choreographer Kenneth MacMillan, would replace me as chair of the dance panel) and, as lottery projects director, that of Nicole Penn-Symons, who had trained as both an actress and a lawyer and had been development director at Sadler's Wells under a previous regime.

When I took up the position someone asked me if I thought I would have more friends or enemies at the end of my appointment. At the time I thought it a strange question – around the Council table the lottery usually meant good news and a real sense of change – but I immediately started picking up an undercurrent of discontent. Richard Rogers wrote a letter of congratulation on my new appointment which also outlined his serious concerns about the quality of design and the speed of assessment of many of the lottery projects – he wanted more rigorous appraisal, more use of young architects and more involvement by the RABs, especially in the earlier stages of assessment; he also urged that a ninth criterion be created, of 'vision'. Then there was a meeting with Jon Foulds who, while expressing a desire to stand down from the Panel because of pressure of work, wanted to register his concerns about the lack of experience within the lottery team and the intense political pressure to distribute funds. He felt these were leading to over-hasty assessments which would not stand up to scrutiny later; he also suggested that the assessment scores given to partnership funding should reflect the likelihood of its being achieved rather than the bare amount and potential source of the funds. Failures on this front were beginning to appear and they, combined with indications of some large cost overruns, were potentially putting projects at considerable risk. Mary Allen agreed with him in part but felt that Jeremy Newton had recently done a lot to 'beef up' the lottery team and would be able to offer robust reassurances about the strength of his department, especially now that a monitoring section was being set up. Jon Foulds's business expertise would be replaced on the Panel by the recruitment of Dr Neil Cross, a director of the financial group 3i.

At a meeting I had with Secretary of State Virginia Bottomley and Permanent Secretary Hayden Phillips at the DNH there was much talk of the need to publicise ACE's good deeds with lottery money, but also criticism from Virginia that an award had been given to an amateur theatre in her constituency at a time when the professional theatre there was threatened with closure. My argument that the amateur theatre's bid had been a good one and was in line with the desire to bring the National Lottery to the people, whereas the professional theatre was suffering from revenue cuts caused by drops in the grant-in-aid, did not appear to calm her. I also had an invitation to coffee from Denis Vaughan, the Australian-born conductor who had been a great campaigner for the lottery, wanting its proceeds to go to the arts and sport. He was undoubtedly a catalyst for its formation and a visionary in his desire for all young people to have the chance of involvement in those two sectors, but he was considered too much of a maverick to be embraced by any of the good cause distributors in any kind of advisory role.

Before I'd really started to get to grips with what I'd taken on there was a slap in the face. The Joseph Rowntree Foundation published its first *National Lottery Yearbook*[6] which featured detailed figures and analysis about the National Lottery from the Directory of Social Change. These confirmed that lottery sales had totalled £5.1 billion in the first 13 months of operation (about 3 per cent of retail spending) but pointed out that this had been at the expense of other popular forms of gambling (such as football pools, betting shops and bingo) where 8,500 jobs were at risk. It did, however, recognise that the growth in capital projects was having a positive effect on the building industry. Information gathered by the Family Expenditure Survey for the first three months of 1995 showed that 'amongst

6. *Findings*, Social Policy Research 94, Joseph Rowntree Foundation, York, April 1996.

those buying lottery tickets, families from the poorest 10 per cent spent just under £2 per week, though this represented 30 per cent of their leisure spending. In contrast the top ten per cent of families spent almost £4 each week, just 4 per cent of their leisure spending'; but there was 'as yet no useful evidence on whether the lottery is causing social problems'. The National Lottery Charities Board had succeeded in channelling most of its money to the poorest parts of the country, while London and the south-east had gained far more than their fair shares of cash from ACE and the HLF. The editors did, however, point out that the imbalance was in response to applications received and not to any strategic planning – which, of course, we were forbidden to do.

The real attack came in a trenchant review of the *Yearbook* in *Arts Management Weekly* by John Pick, the cultural historian and commentator. He spoke of the 'monstrous blow' to Britain's national culture delivered by the National Lottery, which

> is in itself tacky, vulgar and crass and debases every aspect of our cultural lives . . . the sad truth is that everything about the lottery is corrupting.[7]

Pick had strong moral and social objections to the lottery which were

> not concerned with the rights and wrongs of gambling, but with the impact that a vast government-promoted money-raising scheme has upon every aspect of the value systems which inform our private, social, religious and cultural lives.

Ian Watson, AMW's editor, invited me to respond as he did not feel that Pick's remarks should be allowed to go unchallenged. They were obviously heartfelt and had to be respected, but my reply (which sadly no longer exists) argued that millions of people were buying tickets with little or no apparent sign of hardship; Pick's desire to achieve the necessary repairs to the heritage and arts infrastructure through philanthropy and charitable endeavour hadn't in the past proved in any way realistic; and already new and refurbished buildings, new technology and other equipment were bringing great change into the heart of communities throughout the country.

7. *Arts Management Weekly*, London, Rhinegold Publishing Ltd, April 1996 edition.

The National Lottery has become part of national life and I think few would now recognise Pick's forecast that

> Far into the new millennium we shall still be struggling to explain to our grandchildren how we came to so re-order things that our churches and cathedrals, our castles and monuments, our parklands, galleries and theatres . . . suddenly became dependent upon handouts from state-promoted gambling.

None the less his views do raise a question about where money to support the arts comes from. At no time do I remember a moral argument against lottery money being had within ACE. We were aware of the need, and the lottery gave us the money to address it. In the 1970s and '80s opera companies in particular accepted huge amounts from tobacco companies; nowadays, debates rage over BP Oil's sponsorship of Tate and other large cultural institutions, and there is some denial about touching money from Russian oligarchs (perhaps vainly, given the unlikelihood of such people being willing to engage in the first place). While it would be good to stand on the moral high ground at all times, the reality is that it is a complicated position to maintain and one that changes over decades. The improvement in the quality of experience when visiting any of the examples given by Pick in the quotation above would not have happened without the National Lottery, and I cannot share his sense of doom about the ethical harm it has done.

*

My first Lottery Panel meeting took place on 30 April 1996; it was also Nicole Penn-Symons's first meeting as lottery projects director. I was suffering from a heavy cold and nervousness at chairing such a gathering of qualified people, but was put at ease by the commitment of everyone sitting around the table and a general pride in what was being asked of us. It was, and would remain, a privilege to lead such a body.

It was thirteen months since the first grants had been given out and it was time to review how it was all working. Although there was still more money coming in than going out, demand was growing, new programmes were being mooted and would need an allocation, and it was clear that some form of policy – or at least prioritisation of demand – was urgently needed. It was agreed that each RAB should be asked to prepare a capital strategy for its region: as autonomous bodies they could do this, whereas ACE as a good cause distributor could not. Sue Robertson, then chief executive of Southern Arts, remembers the problems of forming RAB strategies:

> That was the difficulty and the joy of it really, that we were meant to strategise but we had no decision-making powers. That was a tough thing to do, to try and divide strategy from decisions . . . both a good thing and a bad thing. It really challenged the RABs at their own game. They always claimed to be strategic and about economical investment and planning for the region, and were always, I think, critical of the Arts Council about not being strategically driven in the old days, but that was quite a challenge for them: 'OK, be strategic.'

The only region that had been quick off the mark initially was that for which Northern Arts had responsibility. Its chief executive, Peter Hewitt, his deputy Andrew Dixon, and his predecessor Peter Stark had identified – before the lottery was even a serious proposition – that the north-east suffered seriously compared to other regions outside London because of lack of infrastructure. Not for them the enormous Victorian investment in galleries and concert halls that the textile industry in the north-west and the shipping industry on Merseyside had funded. In 1995 they had produced *Case for Capital*, a genuinely strategic document, compiled in consultation with the local authorities and arts organisations of the area as well as other interested parties such as the education sector. This outlined building needs but also what could be achieved in terms of public art. Northern Arts was hosting a highly successful Year of Visual Arts in 1996 as part of Peter Palumbo's initiative to have a different artform celebrated in a different region in the years leading up to the millennium. As *Case for Capital* was being compiled the lottery had arrived, and the north had thus been well positioned to take full advantage.

Local authorities in the region were quick to grasp the possibilities, particularly in Gateshead where an early application to fund Antony Gormley's massive sculpture *The Angel of the North* had been successfully submitted to ACE by Gateshead Council, despite considerable local opposition. This was one of my favourite pieces of lottery-funded public art, and it was a special pleasure to see at close quarters its 20-metre-long frame being welded at the Hartlepool shipyards shortly before it was mounted on a line of trucks to trundle slowly up the A1 to its present position near Gateshead. Once in place it quickly pacified its detractors. Becoming a major attraction with over 150,000 visitors a year and being seen by over 90,000 drivers a day, it was one of the first projects to enhance the image of public art.

Gateshead Council's ambition remained exemplary: the art gallery Baltic and the Regional Music Centre (later to be known as The Sage Gateshead in tribute to a generous commercial sponsor) would be two further major projects funded. Much of the credit for this goes to two extraordinary councillors – George Gill, the leader of the Council, and Sid Henderson, who chaired its arts and libraries committee. Peter Hewitt remembers Gill in particular as

> A brilliant leader with a fantastic vision and an ability to drive something forward, he had the ability to recognise . . . a good idea and then to back it absolutely resolutely and to bring people around him in his own inimitable way.

Gerry Robinson, who was to become ACE's chair in 1998, also praises the use by the two men of combined City Council and arts lottery funding to make a phenomenal change to the way that Gateshead felt and moved. Between them they brought about the cultural regeneration of what had been a pretty dismal area, tapping into the funding of not only ACE but all the other good cause distributors as well.

There were 144 grant applications at my first meeting, of which 44 were rejected and 100 agreed for recommendation to the Council, to a total of £48.246 million. Substantial amounts were allocated to London's Serpentine Gallery; Cumbria Theatre Trust for Theatre by the Lake, Keswick, whose first application had been rejected on the grounds of design quality but who had listened to advice and reapplied; the Octagon Theatre Bolton; Salisbury Arts Theatre; Bournemouth and Poole College of Further Education; and Darts–Doncaster Community Arts Project. A film, *The Rake's Progress*, was granted £1.1 million but I don't know if it was ever made (the only film of that name seems to be Sidney Gilliat's 1945 one starring Rex Harrison and Lilli Palmer).

*

The largest recommendation was for an application for £22.752 million from the Royal Academy of Dramatic Art (RADA) for the refurbishment of its headquarters which lay between Gower and Malet Streets in London's Bloomsbury. Bryan Avery, the architect appointed by RADA's then chairman, Lord (Richard) Attenborough, remembered the problems of taking on the job of creating a cohesive whole out of the labyrinthine structure:

> The place was leaking, you couldn't get from one side of the building to the other, you had to go through the dressing rooms or over the roof.

There had been an attempt to move RADA to better premises in Hoxton but this had failed because of lack of money: fundraising had stalled when, at a gala starring John Gielgud, there had been an ominous crack and the stage had descended by six inches with several of the evening's dignitaries on it. Bryan stressed the impact that the lottery's arrival made, both financially but even more importantly in terms of architectural quality. He described how his original block-and-tackle design to take scenery down to the workshop level at RADA was rejected by the assessing theatre panel of the Association of British Theatre Technicians, who urged a proper stage lift:

> It was a huge moment because it suddenly revealed to RADA that they'd had to change their thought process and as an architect of course it was a huge blessing. I'd never been faced with a demand for greater quality, normally I'm cost-engineering down to the meanest-spirited thing imaginable so to be forcibly pushed in the direction of quality was hugely important.

Prior to the arrival of the lottery he remembered feeling patronised by the French with their *grands projets*; now the British

> had our own little *projets* which were grandish [specifically the Turbine Hall at Tate Modern and the Great Court at the British Museum], and you can't really over-estimate how important that is, not just for architects but for self-esteem, national confidence and all that sort of stuff that came to be in the 2000s and it's still with us, right through to the Olympics in the sense that you can do these things.

The project was hugely complicated. The unification of the whole building with its many differing levels made access particularly difficult. During the course of building work a long dispute began with ACE about changes to the design of the foyer which considerably reduced disabled access but, it was argued, was essential for its dual role as the interface with the public and as the only communal space for the students when they were not in class. Work was initially hindered by water pouring into the foundations from a source eventually found to be the city's aquaflow flooding into the Northern Line of the tube system, which necessitated the whole base of the building to be tanked like a great ship. Bryan Avery compared the three years it took to rebuild RADA with the eighteen months it took to put up the IMAX cinema in Waterloo which he also designed, the latter being a new-build on a site that was clear (albeit with the London Underground beneath and homeless occupants who had first to be moved to another space). The IMAX was also ACE lottery-funded, the British Film Institute (BFI) having been awarded a £15 million grant in October 1996. One of its particular strengths was a huge facade bright with a work by Howard Hodgkin, promoted by the BFI with the intention that it would be replaced every two years with an artwork of similar quality. Funding problems meant this never happened, and the facade is now used for advertisements, a situation which so upset Bryan Avery that he said he doesn't like passing by it.

There were also financial uncertainties around the RADA bid. It had been running a deficit for several years and part of the partnership funding for the capital bid was to set up an endowment trust for future income. But it was still the years of lottery plenty and, in spite of a low assessment score for financial viability, the need to tackle the site's deficiencies, and optimism about chairman Richard Attenborough's persuasive fundraising skills, got the application through. It was to prove one of the most difficult projects that had to be dealt with in the next few years.

*

Nicole Penn-Symons soon began the monitoring process. Michael Prescott, a consultant brought in originally by Jeremy Newton to create a practice manual for the application assessment, was asked to draw up a similar procedural document. A team had to be recruited and Nicole looked for people who not only appreciated and loved the arts but who had some professional qualification as well. Some of the operations team had been recruited from other departments of ACE after the downsizing which followed the PriceWaterhouse review and she feels that although they were very bright arts officers they did not always have the legal and construction knowledge needed for a capital programme. David Hall also speaks of the initial lack of knowledge within the lottery department as to how to assess a capital project – although all concerned were taking crash courses through experience. The monitoring department[8] had its work cut out: 542 grants had been awarded by the end of March 1996, many of which were already funding projects under construction; such were the demands for space within Great Peter Street that it had to move offices four times until it finally joined the operations team in Portland House. This hardly helped the tensions between the operations and monitoring departments, which were there from the start.

*

By June another contentious application was on the table. A community arts organisation, Jubilee Arts, was requesting £24.15 million for a regeneration project at its base in West Bromwich, named at the time c/plex. The Panel expressed deep concern about the ability of a small organisation to deliver this but none the less recommended a development grant of £400,000. This was the first of many debates about what was to become one of the most notorious of all ACE lottery projects. Its instigator, Sylvia King, was a supreme lobbyist: for years she persuaded politicians and senior management at ACE to continue to back the scheme against the advice of both the Panel and the Council.

It was finally built as The Public[9] – to a design that its renowned architect Will Alsop described as his 'box of delights' – but since its opening in

8. It was officially known as Projects but always referred to as Monitoring, so I have used the familiar name throughout.
9. Although the project was known as c/plex during my time at ACE, I have called it The Public throughout to avoid confusion.

2008 to its closure in 2013 its history was one of constant crisis, as was set out in a full report on the project in 2011 which ACE commissioned from assessor Anthony Blackstock. This noted that out of the final building costs of £52.6 million, ACE's total investment was £31.8 million with a further £4.1 million paid in revenue grants (other funding came from the Regional Development Agency Advantage West Midlands, the European Regional Development Fund [ERDF] and the Metropolitan Borough of Sandwell). Blackstock is deeply critical of the way Council members did not listen to their own Panel which consistently recommended rejection, particularly during the critical years between 2001 and 2003 when the decisions to give the full grant and the green light to the project were made, mainly at the instigation of the then chief executive Peter Hewitt. More positively, Blackstock does note that ACE had promised to tighten up its processes as a result.

The Public seems to have been unique in the support it gained against majority advice, but it stands with the National Centre for Popular Music (see page 109) as a target for critics of the capital progamme. While no one would deny that both had disastrous outcomes, it is surely unfair to highlight them continually, usually without mention of the thousands of projects that delivered great benefit and success. Blackstock's report ended on an optimistic note:

> The people of West Bromwich increasingly make use of the facilities and there is hope for its future enjoyment. In 2010/11 it received 157,000 visits, confirming an upward trend.

However, ACE refused to commit to further funding and in November 2013 The Public's brief life as an arts centre ended following Sandwell Council's withdrawal of its grant. The building was turned into a sixth form college. Peter Hewitt now expresses real regret that he pursued the project with such zeal against so much advice: he cites political pressure and the ambition and commitment of Sandwell Council in what was – and still is – one of the most deprived areas of the country.

*

By the end of June I was writing to all RAB chairs, the first salvo in the battle to establish some kind of national capital strategy. This was still not allowed under the directions, so the letter requested details of all anticipated bids over £1 million for the next five years, as well as a closer look at likely future revenue implications when assessing capital bids. This was a couple of months after the matter had been discussed at the April Panel meeting, so it seems likely that initial soundings to their senior staff had not borne much fruit and it was thought more effective action might be taken at chair level. Or perhaps it was just that throughout the system everyone was busy preparing for the next major stage in the distribution of lottery funds.

At the end of 1995, it had been announced that the Treasury grant to ACE for 1996/97 would suffer a reduction of £5 million, from the £191.1 million welcomed the year before back to £186.1 million. Possibly the impact of the lottery was giving the public the perception that the arts were now well-funded. The contrast between lottery plenty and revenue starvation was beginning to cause real pain to the infrastructure of arts organisations. Lottery income to the end of March 1996 would be £244.194 million. Some immediate alleviation to the squeezed Treasury grant could be found by switching £4.3 million of ACE overheads to the lottery account: a pattern was forming and more accurate forecasts could be made of the amount of time spent on lottery matters by ACE and RAB staff. Still, more drastic action was needed. There was also an instinct that New Labour were going to win the election which had to take place within 18 months. Around this time Graham Hitchen, ACE's director of corporate policy, alerted Mary Allen to talks he was having with David Miliband, then a senior researcher at the Institute for Policy and Public Research, about the need to use lottery money for wider community interests.

The quantity of lottery money coming in on the one hand, and the pressure on revenue on the other, persuaded the DNH to explore with ACE ways of introducing non-capital programmes without usurping the 'additionality' principle. On the same April Fool's Day on which my ACE membership had been renewed, new lottery directions were announced. These would allow for other programmes, in addition to those existing for capital and film, to be developed in the areas of access and participation and the creative abilities of young people. The poor financial health of many of ACE's regular clients could be looked at through a plan which would come to be known as stabilisation. The idea of capital expenditure covering publications, recordings and new technology was widened, and rules for the commissioning of new work were relaxed. The task for ACE was now to forge a symbiotic relationship between Treasury funds, which could be spent strategically, and lottery money which had to be distributed on the basis of open application.

The publication of the new directions immediately caused tensions. The artform departments wanted lottery money for the organisations they supported, but were inhibited by the fact that lottery grants had to be given on a one-off basis without longterm commitment; others, including some of the RAB chief executives and Graham Hitchen, saw a real opportunity for ACE to create more partnership between its existing clients and a broader constituency – in fact, to develop an alternative direction for arts funding. Before joining ACE, Graham had been director of the British Youth Council for five years and brought with him his passion for youth and community work; he wanted to ensure that new organisations benefited rather than, say, the education departments of existing ones. His radicalism contributed to a strategy document from Mary Allen entitled *Future Directions for the National Lottery and the Arts*, which went to the Council in May 1996 and which formed the basis for the ensuing consultation. This included the ambition that

> from being a body concerned almost exclusively with the professional arts . . . [the Arts Council] is now able to respond to ideas from a far wider range of people covering the whole spectrum of artistic activity, including amateur and small community groups, youth groups and commercial arts enterprises in addition to those working in numerous subsidised arts organisations . . . [Its] ambitious option will be to make the funding available to everyone in a way which challenges artificial divisions and, in doing so, encourages a genuinely democratic and accessible culture, led by artists and audiences.

Each new programme would need its own criteria, although common factors would be quality of work, financial stability and strategic relevance. A huge consultation process began to examine the new programmes: two committees of Council (one dealing with overall strategy and programme content and the other with administration); three advisory groups led by external advisors (on new work, access and participation and creative abilities of young people); detailed work on a pilot stabilisation programme; extensive discussions by the Lottery Panel and a two-day meeting of the Council in early April at which the programmes formed a large part of the discussions as we faced up to their implications. The allocation of money between capital and new programmes would have to be agreed and the relationship between ACE and the RABs in assessing them would mean looking again at advisory structures, always a contentious subject between the two sides of the funding system. It was an exciting time: now that the base for lottery funding was being broadened we all felt that a real change in the way that ACE worked and the people it involved lay ahead.

While all this activity was going on, the only concrete decision made was to set up a stabilisation committee of the Lottery Panel. To chair this, David Brierley, who had recently retired as general manager of the RSC, now joined the Panel. Stabilisation was an initiative from North America, originally designed by the Ford Foundation to create endowments for arts organisations. We have seen that ACE wasn't keen on endowments: its immediate problem was the substantial deficits that many organisations carried after many years of standstill funding, together with a general lack of unrestricted reserves to replenish balance sheets and supply working capital. The idea of injecting lottery money into a stabilisation scheme, which would address both the artistic purpose of an organisation and its ability to deliver it, appealed to ministers and, after much discussion about the importance of ensuring that this was a robust process and not one that would simply reward failure, the DNH had prepared a new policy direction to allow it. Consultant David Pratley was given the job of leading a pilot programme with the advisory help of the committee; the first applications for an initial pilot programme were received in September amid complaints that organisations which had already received capital grants were ineligible. The reason for this was that to meet the criterion of financial stability applicants could not show any instability.

Another committee of the Panel was also now established. Architectural design was initially assessed by a committee of the visual arts panel but this had other work to do and did not have time to look properly at the mass of applications pouring in. Patty Hopkins remembers considerable 'muddle' in the early days over the assessment of this essential part of any building, and the architecture advisory committee, now set up under her chairmanship, was able to look at the design element in much more detail than had been done before. Paying tribute to her fellow architects who gave substantial amounts of time to sit on the committee, she remembers it as an exciting moment: at last there was money available for capital projects together with a desire for the schemes to go well and to be a credit to ACE. Nicole Penn-Symons expresses gratitude for her support and found her advice particularly important because she knew the practical implications of design and the build process in contrast to the more programme-based experience of most of the Panel.

*

Problems were arising with another major project: in October 1995 the English Stage Company (ESC) had been awarded a grant of £15.8 million for a total refurbishment of the Royal Court Theatre in London's Sloane Square. By June 1996 the project was in trouble. Protracted negotiations with the landlords, the Cadogan Estate, were not producing confirmation of partnership funding, and complicated discussions were taking place with London Underground and Thames Water over a plan by the architect, Steve Tompkins, to provide space for an income-generating restaurant and bar that wasn't available on the theatre site. This plan was to tunnel under the road and emerge in the middle of Sloane Square, with the entrance where a ladies' loo had once stood. The ESC also needed funding for its closure costs: it was thought imperative to keep two theatres open for the company's work, and they wanted to sign leases with the Duke of York's and Ambassadors theatres in London's West End. The company was now asking for a further £903,000; £477,000 was agreed, the rest deferred pending more information on closure costs. A note to me from Jeremy Newton scribbled at the June Panel meeting said, 'I'm still convinced this is the most dangerous project we're involved in . . . I can see us having to bail this project out at least once or twice more.' He was right: two further applications contributed a further £3.87 million to the scheme.

From the ESC point of view it must have been one of the very hardest projects to manage, and one can only commend the resilience of artistic director Stephen Daldry and general manager Vikki Heywood, on whom the day-to-day responsibility rested. At the time of her appointment Vikki hadn't even been told that a lottery application had been made. She was also working with an inexperienced team: Simon Harper, formerly production manager at London's Almeida Theatre who had now switched to capital project management with the Royal Court as his first construction job, describes how all concerned were wondering

> How do we do this, we've never done this before – we had an architect who'd never designed a theatre before, we had a theatre consultant who wasn't used to dealing with a client who really knew what they wanted and had already designed it in their heads . . . the whole project felt like a wild west frontier town some days.

He didn't find the move from theatre production to construction difficult:

> I've always been interested in the building industry, always been interested in theatre architecture and the fabric of those buildings. You need to understand how a fly-tower works and to do that you need to understand how you build the fly-tower and you just get drawn into the mechanics of it . . . It's quite exciting to work out how you actually deliver things, what's the best way of procuring something, what's the best and most effective way of designing it. Who do you need to consult with to get the right group of people? Theatre is a most fantastically collaborative art and good construction projects are the same.

Some of the dramas were highlighted in a BBC *Omnibus* film of November 1996 by Stephen Daldry and David Lan, then the theatre's writer-in-residence. This shows the long consultation period with the directors and designers who had been most involved with the Royal Court's distinguished history; the high-wire juggling involving delays to the planning process; the urgent need to sign the leases at the West End theatres while ACE dithered about supplying more money; the Kensington and Chelsea Council planning meeting at which permission was only given for half the project (the meeting had to be reconvened to finalise the job); the vain attempts to get corporates interested. Vikki Heywood also remembers the early explorations underneath Sloane Square:

It was like *The Great Escape*, we had a little tent on Sloane Square with inside two men digging down to work out exactly where the Tube line ran, losing the sand out of the bottom of their trousers every evening. And I used to look out of the window and see that it had moved overnight, another three feet to the left or the right!

There were frustrations with ACE's project monitors who, in their attempts to explain the project's problems to their lottery supervisors, were deemed to have 'gone native' and were replaced (although Vikki does pay tribute to the way matters changed when Nicole Penn-Symons took over the monitoring); anxieties about the extreme limitations of the footprint which led to the contractors underestimating the project and causing a year's delay while they altered their whole approach to the construction process; and dramas over the raising of the partnership funds. All seemed lost on this front when the Cadogan Estate's demands proved too onerous; other options finally vanished at a fundraising party at which part of the entertainment consisted of an actress fantasising over being screwed by a man with the biggest dick in the world. The ESC was living up to its subversive reputation but potential donors left quickly.

The morning after this debacle Vikki's despair was relieved by a call from Alan Grieve, chair of the Jerwood Foundation, who suggested that she needed help and said that he was prepared to provide a substantial sum. The downside lay in the fact that in return he wanted proper acknowledgement for his contribution. Alan has always denied the idea that he wanted to call it the Jerwood Royal Court Theatre, as was widely reported in the media at the time. Certainly investigations were made about putting any name before 'Royal' in a title. In his book *The Summer of a Dormouse*, John Mortimer, chair of the Royal Court at the time, humorously describes the progression from Lord Chamberlain to Colonel Somebody at Buckingham Palace, on to Mavis and then Jenny at the Home Office. The request finally arrived on the desk of the Home Secretary, Jack Straw, himself. All agreed that it was a 'grey area' but the final upshot of the controversy was that, though no one knew how the Court Theatre had come to be called Royal, once that prefix was attached it could not be preceded by any other name. It was finally agreed that the two theatres within the Royal Court should become the Jerwood Upstairs and the

Jerwood Downstairs, but playwrights were by now up in arms at what they saw as the noble name of the Royal Court being besmirched. Alan Grieve was summoned to an edgy meeting in Peg's Club in Soho (which he describes as 'having the feel of a brothel') with three playwrights:

> I was eventually ushered into a room where Harold Pinter was sitting in the middle and David Hare was to his right and Caryl Churchill was lying languidly on a sort of chaise-longue . . . And I was then cross-examined: why did I want any acknowledgement of the Jerwood Foundation if we made this grant to the Royal Court? And they took me through it; Pinter didn't say a lot – although I should just say that of course I was offered a drink. It must have been late afternoon and as you know in the arts world time doesn't matter much. I think Harold Pinter had a champagne so we had champagne. And I don't think either David Hare or Caryl Churchill had a drink. I was cross-examined but eventually we were getting nowhere because I wasn't going to abandon my belief that a grant of this sort should be acknowledged by the recipient . . . And Caryl Churchill I think walked with me, or we all walked maybe together and I remember her last remarks were, 'Well, I don't see why, you don't own capital, you use capital, you don't own anything, why should you have your name or anything like that?' Now, Caryl Churchill is a distinguished playwright, she is still writing for the Royal Court with considerable distinction and she is a very radical-thinking lady and her thoughts are still those. She is left-leaning, left-thinking and does not believe that capital has a necessary place in the arts and if it does it should be restricted; actually I don't agree with that because I think capital does have a position and capital has to be acknowledged as capital but in a proper and reasonable way.

The meeting thus ended in stalemate. Alan says that subsequently John Mortimer offered to drop Jerwood if the playwrights were able to come up with the £3 million 'but of course . . .'. The 'naming' battle was seen to have been won by Jerwood, who went on to support – and to be acknowledged by – many other capital projects, including (among ACE lottery projects) the Jerwood Vanbrugh Theatre at RADA, the Jerwood Centre for the Treatment and Prevention of Dance Injuries for Birmingham Royal Ballet at the Birmingham Hippodrome, and Jerwood Hall at LSO St Luke's.

*

An ongoing frustration for the Panel was the Council's delay in agreeing a funding logo which lottery projects would have to display. This requirement had been mentioned the previous autumn but always deferred, and in many of those who had received grants its absence was encouraging a disinclination to credit what was often the major source of their funding. Projects were by now opening all over the country with little, if any, hint that they had been the beneficiaries of substantial lottery funds. As politicians and civil servants were keen to point out, this was hindering the promotion of ACE as a good cause. Authority was finally given to Grey Gowrie, Richard Rogers and myself to approve a design. I am not sure now how any of us, particularly given the high design standards of the first two, allowed the final version – a tormented squiggle that suggested both a musical clef and a sterling pound sign. An apocryphal story has it that Grey's chauffeur, asked about the colour, said, 'Yellow. That's the colour of gold, isn't it?' and so it came about. But not for long: the DNH had always been keen for us to use the Camelot lottery logo of a smiley face doubling as a hand displaying two crossed fingers, and soon after I left ACE their wish (or rather that of their successor, DCMS) was granted. The yellow squiggle disappeared – literally, as I have been unable to track it down either on buildings or within ACE itself. The only image I have been able to retrieve comes from a small credit in a book about the New Art Gallery Walsall which accounts for the rather poor quality of the picture shown here. Aesthetically, this airbrushing of history was probably right but it's sad that its more general replacement doesn't also set a higher standard of design.

It remained difficult to get some projects to acknowledge their lottery support. In March 1997 I attended the unveiling by H.M. The Queen of a statue commemorating Raoul Wallenberg, the Swedish businessman who saved thousands of Jewish lives during the Second World War. It had been commissioned by the Holocaust Educational Trust with a £60,000 lottery grant. Although many sponsors and supporters of this were publicly thanked, no mention was made of ACE, which had put up the majority of the money. My letter to a representative of the Western Marble Arch Synagogue (which was involved in the bid and hosted the opening), asking to know what arrangements were being made for a permanent lottery credit to be placed near to the statue, went unanswered. Religious organisations in particular seemed to think that it was OK to take the money but not to acknowledge where it came from.

There was also a lot of lobbying. Over the summer months of 1996 my diary entries include a lunch with Alan Borg, director of the V&A, and architect Daniel Libeskind who wanted to talk up the advantages of a proposed addition to the V&A Museum. Although an application was eventually submitted it never came to anything, because it arrived when the money was running out.[10] I got paperwork from Professor Anthony Smith (a former Council member) challenging a decision not to fund extensions to Magdalen College, Oxford; and hurt feelings from Bob Scott, the theatre manager who had valiantly attempted to get the Olympic Games to Manchester, over a rejection for refurbishment of the Lyceum Theatre in London's West End. Bob was concerned at what this meant for bids from the rest of the commercial sector, which had been eligible to apply for lottery grants from early on. In spite of policies being drawn up and discussions taking place, theatre owners, particularly those in the West End, found it difficult to meet the criteria, particularly those concerning public access and benefit, a situation not helped by a certain reluctance to open up their accounting books. Furthermore, many of those West End theatres that needed refurbishment were listed, and English Heritage's insistence that they were restored to their original state flew in the face of what was needed from them in the twenty-first century. Although some owners, notably Cameron Mackintosh, are now investing substantial amounts in their buildings, the West End remains a place of long queues for ladies' loos front of house, and cramped dressing rooms often up several flights of stairs (although it was announced in the autumn of 2016 that the Theatres Trust was launching a 'Spend a Penny' project with the financial support of Sue and Simon Ruddick to improve ladies' loos throughout the country, including those in West End theatres). In December 2013 a plaster fall at the Apollo Theatre in Shaftesbury Avenue caused a certain

10. The extension had to wait until 2015 when AL_A architects were commissioned to build it. It opened to the public in the summer of 2017.

amount of injury to its audience, though thankfully no deaths. One area where commercial managers were controversially involved was in taking on the management of lottery-funded theatres: the ATG Group did this at both Milton Keynes Theatre and the Regent Theatre and Victoria Hall, Stoke-on-Trent. The Panel did discuss the proprieties of this in March 1997 but agreed that it was a good way to make the theatres sustainable. These agreements were already well in place by the time Rosemary Squire, executive director of ATG, joined the Panel in May 1999, giving it her considerable experience of theatre, both commercial and subsidised.

There was much challenge and interest in being involved with such a widely varied programme of work, but at times I did feel the stress of not being in complete control, a limitation that often creates tension for non-executives. While comparing Jeremy Newton to a speedboat, Mary Allen had gone on to say that, as a result of being asked to do far too much in far too short a time, she felt there was not always enough attention to the detail that existed under the waves. I too felt this, especially when looking at the conditions that had been attached to lottery grants and whether or not they were being fulfilled.

The lottery department was working under enormous pressure and I'm sure that my quibbles about the quality of the paperwork were as irritating to its staff as they were to me. There was one particular and personal blow: my day job at the time had become running the Arts Foundation, which gave fellowships to artists in a number of artforms. I wanted to widen its activities and, before becoming directly involved in lottery matters, I had submitted an application to set up a musical instrument fund to supply talented young musicians with instruments they could not afford. A lot of work had gone into the application (I'd like to think that being aware of what this actually involved was helpful when I took over chairing the Panel) and the Panel recommended it – I had, of course, left the room during the discussion. The Council, however, while approving its intention, rejected the application because of the close association of both myself and Grey Gowrie, who was also the Foundation's chair. They felt this would have a negative public relations effect. As with the difficulties of completing the application form, the disappointment gave me some empathy with other rejected applicants.

*

Regular gentle pressure also came from Richard Rogers who, in spite of leaving the room when the matter came up, none the less made it clear that his project as architect with the SBC needed urgent attention from the Council. At the time, the SBC was a lumpen pile of grey buildings surrounded by a web of concrete walkways, deserted apart from a trickle of visitors to exhibitions at its Hayward Gallery or audiences arriving for nightly concerts in its Royal Festival and Queen Elizabeth Halls. As already noted, an application to transform the site had been one of the first received by ACE and had immediately undergone rigorous assessment by a range of consultants as well as ACE staff. It was universally acknowledged that something needed to be done both to the grim outer aspect and the uninviting spaces inside, and Richard had come up with an interesting solution which included throwing a glass canopy over the Hayward Gallery, Queen Elizabeth Hall and Purcell Room. However, for all his architectural expertise, he had not resolved what was to happen in the artistic spaces underneath, much to the frustration of the assessors. At ACE we felt that artistically the SBC had lost its way; the bid itself also raised substantial questions about business planning and financial viability. Because of the need to address these issues, the Council had agreed only the development grant of £980,000 in its first awards of March 1995. By June 1996 a full bid for £127 million had come in, but the artistic and financial concerns remained, and now there were question marks over the proposed retail premises as well as the access requirements. After more discussion the Council awarded a further development grant of £1.2 million, asserting that more work was needed on many aspects of the bid and warning that the overall cost of the scheme needed to be significantly brought down.

*

One of the final dates of my summer of being lobbied was a lunch with Jeremy Thomas and Wilf Stevenson, respectively chair and director of the BFI. I was nervous in advance about this, as the relationship between ACE and the BFI had not always been cordial (for reasons that will be outlined in the next chapter). But, as I noted afterwards to Jeremy Newton, their late arrival and the fact that at the time they were awaiting our decision on their plan to build the IMAX cinema in London's Waterloo, seemed to keep them on their best behaviour. I hope they felt the same about me.

5

A SHORT BREAK FOR SOME FILM

From the early days of John Major's good idea it was always intended that lottery funding should benefit film. The history of government support for the UK film industry had not been a happy one since 1985, when the Eady Levy, a tax on box office receipts which was reinvested into film production, and capital allowances, which had been used by producers as a form of tax relief, were both abolished. Subsequent lobbying by producers, furious at this dual loss, had persuaded Margaret Thatcher to chair a seminar on the subject in 1990 which led to an in-depth review of all sectors of the film industry. As a result of this, the British Film Commission was set up to support the production of international films in the UK, while another quango, British Screen, received an extra £5 million for European co-productions and a more constructive approach to EU initiatives was adopted. Then the National Lottery arrived. In the film industry it was not popular that ACE would be the distributor in charge of allotting the money. During the months before the lottery went on sale an extensive consultation – greater, apparently, than had been given to the capital programme itself – was put in place. It was not until March 1995 that the Council finally approved the guidelines for supporting film production and introduced an initial year-long pilot with an allocated budget of £10 million.

The consultation was pretty hostile. Of all the bodies that were in various ways connected with the distribution of funds to the industry, the BFI felt most strongly that its position had been usurped, in spite of the conflict of interest that would obviously have existed if it had a role as both producer and investor. The relationship between ACE and the BFI had not been good since the early 1970s when the Institute had complained about ACGB's increasing interest in supporting art films and an enquiry, chaired by Richard Attenborough, had recommended that 'the Arts Council should embrace and encourage film-making as a fine art activity'.[11] British Screen also had a go, intemperately saying that making awards of up to £2 million to a single production (the maximum proposed) was like putting 'pure heroin on the streets'. It was assumed that ACE would be interested only in 'art' films without commercial appeal, and there was general consensus that there wasn't the right level of expertise within ACE to assess the bids. Fair enough: film applications were to be overseen by the Lottery Panel (of which film producer David Puttnam was a member, although it would not be his job to consider the detail) but in the early days there was little specialised knowledge within the lottery department itself.

Individual applications were sent out for assessment to qualified advisors but they did not have an easy brief. Initially, the application form and criteria on which film bids were assessed were the same as those for capital projects and this often led to difficult judgements and decisions: how do you describe public benefit in relation to a commercial film? How does quality of design mesh with quality of artistic activity, and how do you score a film application on local, regional and national development plans? The programme was open to films of widely varying content and budgets; some producers, who themselves had differing levels of experience and taste, apparently found difficulty in 'pitching' their projects so that they would find favour with ACE – and indeed with the BFI and British Screen, now partially mollified by being brought in as external assessors.

*

11. *Report of the Arts Council Film Committee of Enquiry* (London, Arts Council of Great Britain, 1973), p. 6.

The lottery department and Panel struggled to make its decisions, but the climate around ACE's handling of film applications was not helped by a row that blew up in the summer of 1996, shortly after I'd taken over chairing the Panel. This was about the film *Love is the Devil*, whose producers were appealing against an earlier rejection by the Council. Although it had been recommended for funding by the Panel, Grey Gowrie in particular had concerns about its quality and, as he felt, its trivialisation of the life of the artist Francis Bacon; particular pressure to reject the bid was applied to some Council members by the art critic David Sylvester. Following a review process, during which its director John Maybury agreed to some reworking of the script, it was finally approved by a Council vote – one of the few occasions I remember this being used. Starring Derek Jacobi as Francis Bacon and Daniel Craig as his lover George Dyer the film went on to win positive reviews and three awards at the Edinburgh International Film Festival. In spite of it having cost him his friendship with Sylvester (who found out that he had voted in its favour), *Love is the Devil* remains one of Christopher Frayling's favourite lottery-backed films: all the better, he feels, for not showing any of Bacon's paintings – 'usually, very lazily, you get all these montages of the greatest hits'. Another lottery film that achieved some success that year was *True Blue*, directed by Ferdinand Fairfax and starring Dominic West: it was chosen for the Royal Command film performance which it was then a glamorous bonus to attend, with Grey Gowrie, Mary Allen and our 'spice' (as Grey memorably named husbands and wives).

*

Peter Gummer had recognised early on that something needed to be done to put ACE on a better footing with the film industry. He had asked Carolyn Lambert, a civil servant in the DNH with some experience of the film world (she had handled film industry policy for several years in the Department of Trade and Industry's Films branch), to review how this could be done. She had recommended the setting up of a dedicated film unit within the lottery department and successfully applied for the job of running it. She now says she did this out of

> hubris because what the film industry wanted was real film people and although I knew how the film industry worked, linked together and all the rest of it I'd never negotiated a film budget or a deal, nor had the people in my department.

She was unable to recruit a team of specialists (lawyer, creative producer, script reader and accountant) to give the necessary support because such people would demand far higher salaries than ACE could pay. Negotiation experience was vital in the film world because it was on the basis of the final deal that profits were distributed. Weakness in this area would cost ACE dear, especially as its maximum grant of £2 million could have represented at least half of production costs: *Four Weddings and a Funeral,* made in 1994 just before the lottery came onstream, had a $4.4 million budget, *Billy Elliot,* one of the last ACE-funded films of 2000, came in at $5 million. Carolyn does not think ACE's earnings from the latter were commensurate with the level of its investment. She had also recommended the setting up of a separate film advisory panel which came into being in September 1996, with film and television producer Charles Denton joining the Council to chair it. This also did not turn out as Carolyn had hoped: instead of a small group of dedicated experts, ACE had to abide by its own policy of recruiting its panels from a wide background that addressed gender, geography and cultural diversity. This helped add expertise to the range of film work that ACE now supported, but could not provide enough clout for commercial exploitation.

One of the film panel's first jobs was to oversee the process of deciding upon the bidding for 'franchises'. David Puttnam had proposed earlier in 1996 that, rather than the ad hoc approach so far adopted, a substantial part of the money given to commercial film should be handed to organisations who would use it both for project development and to leverage additional investment from the private sector. They would then deliver the whole process of making and distributing a series of films. It seems strange to remember that the decision to proceed with franchises had been taken before the establishment of the film panel but at least that panel would have the responsibility of deciding upon them.

Meanwhile the Council retained its own film, video and broadcasting department, responsible for funding films in those media which were directly concerned with the arts. In December 1996, as part of an exercise to transfer as much money from revenue to lottery as possible, it was suggested that the department be closed and its work transferred to the lottery department, overseen by the film advisory panel. This was not easy to do because the work of the film, video and broadcasting department, particularly in broadcasting, was incompatible with the criteria that had by then been established for lottery-funded film. After extensive lobbying from the sector, it was finally agreed that £2 million should be made available from lottery film budgets for the support of arts broadcasting projects, amid reassurances that the importance of broadcasting considerations should be central to the Council's work.

In April 1999, after yet another film policy review which the Department for Culture, Media & Sport (DCMS, successor to the DNH) had instigated (this time led by film producer Stewart Till), it was decided to transfer responsibility for the distribution of lottery film money to a separate UK Film Council. This was set up in 2000, combining the activities of organisations such as the British Film Commission and British Screen as well as providing funding for the BFI. The initial idea was to subsume the BFI into the Film Council but it managed to maintain its independence while relying on the Film Council for most of its public income. In an ironic twist Jeremy Hunt, when he came to power in 2010 as first Secretary of State at the DCMS in the Tory/Lib Dem coalition, abolished the Film Council – apparently without consultation – and transferred its work to the BFI.

Back in 2000, the Film Council seemed a more natural place for film money to be and I don't think anyone at ACE regretted its loss. I certainly felt some relief that film applications would be in more knowledgeable hands. The commercial imperatives – to say nothing of the constant wranglings with the BFI – never fitted in well with ACE's public funding ethos and the two sides parted without many tears. However, it is a pity to write off ACE's film lottery years as a failure, as some critics have done. Many highly reputable films were produced, and if box office takings rarely covered costs there were many other arguments for the investments: artistic quality, increasing diversity, jobs, commentary on British life and the role of the British cinema. These are analysed in detail in *The People's Pictures: National Lottery Funding and British Cinema* by James Caterer, who worked in the lottery film department of ACE and wrote on the subject as his academic thesis before becoming senior lecturer in film studies at Oxford Brookes University and turning the thesis into this fascinating book.

ROYAL EXCHANGE THEATRE, MANCHESTER

On 15 June 1996 the centre of Manchester was devastated by an IRA bomb. Fortunately the police were given forty minutes' warning and evacuated the busy Saturday morning crowds; no one lost their life. But the damage was huge and in the eye of the storm was the Royal Exchange Theatre. No one realised at first how badly the building had suffered – the executive director Pat Weller telephoned artistic director Braham Murray to say that it was very bad news and they might lose the matinee, little knowing that it would be well over two years before another performance was given in the building. The company had already submitted a lottery bid for general refurbishments (the theatre was twenty years old and there had only been enough funding for basics when it was erected within the old Royal Exchange building); in spite of the circumstances, Braham remembers his initial reaction was one of joy. He realised that any rebuilding would facilitate a much more ambitious capital scheme, eventually providing a studio theatre (which he badly wanted for the kind of work he couldn't do in the main house), a state of the art workshop, a rehearsal room and a floor for office space that didn't have to be shared with the dressing rooms. He also remembers Thelma Holt calling and saying, 'Braham darling, I knew you were clever, I didn't know you were this clever!' His only retrospective regret was that the scope and duration of the work meant laying off a number of staff. With the help of Howard Bernstein (chief executive of a council task force appointed to oversee the redesign and rebuilding of the city centre), he immediately installed the company in a mobile theatre that they had been using for touring and, together with Pat Weller, got down to re-submitting a lottery application for a much larger amount. He recalls that this meant battles with the Prudential who owned the building and who were obliged to send in experts to examine the foundations: these apparently caused more damage than the bomb (interestingly, the auditorium, which was suspended from great pillars rather than resting on the ground, was almost unharmed by the initial blast). But they found nothing and the Panel minutes for 16 July show that the Prudential did immediately undertake to repair the dome and the roof. ACE made an initial grant of £3.2 million to allow the capital programme to begin and thus avert a revenue crisis. When submitted, the actual bid was quickly assessed and two further grants totalling £19.86 million were given in early 1997.

The refurbished theatre re-opened on time and on budget on 12 December 1998. Braham Murray had agonised over what should be the opening show when, in a flash of inspiration, he decided to continue the run of *Hindle Wakes* which had been so rudely interrupted by the bomb. He managed to get together most of the original cast and led the company back into the theatre from its peripatetic wanderings – first in a BBC Nissen hut and then offices which had been lent by the Hallé orchestra. He pays tribute to the way that organisations in Manchester supported each other during that difficult time – as indeed they did after another terrible Manchester bombing in May 2017. He does not, however, share my clear memory of his threat to open the proceedings of the night with a performance of the lottery monitoring conditions set to music . . .

6

AN ACTIVE AUTUMN

*The Rogers revolt – advent of the new programmes – changes
to the capital programme – National Centre for Popular Music –
back to the ROH – the consultancy culture – back to
Panel business – general re-ordering – The Lowry*

It was more than just the SBC project that was concerning Richard Rogers. In early September 1996 he arranged a lunch at his Hammersmith offices (catering courtesy of the River Café) to discuss how the whole operation of the arts lottery distribution could be improved. He wanted to see how Council members could get more incisive and relevant information so as to make more informed decisions; how lottery money could change and not just reinforce cultural attitudes; how the economic aspects, including partnership funding, could be improved by lease-back strategies and commercial development; how the RABs could become more involved and be given a clearer vision of what was possible; and how to lift the standard of applications of both small and large projects. In attendance were Richard Cork, Andrew Motion (now chair of the literature panel), Ernest Hall, David Reid (chair of Southern Arts and of the Council's finance committee), Peter Gummer (the only non-Council member present) and me. The outcome was a velvet revolution: it was felt that the Council members needed to be reduced to a maximum of fifteen, that the regions should be given more power under the strategic direction of the central Council, that a new and more efficient headquarters should be found for ACE, not necessarily in London, and that both capital and revenue funds should be used to reinforce and change the nation's cultural attitudes. Bureaucracy should also be reduced. After some pressure from David Reid and others who felt uneasy about being part of a 'cabal', it was agreed that Richard should inform Grey Gowrie that he was working on a brief report on the structure of ACE and holding a number of meetings about it.

The pity was that while many of us agreed that something needed fixing, these essential concerns were never brought to the Council table. There always seemed to be too much to do, the volume of business preventing serious strategic discussion. And it wasn't for want of time: by the autumn of 1996 Council meetings were being held over two-day periods, 6–10 p.m. on the first day and 9 a.m. to early afternoon on the second. As these were usually monthly events the commitment demanded of Council members – the majority of whom also had either RABs or panels to chair – was considerable, not to mention the paperwork that needed to be read for each meeting. Christopher Frayling remembers once being at his holiday home in Ireland and coming back from fishing to find the whole room filled with paper spewed out of his fax machine. My Lottery Panel also met monthly: the reading material for each meeting covered details of well over a hundred assessments together with reports, monitoring updates and policies for new genres of applicants; this was condensed for the Council but was none the less a substantial addition to its normal business.

One reason for the long meetings was the fact that Council members were more hands-on than should really be expected from a non-executive, unpaid body. Although there was a seemingly competent and committed executive, almost all of us Council members seemed hungry for real involvement: the opportunities for expanding the work of ACE being offered through the new lottery funding made us keen to take an active part. I was only working part-time but how I still managed to put in all the hours remains a mystery. There were Panel and Council meetings as well as those of the integrated working group (which met regularly, if to relatively little effect) and of the splendidly named preparation of business committee which had been formed in early 1995. This met before each Council meeting to help Grey Gowrie come to terms with the inordinately long agendas. I sat on this together with Grey, David Reid, Thelma Holt and Mary Allen; it was attended by other members of the senior management team when necessary. I think there was a certain amount of resentment in the Council at the cosy 'kitchen cabinet' at which, it must be admitted, some deals were done; on a personal level it was good to have the chance to thrash things out practically in a smaller circle than the 23 sitting around the Council table. But I would not have liked being outside this small frame, and I would never recommend such an inner sanctum because of its divisive effect on other board members.

In addition to all the meetings, the Council was encouraged to visit projects and sites whenever we could. I insisted on setting up a diary of lottery-funded openings so that ACE could be represented whenever possible. Because of pressure on time (and commitments to other events funded through the Treasury grant) this sadly didn't happen as much as it could have done for many Council members but, as far as I was concerned, such events were a really pleasurable part of the job. It was wonderful to see projects rise from the reams of paperwork and become living, breathing things. As examples of the range throughout the country at this time, I attended the openings of the Chequer Mead Community Arts Centre in East Grinstead, a new digital sound suite at the Studio in Beckenham and a drama studio and theatre at Sedgefield Community College, County Durham. The champions of all three gave me a very warm welcome, were intensely proud of what they had achieved and wrote appreciative letters of thanks for the lottery support. Visits to projects during their construction phase were also enjoyable and the donning of the hard hat and hi-vis jacket made a welcome change from the hours spent in committee rooms. I tried to do as many visits as I could because they really brought home the improvements that the lottery was making to people's lives.

Richard Rogers's incentive persisted through the autumn and in December David Puttnam sent me, apparently at Richard's request, a draft structural plan for ACE, set out in a series of rings like a dartboard. At its very centre was a minister, ringed by strategy; the next ring was a chiefs of staff/cabinet consisting of five independent members operating on majority decision without a chair but with ACE's chief executive as its secretary; circles of artforms and then of regions completed the diagram, the one to implement strategy with assistance from expert panels, the other boasting a high degree of autonomy but working with national strategy. In my response I described placing a minister at the centre as 'a huge – and dangerous – mistake' as I felt it breached our all-important arm's-length principle. A general election was looming in the spring of 1997 and David, supported by his advisor John Newbigin (who had worked for Neil Kinnock in the run-up to the 1992 election), was leading a group to formulate New Labour's cultural policy. Their discussions apparently took place informally and the structural plan itself seems to have been initially devised by Ben Evans, who had worked for shadow spokesman for the arts Mark Fisher, and Graham Hitchen, who was continuing to stress ACE's need to get closer to the likely incoming government.

If this was the way outside thinking was going it didn't reach the Council table. The structural plan was never officially discussed and seems to have evaporated. In early 1997 it was agreed that, in view of the election, it would be desirable for ACE to begin discussions with the DNH about longer-term funding. Good relationships with civil servants were obviously important but the need to get closer to the New Labour politicians who were likely soon to have their own say about a cultural future seems to have been officially ignored. In the lists of meetings and events undertaken by Grey Gowrie and Mary Allen there is barely a mention of the shadow team, let alone its advisors, although I know that Mary had good informal contacts with several of the New Labour team.

David Puttnam himself was also campaigning actively for change to the lottery distribution. He had made a presentation to Secretary of State Virginia Bottomley earlier in 1996 arguing for three additional distributors to be added to the original five. This would mean all distributors receiving 12.5 per cent of the good cause money as opposed to the existing 20 per cent. He put forward four suggestions: NESTA (a National Endowment for Science, Technology and the Arts) would promote new thinking by investing in individuals working in those areas who showed particular talent or skills, with a primary focus on young people – the idea was described to me by David as an endowment which would be swelled by royalties from those it supported. A national children's play programme would invest in spaces and equipment as well as general research into all aspects of play. An environmental technologies fund would support research and projects which could lead to breaking the back of the national energy inefficiency problem with three to five years' funding. Finally, a multi-media council would support new ways to use multi-media skills in education. The presentation, made before ACE launched its new programmes, was an attempt to see lottery funds invested in people as well as buildings and equipment. David says that Virginia Bottomley seemed keen but her officials shied away from introducing more changes to lottery legislation with an election looming: new directions were one thing, changes to the structure of good cause distribution another.

*

Meanwhile the big event of the September 1996 Council meeting was the confirmation of those new programmes. A budget for all strands of lottery funding within a total annual allocation of £240 million for the years 1997/8 to 2000/01 was agreed: this amount was thought to be conservative and the actual allocation would be reviewed each November. The capital programme was badly affected, reduced to £180 million in 1997/98 and then to £150 million by 2000/01 (a total over the four years of £640 million), while the annual figure for film (already grown from the initial £10 million awarded in March 1995) rose from £25 million to £30 million over the same period. Although I was aware of the pressure of continuing demand (pending applications now amounted to £1.2 billion) I had to accept this because support for broadening the lottery base among the rest of the Council was overwhelming. The new programmes would be:

- Arts for Everyone: the result of the consultation process was a strong recommendation that the three strands of work being developed by advisory groups should be managed as a single scheme. A new lottery programme would present opportunities to engage with arts activity for both audiences and participants, ease access to lottery funds for young people and amateur groups, and support new work. Its total allocation would be £22.5 million for 1997/98 rising to £40 million by 2000/01, and it would be promoted under the title A4E (Arts for Everyone, an acronym suggested by Christopher Frayling based on the Channel 4 logo designed by Martin Lambie-Nairn). The RABs would play a significant part in stimulating and assisting applications and the artform departments would keep a grip on the assessment process. A special fast-track approach called A4E Express would offer youth and community groups a first-time opportunity to apply for smaller-scale projects under £5,000. This was all new territory and really seemed to offer a revolution in the way that the arts were funded. While the regular clients weren't disbarred from applying for A4E grants on a one-off basis, the doors were open for many more to enter.

- Discretionary grants: local authorities were increasingly reluctant to provide discretionary grants for vocational training for dance and drama students and this had been exercising the dance and drama departments of the Council for some time. Thelma Holt had been particularly vociferous in insisting that the problem be resolved. We had thought that the new direction about the creative abilities of young people would address this, but lottery rules required the Council to avoid entering into longterm commitments or creating longterm expectations. There was also a general feeling that this area was more properly the responsibility of the Department for Education and Employment (DEE) but that body seemed reluctant to act. Meanwhile, students and the dance and drama schools were suffering. London Arts chair Clive Priestley was thought the ideal person to take this forward: his forensic mind could unpick the web of problems and as a former civil servant he knew how to deal with the various departments involved. As a result of his negotiations ACE now agreed to contribute £7.5 million a year for the three-year period 1997–2000 to accredited dance and drama schools, in addition to funding from the DEE of £3 million a year. The time limit would allow lottery funds to be used but would also put pressure on the DEE to find a longterm solution.

- Stabilisation: this would start with a relatively small allocation of £5 million in 1997/98 but would rise to £20 million by 2000/01.

As for management, a dedicated unit within the lottery department would deal with stabilisation, and the drama and dance departments would oversee discretionary grants (likely to be fewer applications in comparison to the other programmes). In contrast to the capital programme, no new department would be set up for handling A4E applications, and there was an assumption that with a few extra staff the artform departments would be able to cope. Grey Gowrie wrote to all Council members on 23 October recommending a 'light touch' approach to assessment, especially for A4E Express grants. For these there would be no qualitative assessment: the aim of the programme was to get to groups whose work was unknown to ACE, inviting them to make their own case for support. Each application would be endorsed by a referee whose comments would be crucial; artform departments and RABs would only be able to comment on a project's eligibility. His letter also stated that other organisations launching similar programmes (the Gulbenkian Foundation, the Prince's Trust and the National Lottery Charities Board), although initially nervous of a 'light touch' approach, had found their schemes robust, attracting genuinely new applicants and enabling them to support new types of work. They had also received fewer applications than expected. It was therefore felt that, rather than adopt a 'first past the post' system, ACE would be able to fund all eligible applications. The pilot A4E programme would be launched on 21 November.

*

While the function of the Council was being debated at Richard Rogers's meetings, the Lottery Panel was overseeing change at a practical level. In spite of the drop in capital budgets necessitated by the introduction of new programmes, there still seemed to be a lot of money around. Future planning focused on keeping up the pressure on the RABs to supply the lists that would help in forming an orderly queue. But the need for some tightening up of the processes had been acknowledged. Adrian Ellis, a cultural policy consultant, had been commissioned by Jeremy Newton to look into lottery procedures so far and recommend necessary changes. While he felt that there were no grounds for – and, with so many projects successfully completed, strong arguments against – any radical overhaul of the capital programme, he did point out that our ability to fund all eligible applications was no longer sustainable. However, any change would need careful handling. The strongest of his recommendations (all subsequently accepted by the Council) was that capital bids, especially those for £500,000 or more, should now be applied for in three stages – feasibility study, project development and construction. This would ensure that their development could be more carefully considered and funded. The marking of bids against the eight criteria should be tightened, especially when it came to financial viability, and all assessors should be given much stricter guidelines. Richard Rogers's suggestion of adding a ninth criterion, for vision, had been welcomed by the Council and Richard made it a feature of his farewell speech when he stepped down that December. Rather surprisingly, in view of the general enthusiasm, the Panel subsequently decided that, rather than adding a further criterion, recommendations to Council should be accompanied by a box with the Panel's additional comments about the vision of a project. No more seems to have been heard – or done – on the subject.

The capital programme was relaunched the following spring with new application packs. These reflected the capital review which had started with the recommendations in the Ellis report, been the subject of long papers by both Jeremy Newton and Moss Cooper and discussed intensely by the Panel at its February and March meetings. The outcome was that all eight criteria, particularly those regarding financial viability and capacity to deliver, were tightened, the environmental impact of bids was highlighted and the three-stage process was insisted on. Future applicants were informed of the changes through a series of road-shows which lottery staff presented around the country.

*

While all this was being discussed applications continued to flow in. Over two September meetings the Panel considered 225 applications of which 154 were recommended at a cost of £69.9 million. The application that caused most disagreement was the funding of a National Centre for Popular Music in Sheffield. The Panel's initial reaction, mainly voiced by David Puttnam, was that if popular music needed a national centre the pop industry itself should pay for it. But at a second meeting Ruth Mackenzie argued strongly in its favour and it went forward for a recommended grant of £9.5 million. After some querying by the Council about both the artistic contact and the financial stability of the project, the grant went through, although against Grey Gowrie's better judgement. As Arts Minister he had been instrumental in closing the Theatre Museum at the V&A and he sensed similarities:

> No one wants to see Edith Evans's knickers. They want to go and see a show. A pop museum without a venue for a pop concert . . . I couldn't see how this was going to work.

In hindsight it was a pity that the Panel's original instinct to reject wasn't heeded. The National Centre for Popular Music failed to attract visitors and became a white elephant on whose ample body critics of arts lottery funding have feasted for many a year. It opened in March 1999 and closed in June 2000. The building, designed by Nigel Coates, ironically one of the few large new buildings of architectural interest funded by arts lottery money, was taken over by Sheffield Hallam University and now houses its students' union.

Several projects around this time failed to achieve their desired visitor numbers, particularly those funded by the Millennium Commission. David Hall points out that the Commission's ambition to give all the large cities of Britain some sort of major new facility created something of a crisis in that too much was offered within relatively short distances. The awards of all the good cause distributors (with the exception of the Charities Board which wasn't limited to capital projects) were stoking a huge lottery building boom and the high numbers of attendees forecast in elaborate business plans were often little more than fictional. Some kind of national strategy or plan entered into by all the distributors would have been very useful – but this, of course, was forbidden by lottery directions.

*

Meanwhile the ROH was still causing problems. During the autumn ACE monitor Richard Pulford produced two substantial reports, one on the financial position and the other on whether the supplementary conditions were being met. The former highlighted another deficit close to £1 million for 1996/97: although urgent remedial action was promised by the chair (Peter Gummer, who had been given a peerage in October 1996 and was now Lord Chadlington), a Panel discussion in October described the ROH's financial forecasting as 'vague and over-optimistic'.

The second report highlighted that negotiations between the ROH and Sadler's Wells were in trouble and the condition relating to the closure period was not being met. This had long been a real concern at ACE – hence the supplementary condition – because none of us had any faith in the solution favoured by the ROH, and particularly by its general director Jeremy Isaacs. This was the building of a second, temporary, theatre by London's Tower Bridge in which to house the two performing companies while the ROH was closed. This plan occupied the ROH for many months until it all fell through. By that time possible West End theatres, including the Theatre Royal Drury Lane and the Lyceum, were no longer available for negotiation and the ROH started discussing with ACE a back-up plan to use the new Sadler's Wells, scheduled to be open by the time of the ROH's closure. Ian Albery remained in the dark about this until, he says, he was summoned to an ACE meeting and told that ACE 'expected' him to accommodate the ROH for over thirty weeks, thus delaying an exciting opening programme put in place by his arts programming director, Nigel Hinds, which he says ACE had already approved. His dismay was shared by many of us in the dance world who had been looking forward to seeing a wide variety of international dance companies. Ian also felt patronised by the ROH board: 'a lot of sort of talking down and looking down their noses' and not wanting to go to Islington because of the 'lack of good restaurants in the area'. According to Ian, ACE intimated that any future revenue funding would be withdrawn if he didn't agree to this deal so he reluctantly caved in on the condition that he would be able to charge the ROH the equivalent weekly rental for a West End musical.

A deal was finally reached and on its basis ACE finally approved the second tranche of its lottery grant to the ROH at its 19 March 1997 meeting. The agreement didn't last, however: Jeremy Isaacs, having negotiated a satisfactory deal with Ian Albery, retired and Peter Chadlington, as ROH chair, decided that Ian's terms were unacceptable and wanted to intervene personally. This appalled Ian Albery who didn't like the way it sidelined Jenny McIntosh, who had replaced Isaacs (she had previously been executive director of the National Theatre). He says he offered to hand back to her the additional £200,000 in rental that he had managed to obtain from Chadlington, 'taking him for a ride because he didn't know what he was doing'. All negotiation eventually broke down that summer. The ROH was by that time on the brink of insolvency and in a staffing crisis. Because of their disarray, they were unable to fulfil their thirty-week contract with Sadler's Wells and, at very short notice, Nigel Hinds had to re-open discussions with international and UK companies to fill the yawning programming gap thus caused. Ian Albery successfully negotiated with ACE for full financial compensation for the extra costs and loss of revenue and he is sure that this came from the closure budget for the ROH, although I have no memory nor record of this – it was probably done quietly, with neither the Council's nor the Panel's knowledge. The eventual outcome for the ROH closure period – short seasons in a variety of London venues – lost money and did little to enhance the reputations of the Royal Ballet and Opera companies.

*

Specialists such as Adrian Ellis and Richard Pulford were doing excellent jobs, but the increasing use of consultants and their growing involvement in all sorts of arts funding was beginning to cause concern. In the early days the staff of the lottery department – not, as we have seen, very experienced in capital work – assessed the smaller applications, but outside help was needed to cope with the volume and complexity of material submitted for the larger bids. Freelancers were recruited in great numbers to cope with demand. Some, such as David Hall, were invaluable; his particular skill was extrapolating the key issues from the mountain of paperwork. But as far as ACE was concerned, this was the start of a gradual – and expensive – change in the nature of its advisors: before the start of the lottery, paid independents were rare creatures. The staff did the work and the panels, which contained artists and practitioners of the highest calibre, working *pro bono*, gave the advice. The new lottery programmes stoked the demand for additional review, and arts managers in employment and many who had lost jobs during the recession years of the early 1990s suddenly found new, green pastures; management consultants, both firms and individuals, also joined the party. Professionals in the building business – architects, engineers, contracting specialists – were needed as assessors and they demanded fees at commercial levels; arts practitioners found their own fees rising accordingly, creating a notable imbalance with artists' remuneration, a scandal that persists to this day. The gap between what artists and managers earn has been increased further by a fairly recent trend of senior managers in heavily subsidised organisations receiving salaries at commercial levels. While Tony Hall's salary package as chief executive of the ROH was in the region of £450,000 a year, anecdotally the salary bands of principal dancers in the Royal Ballet actually went down. Highly trained dancers who appear in Royal Opera productions claimed in November 2014 (admittedly some eighteen months after Tony Hall had left the organisation) that their rehearsal rate was less than that of a box office assistant.

Grey Gowrie justifies the level of consultancy use that began in the early years of the lottery because of his

> personal mortal terror of fraud. If you bring that amount of money into a public system, some of it is going to stick to some dodgy fingers. Surely somebody might walk off with the swag because human beings are ingenious when it comes to money. I think we did well not to have money going AWOL in those first years – but it was costly.

It was not only ACE that was using consultants, the applicants were doing it themselves. Grey also points out that

> Every project felt very vulnerable and so did accountability. Because of being accountable, and being transparent, all good words, people forget that these are also very expensive words. People cover their backsides by hiring top City accountancy firms to determine whether a project is viable or not. Government and Parliament are still at this, in spades. Millions of NHS pounds are spent on it.

In view of some of the subsequent financial problems suffered by bids in both capital and revenue terms, this was not always money well spent.

The growing use of consultants was brought up regularly at Council meetings. In September 1996 Mary Allen wrote to me that consultants were nearly always suitably qualified freelance individuals and we have only exceptionally and occasionally made use of sizeable firms which provide consultancy services.

But this situation wasn't maintained, and high fees were regularly paid to both individual consultants and those attached to large firms; concern about this 'consultancy culture' remained a *leitmotif* all my time on the Council. Nothing seemed able to stop its growth, and on one occasion the ACE auditors would point out to the finance committee that one member of staff, paid on a consultancy basis, was earning more than the chief executive himself.

The arrival of the lottery meant that figures under discussion very quickly jumped from thousands to millions, and the jobs of chief executives working in the arts began to become much more complicated – justification, some would argue, for the rise in salary levels. Not only did they have to contemplate and manage capital bids but a growing emphasis on turning arts organisations into business ventures, started during the Thatcher years and peaking during the 'target' culture of New Labour, was an additional strain. Looking back on my own time at Rambert and the English Shakespeare Company I can see that in the new climate I would have needed much more support than the tiny staffs I had then. And there were a lot of people offering it: the increasing number of arts managers who worked on a freelance basis and were good at making a pitch explains why the industry that sprung up at the time of the arrival of the lottery remains today. But John Newbigin (who was to become special advisor to Chris Smith when the latter was appointed as Secretary of State in 1997) sees reliance on consultants as an abnegation of executive responsibility and a serious structural issue, especially in terms of strategy development. He acknowledges that New Labour contributed to the climate:

> A lot of the policy ideas that were implemented by the Labour government were being brewed in little back rooms in informal ways, the way these things are, so after 1997 there was a feeling 'the civil servants don't get it' . . . so the whole thing about having outside consultants and outside people writing these papers, I think over the last twenty years – and it's a fault, it's a sin that can be laid very largely at New Labour's door – has absolutely

undermined the confidence of the civil service and of a lot of these public agencies because there's no point in them doing any strategic thinking because some smart-arse from PriceWaterhouseCoopers or David Puttnam's office is going to come along and tell them something different . . . Once you've lost that capacity and confidence from inside the government machine – and I mean government in the larger sense, including the Arts Council – how you reinvent that is incredibly tricky.

In his report on The Public (the West Bromwich project that went disastrously wrong) Anthony Blackstock fears that over-dependence on consultants 'may have distracted officers from a close enough real engagement with the issues' and commends the more detailed personal engagement of ACE senior officers that he says has been evident since 2006. The consultancy culture is still with us but its effectiveness is increasingly questionable. One example is data collection, especially financial. ACE pays large sums to outside consultants for this in addition to receiving regular financial information from its funded organisations, but the results often remain unobtainable; any report that is issued on cultural matters continues to rue the lack of concrete data. The same climate allows two cultural commentators, highly respected in their own fields, to write a book on how to run a cultural organisation when neither of them has ever done so. I would be a hypocrite not to admit that I am one of many who have been paid to advise and been commissioned to write reports which have joined others on dusty shelves. The strangest thing of all is the fact that such reports go on being regularly commissioned although the recommendations contained within them hardly ever get acted upon.

There remains the question of how ACE itself takes its artistic advice. Since advisory panels for each artform were removed in the early 2000s, paid assessors have taken their place who apply a more rigorously transparent reporting process. And the future will contain a new method with the introduction of quality metrics, described as 'a sector-led project that uses self, peer and public assessment to capture the quality of art and cultural work'.[12] This seems to have been devised from a consultant's desk and has raised much consternation among the arts community: the

12. http://www.artscouncil.org.uk/quality-metrics/quality-metrics.

prescriptive language and insistence on a format seems completely at odds with the passion, the joy, the risk and the sheer unexpectedness that good art can supply.[13] Perhaps for me it's a question of fighting off nostalgia for a time when grants were debated by peers who were not only highly respected in their own fields but who also, by their association, gave ACE credibility.

*

During the autumn of 1996 the Panel began to examine the RABs' lists of proposed projects over £1 million likely to be submitted over the next five years. They were long, and in many cases not very specific, but it was a start as we tried to forecast and prioritise likely future demand. An overall lack of vision was lamented (ironically, given that we had dismissed the Rogers 'vision box'); there were few new-builds and a dearth of culturally diverse or disability projects. It was also felt that the RABs were promoting their existing clients rather than looking at a wider field, another ironic contrast to the fighting that had taken place over the new A4E programmes. The production of these lists was only the start of a long process: by February 1997, artform departments had added their comments, the lists then went back to the RABs and that April the Panel was told that the RABs would not be able to produce revised plans before the following September. It seems extraordinary now that there was so little sense of urgency given the reduction in capital budgets. But at that stage there still seemed to be plenty of money even if there was no slackening in demand – to deal with which, rather than any drawing in of resources, more staff were recruited over the next few months.

At the end of November it was announced that the grant-in-aid for 1997/8 would be standstill at £186.1 million – something of a relief as ACE had been told by the DNH to expect a cut of £3.2 million. But in real terms, the grant's value had reduced by £25 million over five years. The allocation of this Treasury money was discussed by the Council at its December meeting. The lottery was to some extent alleviating the pressure

13. ACE subsequently postponed the introduction of the plan (https://www.thestage. co.uk/news/2017/arts-council-delays-2-7m-quality-metrics-decision/).

on revenue funding and every attempt was being made to increase this: more overheads could be transferred to the lottery accounts; increasing the number of clients on the stabilisation programme was suggested; a publications and recordings programme was proposed which could form part of the capital programme and help artists' commissions. It was also at this time that the proposal to transfer the film, video and broadcasting department to the film section of the lottery department was made.

December 1996 arrived with a resignation letter, into which I was copied, from one of the operations team, outlining a slew of concerns about the serious underestimation of the scale of the whole capital undertaking. She criticised what she saw as the lack of executive appreciation about the range of the skills needed to manage the funding and its distribution as well as the monitoring of the projects. The letter warned about the likelihood of diminishing funds in the future and the fact that applications were continuing to be accepted regardless of the need to cut back to a more strategic level. Looking back on it now it seems a reasonable, if frightening, appraisal of the situation eighteen months after the first awards had been given out; as a prediction it had some accuracy. Its author did acknowledge that some of her concerns had been addressed through the Ellis review; moreover, at this time, the monitoring department was still recruiting and training staff and would not really be up and running until the early months of 1997. In my reply I noted politely that it was helpful to have the concerns raised and went on:

> Obviously it has not been easy to develop a department dealing with such major sums of money and such substantial issues without the research and development time that any commercial institution would have engaged in.

That was really the crux of it. Political pressure to get the money out, the absence of any planned strategy and the lack of proper experience within the team had all contributed to hasty systems being set up to deal with unknown and complicated demand. None the less, in spite of all the brickbats and difficulties, many projects all over the country were now coming into bloom and the country's cultural infrastructure was gradually being strengthened.

*

Before what seemed to be a well-earned Christmas break, and as a change from board rooms and paperwork, I made a journey north to look at progress on various projects – including a visit to Salford Quays where Salford City Council (SCC)'s vision for an international arts centre was being realised. The SCC saw this as a catalyst for regeneration and a means of giving aspiration to a populace that was one of the poorest in the country. It would also house the SCC's formidable collection of the works of L. S. Lowry. Once again, an exemplary local authority man was behind it. John Willis, chief executive of the SCC, had launched an international architectural competition in 1991 from which the partnership of James Stirling and Michael Wilford had been selected (the project was continued by Wilford after Stirling's death in 1992). Willis had then started to build up a team under the chairmanship of Felicity Goodey, a former BBC journalist. Other sites on the Quays were to be reserved for commercial ventures and their rents would in the long term both support the revenue needs of this new Lowry Centre and, of more immediate importance, act as the 50 per cent partnership funding then demanded by the Millennium Commission, who looked with favour on the project as one of their landmarks for the north-west. It was something of a shock to all concerned when the Millennium Commissioners ruled, quite contrarily, that partnership funding could not be allowed to come from commercial sources. At this point, in the latter part of 1995, Jennie Page, the Commission's chief executive, called an urgent meeting with representatives of ACE and the HLF to persuade these other distributors to join the Commission in the project's funding.

David Hall was one of the assessors who looked at the bid at this early stage for ACE. He and his team advised that it was a good idea in principle but that there were far too many unanswered questions, including severe underestimation on the revenue side; they recommended that it go back to the drawing board before any commitments were made. So he was astonished, about six weeks later, to see an announcement on television that ACE had agreed to award £41 million, with the Millennium Commission contributing £15.65 million and the HLF £7.65 million. In spite of the imbalance of funding, it was promoted from the start very much as a Millennium project (Virginia Bottomley, who chaired the Millennium

Commission as Secretary of State, says that it was 'thrilling and wonderful and a fantastic statement for the millennium'). Felicity Goodey describes her relationship with ACE during those early years as extremely difficult and is sure that this was because ACE officers resented being bounced into the deal by the Millennium Commission. It certainly didn't help that ACE had come late into discussions about the vision: in addition to the assessors' concerns about the business planning there were many queries from artform departments and their respective chairs about the size of the proposed auditoria and what programming they would be filled with, as well as an awareness about competition with other large-scale theatres in Manchester with whom touring companies had their arrangements. Sure enough, pressure would subsequently be put on ACE by Apollo Leisure, then owners of the Opera House and Palace Theatre, the major touring theatres in Manchester, anxious about the Lowry's proposed artistic programme. They tried to insist that no ACE subsidised companies should perform at the new venue.

Felicity feels that a great deal of research and careful planning had gone into a project designed as though it were

> a 'department' store, different departments, each one a self-contained business centre. From the outset we wanted the ability to 'push the boundaries' artistically, and that meant we needed to be able to cross-subsidise the non-commercial elements with 'business centres' which made a profit.

While she is critical that none of this was taken on board by the artform departments, the fact is that ACE was being advised by specialised experts who were raising substantial concerns. There was to be a string of sour exchanges in the future and, as with the ROH, feelings of deep frustration on both sides as ACE struggled to get information and the Lowry team railed at what they saw as interference based on the lack of comprehension of a vision. Felicity feels particularly strongly about the relationship with ACE, but future meetings would show that all the good cause distributors concerned expressed considerable unease about business planning and partnership funding as the building slowly materialised.

However, on the cold December morning I met Felicity Goodey and John Willis in a small office on the edge of Salford Quays, all was amicable (as indeed it would remain between us on a personal basis). It required a wide stretch of the imagination to look out on a scene of empty desolation – echoing some of L. S. Lowry's bleakest cityscapes – to visualise the vibrant centre of a Salford that now hosts not only the Lowry but also the northern branch of the Imperial War Museum and the BBC's MediaCity, as well as shopping malls, car parks and new residential estates. But it felt good that ACE was involved with such a vision, and it was one of the pleasures of the job to be working with two of its passionate advocates.

THE NEW ART GALLERY WALSALL

All successful projects have relied on at least one visionary champion, and Walsall, historically a deprived area in the West Midlands, had Peter Jenkinson. In 1989 Peter had been appointed director of the Walsall Museum and Art Gallery (where the Garman Ryan Collection was being housed in dire surroundings, see page 24). He had been disappointed when Walsall Council's plans to build a new art gallery, designed by Levitt Bernstein on a site opposite the Museum and Art Gallery, had to be cancelled when budgets were slashed at the time of the poll tax. But he had not given up, and some City Challenge money arrived, to be supplemented by European (ERDF) funds, and these coincided with the birth of the National Lottery. A prime site in the centre of the town was selected for the building of a new art gallery as the cornerstone of the regeneration programme, and Peter remembers inviting Grey Gowrie to see this and to meet councillors and other local VIPs; he was astonished when Gowrie advised them to be ambitious and to double the budget they were thinking of: 'It was that moment, I know, which completely changed the politicians' minds.' He praises the support given at that time by Mike Bird, the leader of Walsall Council, and by many other councillors from all parties during the intensive two-year consultation programme with local communities. Peter was determined to deliver a building of the highest quality, in terms of design and architecture and of maximised community involvement 'for people in this area of the country that had been bashed about, whose aspirations were through the floor'. After an international architectural ideas competition, a firm of new and untried architects, Caruso St John, were selected and by March 1996 the bid to ACE was ready:

> We had the People's Launch and the lottery bid was handed down, in a human chain, from the Mayor's Parlour with all his regalia on, with people of all ages, children, babies, all the way down three staircases to the front door with a huge crowd waiting with 'Postman Pat' who was there to put it into his post van to take the bid to London. And it was small things like that . . . that were important, people on the landings in wheelchairs . . . people from the Asian community, people from the African-Caribbean community . . . it was very joyful. It was such a hot day that Postman Pat was falling over: I had to take him round the corner to take his head off because he was sort of wavering!

Peter found the assessment process rigorous, particularly a grilling by the architecture advisory committee, some of whom questioned the philosophy of leaving the public to explore the building rather than being pointed in a fixed and defined route. However, an award of £15.75 million was finally made In October 1996 and construction began in January 1997. Then followed some typical stresses, particularly with the contractors, McAlpines, who at one stage threatened a £4.5 million overspend; legal action seemed imminent until a settlement was agreed which saw Walsall Council paying about £500,000 of the extra cost, the rest presumably being borne by McAlpines. Peter's insistence on quality also caused him and the team many fights with the main contractor: he felt among them a disregard to make good use of money that came from the public (and often poorer parts of the public, who were allegedly the majority of lottery ticket buyers), though he is full of praise for many of the skilled sub-contractors who became deeply committed to delivering excellence for Walsall.

His persistence paid off because The New Art Gallery Walsall is one of the relatively few large and architecturally admired buildings of this time. Peter acknowledges that, like so many of the other arts managers delivering capital projects, he was 'an architectural and building virgin': the physical strain resulted in his getting shingles, losing his eyesight for over twenty-four hours and twice being hospitalised after collapsing on train journeys. He pays glowing tribute to Simon Whelan, his project manager; to Sheila McGregor, his deputy who continued running the old Gallery until the move; and to the rest of his team, to many local councillors in all parties, to the gallery's trustees, the architectural competition judges, the architects, engineers and designers, the wide range of craftsmen and women who built the gallery and, most of all, the community itself to whom the project was always dedicated. Above all, he is one of the exemplary champions to whom this book is dedicated. In *The New Art Gallery Walsall*, a comprehensive book of essays, photographs and drawings on its making, Rowan Moore pays tribute to his

> passion, energy, infectious enthusiasm and personal and political skills, his ability to spot rocks and reefs in the uncharted waters of public funding . . .

The Gallery, which was nominated for a Stirling Prize for architecture, continued to attract around 200,000 visitors a year and maintain what Peter (although he himself moved on) described as 'those really core philosophical commitments' of acting as a community and civic space as much as an arts centre and an investment in education:

> Education is going to be the driver of the regeneration of the area of which the gallery, passionately from the beginning, was part.

These words, spoken in 2013, ring hollow now. Because of the austerity cuts to local authority budgets, Walsall Metropolitan Borough Council is threatening to withdraw its grant by 2020, a proposal that is currently (March 2017) undergoing public consultation. This would mean that the Gallery would have to close – a tragic end to a project that began with such commitment, passion and vision.

7

A BOISTEROUS SPRING

More SBC – my Bath lecture – crisis over A4E applications – stabilisation – ENO – Bristol Harbourside – public relations and some openings

While dealing with the likes of Peter Jenkinson was always an inspiring pleasure, I didn't feel as warmly about the champions of the SBC bid. A revised version, for £80–£90 million, had been received in late autumn 1996. By February 1997 heavy pressure for a decision on it before pre-election purdah set in was being put on ACE by politicians who had nothing directly to do with the project, such as Michael Heseltine and John Gummer. I reluctantly called a special Panel meeting to discuss it on 17 March. This turned out to be a waste of time because the bid remained inadequate in many practical features including financial viability. Deferment was recommended, and the bid did not feature on the agenda of the next Council meeting because of a convention that the Council did not discuss Panel deferments. To confront the Panel's concerns, it was agreed that Grey Gowrie should meet Sir Brian Corby, chair of the SBC. This meeting soon took place, also attended by Mary Allen, Jeremy Newton and me from ACE and by another SBC board member, Martin Smith, and Nicholas Snowman, chief executive. There was a lot of bluster and mutual blame: Jeremy and I in particular were impatient that the assessors were not being listened to after nearly two years and the investment of £1.2 million of development money. The meeting did not get anywhere and was followed by another one a fortnight later with Grey, Mary, Sir Brian and me. Once more we went round and round about the inadequacies of the bid; eventually Grey had to throw us out of his office because of another meeting. That didn't stop Sir Brian, who pursued me into another room, then to the lift and out into the reception area, trying to insist that we got out our diaries there and then to plan another meeting. During all this badgering he seemed to refuse to acknowledge my reiterated concerns about the management of the project. He and other board members continued to lobby both ACE and the DNH. Melanie Leech, then head of arts policy at the department, remembers persistent telephone calls. The government had ownership control of the site and would have had to give its own permission for any development to go ahead; Melanie recalls that the DNH's own assessors were insistent that the bid was not ready.

And so it dragged on: the application was brought up at both the April and May meetings of the Panel and still deferment was recommended, amid stupefaction among Panel members and assessors alike that no one at the SBC seemed to be listening. Meanwhile the bid was growing: in July it again came before the Panel at £112.9 million. The Panel continued to think that some major issues had not been resolved; if a bid was granted it would have to be accompanied by thirty-eight conditions and so we recommended a fourth deferral. We had heard that the newly elected Prime Minister, Tony Blair, was keen to announce a £12 million offer to the scheme from the publisher and philanthropist Paul Hamlyn, but at the meeting's lunchtime break David Puttnam passed me a handwritten note saying 'No. 10 [Downing Street] will be "V comfortable" with a reasoned deferment on SBC . . . someone v. senior will be delegated to talk to Paul H.' I haven't been able to track down who this 'v. senior' person might have been.

As a result of the lack of progress I was then invited to accompany Grey Gowrie to a meeting at the DNH to discuss the Panel's concerns. Hayden Phillips and Melanie Leech showed sympathy with our position – which remained shared by their own assessors – and it was suggested that the SBC be offered the help of a temporary supremo with some artistic vision. As no appointment took place, I assume this idea was vetoed by the SBC's board.

*

Early in 1997 I gave a talk at the University of Bath on 'The Arts Council of England and the National Lottery' which gave a snapshot of where things stood some two years after the first grants had been given out. Awarded grants numbered 1,309, to a total of £703.6 million, 75 per cent of which had been for less than £100,000. A network of theatres, art galleries, community centres and village halls had been built or refurbished throughout the country; nearly two hundred brass and silver bands had received new instruments; a fleet of vehicles for transporting touring companies and their sets had been provided; and new computers, editing suites and multi-media centres would lead the arts technically into the twenty-first century. One example of this was the £98,000 given to a group of twenty arts centres and small theatres coming together to develop a computerised box office network. Lighting and sound equipment was being upgraded, as project manager Simon Harper points out:

> The kit we have now is ten times better than anything we had before the lottery started because we were able to buy more, the kit manufacturers were able to invest more R&D in it, there was a demand for more efficient, better equipment, everything got better, even got a bit cheaper in some cases. People were buying more of it so unit prices came down.

Having outlined the new programmes to be introduced I then referred to investment in film: several major features been financed, including *The Woodlanders* starring Rufus Sewell, *Wilde* with Stephen Fry, and Sally Potter's *The Tango Lesson*. So too had seventeen short films – vital training grounds for incipient filmmakers.

I also stressed the importance of maintaining both streams of ACE income. The Treasury grant ensured that a network of arts organisations throughout England had a relative amount of security and could provide consistency and growth; lottery income supported necessary capital work and, through its A4E and other programmes, widened the cultural embrace through being open to any arts project on a one-off basis.

I ended by highlighting the case for supporting the arts, both through Treasury and lottery funding, quoting from words recently spoken by Richard Rogers:

> Today wealth comes from our capacity to be creative. Raw materials and brawn are being replaced by imagination, solid matter by grey matter . . . So let's start to think about how in our changing society we can use culture to prepare ourselves for a bumpy future. By culture I mean anything that expands the brain, knowledge which is not merely aimed at maximising profit. It should be something that is nurtured within all of us from cradle to grave.

With all this enthusiasm it was a pity that the audience was tiny. But Richard's words sum up what I think drives all of us who work in the arts today. They echo hollowly as threats to arts education in schools have become a reality and a Tory government is introducing an EBacc curriculum that does not feature any art as a mandatory subject.

*

The achievements I had so proudly set out in my lecture were soon to be threatened by another drama. A4E Express grants were small grants of less than £5,000 to be given to people who had never previously applied to the arts funding system; in order to reach them there had been a campaign of information days, telephone advice and extensive mailings, mainly carried out by the RABs. This meant, however, that, contrary to the advice we had been given in the autumn, the demand for A4E Express grants was much higher than anticipated. By the January deadline for the first round, some 4,450 applications had been received of which about 2,700 were ineligible or likely to be rejected because of negative or incomplete reports from referees. The remaining 1,750 required total funding of £8-9 million, substantially more than the £4 million budgeted for the two proposed rounds. No selection criteria had been advertised and, if introduced retrospectively, would be considered unfair. After some frantic scribblings between Jeremy Newton and myself at the March 1997 Council table about whether the budgets could stretched over a four-year period, it was finally agreed that the demand be met because of raised expectations, with a caveat that in future the situation should be much more firmly controlled from the outset. However, this was too late for the second round of A4E Express which was already being applied for: the eligible applications for that totaled £15.4 million, a figure that the Council was similarly forced to agree to at its June 1997 meeting.

The A4E Express programme was not repeated. Annabel Jackson Associates, who evaluated it in November 1997, recommended that it should continue, although with strict conditions about its objectives and management, but this wasn't taken up by the Council, scared off perhaps by the huge over-demand that had been generated. A pity: no programme with quite its immediacy and its targeting of small groups and individuals with no previous contact with the arts funding system has replaced it. Graham Hitchen regrets that A4E Express was not introduced as a rolling programme over a period of time to avoid the overload of the first two rounds. He points out the impact that it made, not least on those working on a cultural policy for New Labour who were struck by the enthusiasm from youth and community groups for the support they were getting. Perhaps ACE was not as out of touch and in need of a massive shake-up as they had suspected.

At the beginning of April Graham Devlin replaced Sue Hoyle as deputy secretary-general. He remembers that his immediate concern was the chaos surrounding the plethora of applications for the main A4E programme which were now flooding the building: the boardroom was like a sweatshop and extra staff were being urgently recruited to cope with the assessments. Sue Hoyle feels that a new team, similar to that for capital projects, should have been set up to run the new programme. Instead it was bolted on to existing artform departmental structures that were under-equipped to deal with the volume of work.

*

The stabilisation programme was getting under way in much more controlled circumstances. Eighteen organisations had been put forward for entry into the pilot programme and at its January 1997 meeting it was a hard choice for the Panel to take this number down to the fifteen that had been stipulated by the Council. Both Welsh National Opera and Opera North were strong contenders but in the final list opera was represented by ENO. Birmingham Royal Ballet (BRB) was preferred to the LSO (a very worthy candidate but not an unstable one); however, this decision was almost immediately reversed by the Council when a query arose over BRB's close relationship with the ROH (a toxic contamination!) and the LSO was confirmed in its place. David Pratley subsequently felt that that was always going to be the decision

> Because of ministers' and the Arts Council's understandable anxiety not to be seen spending lottery money on 'lame ducks', the programme was asked deliberately to select at least one organisation of demonstrable quality in artistic work and management.[14]

The others admitted to the programme were Birmingham Repertory Theatre, Junction Arts Centre Cambridge, West Yorkshire Playhouse, Norfolk and Norwich Film Theatre, Northern Sinfonia, Bristol City Council Consortium, Tara Arts Group, Embroiderers' Guild, Blackheath Concert Hall, Bournemouth Orchestras, Inner City Music Manchester, Hampshire County Arts Centres Consortium and Sheffield Museums and Galleries Consortium. In good lottery fashion, they represented a range of cultural organisations, not all of them among ACE's normal clients.

The actual process of stabilisation certainly wasn't an easy ride for the organisations involved. To wipe out deficits and inject investment into their balance sheets, every aspect of their work was subjected to a strategic stocktake by two lead advisors. This resulted in a technical assistance briefing which led to agreed stabilisation objectives and then strategies for their implementation over five years. Far more detail and insight was asked of arts organisations in stabilisation than those going through a capital project. David Pratley agrees, pointing out that the process was heavily influenced by the accountancy firm Coopers & Lybrand who had been recruited in the early stages. They

---

14. *Organisations in Renewal: A Review of Arts Council England's Stabilisation Programmes 1996–2004*, David Pratley Associates, London 2006.

wanted to create a good model for organisational development which they'd thought would work. And I think that process was vindicated . . . by all the clients who went through it, many of whom said that the process had been at least as important as the money . . . There will never ever be such a thing as stability within the arts – by their very nature and by the exigencies of the funding system that can never be guaranteed. The bit that we can improve is the organisation's capacity to be capable of change in terms of its leadership and openness and its systems and so forth.

During the pilot programme some stakeholders did renege on their obligations, some other potential funders withdrew and there was a failure to meet financial targets. David feels now that problems occurred when organisations failed to take responsibility for their own destiny, particularly by discarding the objectives that they had set down in their organisational plan. I have already mentioned over-reliance on the consultancy culture and I feel that this is a good example of such organisations being over-advised and not having real ownership of their plans in the first place. It also soon became clear that it was unrealistic to have excluded capital needs from the original applications as in several cases these were an urgent and vital part of stabilising the organisation.

The organisations admitted to the pilot programme held their own meetings to discuss progress. A stabilisation forum in April 1999 agreed that while the programme had much to offer no one seemed very clear about what stabilisation actually was. The quality and experience of the consultants and the benchmarking had been inconsistent, and the failure to involve organisations more fully in the monitoring and assessment of the pilot programme had had the effect of excluding much critical comment. It was felt that more clarity and strategic involvement by ACE and the RABs was needed if organisations were to remain stable.[15]

None the less the pilot programme did get more money into revenue streams and it attracted political approval. By July 1997 a longterm extension was agreed and the interim life of the stabilisation committee continued. A main programme aimed at improving the stability and

15. From confidential notes sent to the author from the stabilisation forum held on 4 February 1999.

sustainability of large-scale arts organisations was launched in 1999: nineteen were admitted in three groups during 1999 to 2001, receiving in total £42.6 million of lottery funding. A recovery programme provided speedy assistance to those of a smaller scale. Between 1999 and 2006 this provided £78.778 million to sixty-five organisations and together these programmes contributed a major boost to the revenue side of ACE's work. Although a stabilisation programme no longer exists, it can claim credit for tightening up managerial procedures and the fact that most arts organisations now have some level of reserves. The huge deficits of the mid-1990s seem to be a thing of the past.

The process of stabilisation certainly helped to introduce a more businesslike approach to arts management. Obviously this is a good thing, although the accompanying language becomes tiresome. As mentioned on page 46, ACE now heavily relies on 'resilience', 'investment', 'sustainability' and 'learning objectives' to prod organisations along the route which stabilisation first trod. One has the feeling that much of this is to satisfy political masters but it's a pity that art for art's sake doesn't get more of a look-in.

There's also the obsession with assessment and evaluation. Any good grant-giver will obviously want to know how successful their funding has been, but it's only worth spending thousands of pounds evaluating every scheme if the learning is going to be put to practical use in the future. But so often it isn't. A recent cultural enquiry by King's College London entitled *Step by Step: arts policy and young people 1944–2014* found that many government and ACE policies concerning young people had been formulated without reference to what had gone before and lessons had not been learnt. Its first recommendation suggests that the Department for Education, the DCMS and ACE

> should evaluate historical precedents when formulating new policy in the area of arts engagement by children and young people, auditing the historical record and incorporating insights into the policy development process.

The second recommendation refers to the regular re-structuring of ACE to which I have already referred in the context of the PriceWaterhouse review back in 1992. It urges those same bodies to

> recognise that the cost of organisational restructures is greater than simply the financial burden of severances and recruitment. To address the loss of

insight and experience that comes with change we recommend that they
embody best practice in information management at all times, but especially in the lead-up to any restructuring.

Even if the language requires some unpicking, experience causes me to
agree completely.

*

The most demanding organisation in the pilot programme was ENO, who
had applied because of its deficit and also because ACE's 1995 lyric theatre
review had thwarted its immediate desire to apply to the capital programme. The review's recommendation that the organisation wait to
address the considerable deficiencies of its London home, the Coliseum,
until the ROH redevelopment was complete put its nose right out of joint.
So too did the review's other recommendation that more dance should be
presented at the Coliseum. This was something that the ACE's dance
department had long lobbied for, feeling that the London auditorium with
the best sightlines for large-scale dance shouldn't just be the preserve of
opera. Although Sadler's Wells would fulfil many dance ambitions, the
Coliseum provided the scale necessary for major classical work. In spite (or
perhaps because) of it being a recommendation of the lyric theatre review,
ENO's board and general director, Dennis Marks, had consistently refused
to make it any sort of priority.

Almost as soon as it was admitted to the stabilisation programme the
company was demanding early consideration of its bid, which the Council
was reluctant to give. Not only would it be unfair to the other stabilisation
clients but ENO's attitude was considered generally uncooperative.
Council members were also cross about a letter sent by the company to its
subscribers which implied that its decision to postpone a new commission,
Dr Ox's Experiment by composer Gavin Bryars, was due to the conditions
imposed by the stabilisation programme rather than its own shaky finances.
ENO had to go through the full Coopers & Lybrand recommended
process for nine months until in October 1997 an interim stabilisation
grant of £4.5 million was approved, one condition being that dance should
be a clearly identified feature of its strategy at the Coliseum. The company
finally received £9.45 million of stabilisation money.

ENO seems to have figured prominently on every subsequent pro-gramme introduced by ACE to give extra help to its regular clients. It has received millions of pounds in addition to its core grants. It finally seemed to have turned a corner with a small surplus in 2012/13 but remained in the sick bay, in spite of generally producing much more original and exciting opera productions than its immediate rival, the Royal Opera. In 2015 it found itself in the curious position of having its ACE annual grant cut by £5 million but being offered a one-off grant of up to £7.6 million to help it re-plan its business model, something that all the other extra grants never seem to have accomplished. A consultant from McKinsey & Com-pany, Cressida Pollock, was brought in and subsequently appointed as chief executive in March 2015; the business plan she drew up suggested reducing the chorus's weeks under contract by 25 per cent, whereupon strike action was threatened. A compromise was finally agreed in which the chorus would in future work (and be paid) for only nine months a year instead of the previous twelve; their pro rata pay for those months would be raised. Under this agreement the average loss to each member would be £5,900 a year as opposed to the £10,215 originally proposed. The hope was that the money could be made up by their taking on teaching and freelance engagements. Perhaps it was no surprise when the music director Mark Wigglesworth announced in March 2016 – after only six months in the job – that he would step down at the end of that season, his resignation letter to the musicians apparently stating that the company was evolving into something he did not recognise. A further row broke out in November 2016 when ENO announced that its planned visit to Blackpool in May 2017 would not now take place because it had not entered into a contract with the Winter Gardens there and the theatre had found a preferred booker. This meant, as journalists were quick to point out, with only eighty performances scheduled for its 2016/17 London season, ENO would be receiving public subsidy of £153,750 per performance.

A coda to the tale lies in the Coliseum now including in its program-ming semi-staged versions of popular musicals which could mean that it would be less available to, for example, English National Ballet (ENB) to present its annual – and profitable – *Nutcracker* seasons over Christmas. It will be interesting to see how strongly ACE continues to argue for the importance of dance at the Coliseum. Certainly in its 2014 analysis of its investment in large-scale opera and ballet[16] it suggested that ENO explore ways to make the Coliseum into a more viable operation, 'recognising the important national role the Coliseum plays as a venue for both opera and ballet'; at the same time it warns that ENO's proposed new business model represents considerable challenges to ENB's own operating model and pledges support to both companies to work together to resolve this.

*

Another bid was on its way that would hit the headlines in a negative way. In September 1995 Bristol City Council had been awarded £375,000 by ACE for a feasibility study and architectural competition costs for the Harbourside Centre,[17] a proposed new concert hall estimated to cost over £80 million. Although much of the feasibility work was still unfinished, they applied for the full amount of £74.606 million in August 1996. In April 1997 the assessors delivered their report, which raised substantial questions over the management of the project, its artistic purpose, its financial viability and its partnership funding. All the Panel felt able to recommend was a development grant of £300,000 to cover further work in these areas. Their concern was echoed at the subsequent Council meeting by one member describing the scheme as 'half-baked'. The further amount was deferred until the feasibility study was completed.

In hindsight it would have been best to reject the bid at this moment. But there was a feeling that the concert hall would be a good thing for Bristol: the south-west as a region was low on *grands projets.* South West Arts chair and fellow Council member Maggie Guillebaud was often on the phone: although professional about it, she was obviously in a difficult position as she had close local connections with the board of the Harbourside Centre and wanted to do her best for the region. She asked if the Panel could recommend an 'in principle' grant for the full amount but I had to explain to her that this wasn't possible because of the bid's inadequacies. In spite of feasibility work that was still outstanding and against the Panel's

16. http://www.artscouncil.org.uk/sites/default/files/download-file/Analysis_of_Opera_and_Ballet.pdf
17. This was originally submitted under the title of Centre for Performing Arts (cpa) but was renamed the Harbourside Centre, which I have used throughout for clarity.

advice, the Council awarded two development grants, for £300,000 and £4.346 million, in June and September respectively; both were accompanied by warnings that the overall costs of the project should be reduced substantially.

The announcement of the second development grant turned out to be a spectacularly bad public relations move. Grey Gowrie was helicoptered into Bristol waving a cheque, which gave the impression that the whole bid had now got the green light. Grey remembers that the ACE press office

> persuaded a rather reluctant me, it wasn't my wheeze, but I do take responsibility. I should have asked ACE to veto it. I cheered up the burghers of Bristol by appearing to descend with a cheque from a helicopter, like Father Christmas. But the cheque could not be cashed as the project did not get off the ground . . .

The assessments rumbled on, mixed messages being sent to the trust that had now been set up to take on the project. While I was meeting and corresponding with its chair, Louis Sherwood, to point out the bid's deficiencies, the lottery department were apparently giving assurances (unbeknownst to the Panel or Council) that ACE would back a £58 million bid. An application for that amount was eventually made and came up for discussion at the July 1998 Council meeting. Despite the project featuring on the priority lists and having received over £5 million in development grants, there remained substantial concerns over financial viability, partnership funding, management and design planning. There was no option but finally to reject it.

Bristol City Council were furious and demanded meetings with ACE and other stakeholders to explain the decision. Peter Hewitt remembers protestors greeting him off the London train, and the fall-out within the city council led to the resignation of its chief executive, Lucy de Groot, who, ironically, seemed to be one of the saner heads around the project. The Centre went into administration and long-drawn negotiations began, accompanied by political pressure from some of its creditors. The matter was finally resolved only in November 1999 when a joint press statement was issued by ACE and the Centre, stating that their dispute had reached full and final settlement of all claims between them. To achieve this, ACE had had to pay out a further £1.4 million from the balance of the agreed development grants.

It was a regrettable outcome: the south-west still lacks an adequate concert hall and the proposed location at Bristol harbour could have made the siting spectacular. But it was never properly thought through, its management was inexperienced and those in charge tended to replace listening with banging on the table and saying 'You will give us the money and you will give it to us now', a negotiating stance that was utterly resistible. As a Bath inhabitant, I had to avoid social gatherings in Bristol for some time afterwards, so palpable was the anger directed towards me when my connection with the lottery became known. There was a lot of accusation that ACE had pulled the bid because it had run out of money, but this was not true: the project had featured in all the national priority lists with an allocation of £58 million up to that point.

Too many expectations had been raised by the decision to feed the scheme with development money instead of simply rejecting the bid early on. In cases where rejection led to a proper re-think (such as with the Laban Centre in Deptford), the resulting applications were often successful. Where high-level – often political – support was at its most extreme, drawn-out negotiations and the eking of development money caused the greatest waste, disappointment and fury. The SBC, The Public and Bristol's Harbourside Centre are all fine examples of the way not to do things. This enormous pot of money had appeared, but it still had to be bid for and the criteria set up to assess applications had to be met. It was mostly in the bigger projects that a bullying – and often misogynist – attitude and an assumption of entitlement to the money was most evident.

*

Meanwhile I was continuing to experience the highs of seeing projects completed but also some lows, often in tackling a general grouch and scepticism that has surrounded the lottery ever since its early days when the Churchill Papers, the ROH and the Millennium Dome all received a good public whacking. I felt proud of what it was achieving. The infrastructure of the country was being strengthened by substantial investment, and new participants and audiences were being reached. If some people railed against it there were many others who were appreciating its benefits, even if they had had to put in a lot of hard work in applying and then in actually delivering their projects. On the whole it was national commentators who were continually having a swipe at the lottery, while local press welcomed the projects involving their own areas. Finally, in January 1999, a piece in *The Financial Times* by Antony Thorncroft, entitled 'The Whingers are Silenced', lifted my spirits. He regretted the instinct of the arts community to complain and listed several big capital projects coming to fruition or already producing positive results; he commended the way other lottery programmes (such as A4E) were promoting access and new artistic approaches to audiences.

It was often the smaller projects that were most appreciative. When I attended openings such as a new bandroom for Swindon Pegasus Brass and a concert platform at Crystal Palace the sense of accomplishment was tangible. An unusual completion was a tapestry for the British Library, commissioned from the artist R. B. Kitaj. Called *If Not, Not*, and based on the artist's painting of the same name, it was the largest tapestry to be woven in Britain, measuring 22 square feet. Its hanging in the main entrance hall of the library was part of the original design by architect Colin St John Wilson, but it was threatened when long delays to the building of the library demanded cuts. It was rescued by the arrival of the National Lottery and a grant from ACE of £139,000. Tradition demanded that it be 'cut off' from the loom by a woman – it was a delightful surprise to be asked, and I duly went up to the Edinburgh Tapestry Company's huge Dovecot Studios for this ceremony. It was a tough job to cut 22 feet of heavy threads with what looked like kitchen scissors, but I had the support of master weaver Harry Wright, who had headed a team of four working on the tapestry for four years. Also in attendance were Brian Lang, the British Library's chief executive, and a collection of other dignitaries. Mission accomplished, my most vivid memory, as I posed for photographs against the loom while the champagne circulated, is of a disapproving Edinburgh matron tugging down the rather short skirt I was wearing. Perhaps the resulting images do show an unseemly expanse of thigh but it was a Christian Lacroix suit bought in a recent sale which I thought was the height of chic.

8

STORMY DAYS

New Labour and the Mary Allen affair – forecasts and figures –
the Sage and the Baltic – more plotting – back to the ROH –
A4E awards and their long-term effect

At the general election of 1 May 1997, Tony Blair's New Labour Party got in with a huge majority. Chris Smith was appointed Secretary of State for National Heritage – his department changed its title to Culture, Media & Sport (DCMS)[18] on 14 July. The choice was unexpected – he had been shadow Health Secretary before the election – but welcomed by the arts community: he was considered a cultured man with a practical interest in the arts. He walked straight into a storm. In early May Jenny McIntosh, after only five months as chief executive of the ROH, resigned, citing ill-health. ROH chair Peter Chadlington asked for a conversation with the new Secretary of State, at which no officials were present. He wanted to offer the job immediately to Mary Allen, sidestepping the required advertising process, and to this Chris Smith agreed. I first heard of the situation in a telephone call from Grey Gowrie on 12 May in which he announced

18. The name was changed again in July 2017 to the Department for Digital, Culture, Media & Sport.

the news but said that Mary would not leave ACE until September, thus giving the Council sufficient time to find her replacement. My immediate reaction – shared by other Council members – was shock. Not only would we be losing our chief executive to a fractious client, but New Labour, so optimistically greeted only a few days before, had immediately shown itself to be partial to the same sort of backroom arrangements for which its predecessors were notorious. At the DNH, where the civil servants were coming to terms with a new, and keen, administration after eighteen years of the Tories, initial consternation about the private meeting in fact turned into something positive. Melanie Leech remembers that she and her colleagues had concerns about whether Chris Smith, with his personal interest in the arts, would have problems in being as dispassionate as his position demanded:

> That was a big fear for us and in that respect the disaster around Mary moving to the Opera House was the best thing that happened because in one fell swoop, from our departmental perspective, the scales fell from Chris's eyes . . . I am prepared to believe it was well intentioned, it was all done for the right reasons but he was done over, he was taken to a private meeting, no officials were allowed to be there, he was told this had to happen, and he came back and we said WHAT? You told Peter WHAT? . . . And it probably would have taken us a year, through giving our best advice and debating with him and working matters through with him, to get to the same place that we got to overnight.

On the following day, 13 May, Mary's new appointment was announced. That evening the Council met in Nottingham for an open forum, everyone abuzz about who knew what and who had said what to whom when, Grey's role in the timetable of events being particularly unclear. The Council meeting the next morning was chaired by David Reid (in Grey's absence at the state opening of Parliament). Some members had asked for a closed session without staff present in order to discuss the situation but David refused. He read out a statement saying that Lord Gowrie and the secretary-general had had a successful initial meeting with the new Secretary of State; the same statement referred to Mary's ROH appointment. Members congratulated her but 'recorded their dismay and strong reservations about the way in which the appointment had been made'. Peter Chadlington had angered Council members anyway by a recent speech in which he championed direct government funding for national organisations such as the ROH, thus taking them out of ACE's portfolio; we were now infuriated by his approach to the Secretary of State without notification to the Council. There were various versions of events. The minutes state that Mary herself confirmed that she had advocated this course of action, although my diary note says that she had told Peter that she was not in a position to advise him but that he would have to ask the DNH. A statement by Thelma Holt saying that it was a splendid appointment but that the ROH had behaved disgracefully got unanimous support. It was agreed that a scrupulous procedure was needed for the appointment of a new secretary-general.

Over the next few days there was a great flurry of meetings. The situation was not helped by a photograph of Mary on the front page of *The Times*, cheerfully drinking champagne at the Cannes film festival where she had immediately gone to announce the recently agreed film franchises. (These had also caused some consternation in film circles as four had been forecast and only three awarded, to a total of £92.520 million. But at least one of our lottery-funded films, *Love and Death on Long Island*, starring John Hurt, was showing at the festival.)

Council members' dismay at the whole situation was mirrored among ACE staff who were furious and demoralised at what they saw as a stitch-up, moreover one that would make it very difficult in future for ACE to insist that its clients had proper appointment procedures. There were reports of Graham Devlin having to calm down artform directors about to mutiny. Another confusion lay in who had given permission for Mary not to serve her full six months' notice at the Council: it had been reported at our meeting on 14 May that she would now be leaving us on 1 August. There was ambiguity around this anyway, as one of the reasons Peter Chadlington gave for not having an appointment process was the fragility of the ROH finances and the urgent need for a chief executive to be in place.

Over the weekend at home the telephone rarely stopped ringing as various Council members shared their anger. Colin Nears (former chair of the dance panel) and choreographer Peter Wright were staying with me and my husband Brian, and it was difficult to maintain some discretion in front of them. This became even harder when Pamela Harlech (chair of ENB at the time) arrived for Sunday lunch positively steaming with indignation at the whole situation, about which *The Sunday Times* had published a surprisingly well-informed article which seemed to know as much as we, the Council members, did. The matter thus brought into the open was minutely dissected without anyone really knowing how it had all come about. Visitors departed, the telephone continued ringing and, in a series of calls between David Reid, Christopher Frayling and me, a suggestion arose that the former, as a retired businessman, should take over as acting secretary-general and oversee the appointment of Mary's successor. This seemed a good idea because Graham Devlin had only recently been appointed deputy secretary-general; although held in regard as a consultant and artistic director of the small theatre company Major Road, he lacked top-level executive experience. When David himself suggested the idea to Grey Gowrie the latter seemed enormously relieved; this appeared to be the way to calm the situation down and get both himself and the secretary of state off the hook. Over the next few days I received a call from Peter Chadlington, asking why everyone was so upset. He went on to say that the ROH was close to bankruptcy, that its technical union was threatening a strike, and that any criticism by ACE could prejudice an already delicate situation. I wasn't in a mood to listen.

The ROH came up again at the 21 May Panel meeting. Amid the furore surrounding Mary Allen's appointment, its management and finance team had apparently left. And, in spite of the emphasis put on access within the development bid, the organisation was still failing to produce an equal opportunities policy. While in the circumstances this couldn't be at the top of the priority list, any backsliding on such conditions was anathema to the Panel who were getting as sick of the ROH as the Council members were.

The Panel meeting was immediately followed by an emergency Council session. It was unanimously agreed that, given the consternation about the manner of her ROH appointment, Mary could not remain as our secretary-general. Her immediate resignation from ACE was sought, although because of the conflict of interest between the two jobs she would have to take a few months' 'gardening leave' before arriving at the ROH. Our fury with that organisation made us determined to issue a press release stating the Council's feelings. As senior appointments had to be agreed with the government, Grey Gowrie and I then set off for the DNH where we met Mark Fisher, the new minister for the arts, and permanent secretary Hayden Phillips. We told them of the suggestion that David Reid should become acting secretary-general (to which the full Council had agreed), and also mentioned our intention about the press release. Neither proposal received a warm welcome. It was finally agreed that the David Reid suggestion would have to be referred to the secretary of state; any public statement from ACE about the ROH should look to a positive future rather than rake over the past. In order to provide some departmental control over its drafting, Melanie Leech accompanied Grey and me back to ACE's headquarters where we, together with David Reid, spent the next two hours trying to find the right words. Concentration wasn't helped by Grey diving in and out of his private loo to change into a dinner jacket for a dinner with HRH Princess Margaret. The problem was how to devise a statement that would discourage Council members from resigning while satisfying a department wanting to protect their own position and that of the secretary of state. The result was phoned through to Mark Fisher who felt it should first be cleared with Chris Smith, so no immediate action could be taken. I took a late train back home to Bath and my long-suffering husband.

Word leaked out that a press release was being prepared. The next day I received a furious call from an ROH board member saying that if anything critical of the ROH was said it could bring down the whole development project – in which case the ROH would sue ACE. The lines started overheating again as aghast Council members telephoned each other and threatened to resign, aware of the disrepute into which the situation had brought ACE. A further emergency Council meeting was called on the afternoon of 22 May. We were told that the secretary of state had refused to endorse David Reid's appointment because of the need to follow proper procedures: as Graham Devlin was the deputy, he, and not a Council member, should become acting secretary-general. It was also reported that Peter Chadlington was preparing to come and explain to us what had happened but we felt this was inappropriate; nobody wanted to hear excuses. Instead, he and other members of the ROH board would be invited for a discussion on the current situation and an update on the development in progress at the June meeting of the Council. The press release was dropped: Grey Gowrie would issue a personal statement expressing regret at Mary's departure. It was also agreed that ACE should conduct an independent enquiry into the relationship between itself and the ROH; a lawyer, Edward Walker-Arnott, was commissioned to undertake this as a matter of urgency.

*

The 11 June Council meeting was held in a rather sombre room at the Grosvenor Hotel, next to London's Victoria station. Council meetings were sometimes held in venues other than the ACE headquarters at Great Peter Street but this was usually when they were seen as an annual 'retreat' and took place at some country hotel. It was unclear whether neutral ground had been found for our conversation with the representatives of the ROH board. These were Peter Chadlington, Vivien Duffield, James Butler and Robert Gavron; their arrival was somewhat confused. Grey left the room – we assumed to greet them but actually to go to the lavatory, so there was some consternation when he returned without them. When they were finally ushered in, the discussion was superficially cordial but Christopher Frayling says he learned a lesson that day:

> We all agreed who was going to say what [several of us had met earlier that morning] and I was going to kick off, and I remember going for it because we'd agreed to do that, and of course afterwards one member of the Council, who had said she was really going to go for them, collapsed completely and said, 'Of course we all love Covent Garden,' and Grey said the same. I was completely isolated. Bob Gavron that evening, it was reported to me, called me the biggest shit in London for having gone for them in front of the full Council. It was just naive of me to imagine that anyone would actually stick to what they said they were going to do, but they all collapsed like a pack of cards when it came to the personal confrontation.

The minutes of Council meetings were always exquisitely written by head of secretariat Lawrence Mackintosh, a delightful *eminence gris* who knew all the secrets but was discretion personified. Those for 11 June do not record individual contributions but they do note the need for the ROH to meet the conditions of its lottery grant – this had been my allocated script at the pre-meeting so I hope I didn't let Christopher down. There was regret over the way in which senior appointments had been made. Council feathers were ruffled over a remark by Vivien Duffield that special allowance should be given to the ROH because of the amount of private funding they were raising; likewise those of the ROH representatives, when they learned that ACE had already issued a press release announcing the independent enquiry. Peter Chadlington told me the next day that they had already lost one donor because of this; I retorted that it had to be that way because no one at ACE trusted the ROH's spin doctors. He also felt that ACE was not taking on board the seriousness of the ROH's financial situation: I said that we were aware of it, but there was no way that we could give them more money.

*

Since I had taken over as chair of the Panel I had felt increasingly irritated by the projection figures for future income. At that time (April 1996), the total amount available for immediate commitment was around £210 million, with £280 million predicted for 1997/98 and £300 million by 2000, providing the rules governing the lottery were not changed. This seemed reasonable: for the year ended March 1996 ACE's lottery proceeds had totalled £244.94 million. But since then the new programmes had been introduced, which had made a substantial inroad into the capital allocation. The total of £640 million allocated for the capital programme over the four years 1997–2001 in September 1996 dropped in early 1997 to £500 million because of the demands of the new programmes. A suggested ceiling of £15 million was then given to the Panel to recommend at each of its meetings. Although this was raised to £19–20 million in March 1997 when Camelot produced better figures than expected, no particular consternation about our diminishing income was expressed, in spite of the fact that some big applications were still in the pipeline. Overspends were also beginning to occur. Although additional money was provided to projects only after considerable scrutiny, we decided to establish a contingency fund of 10 per cent of the cost of uncompleted medium and large-scale building projects. Now that the monitoring department was up and running we could have a progress report at each meeting on all projects over £5 million.

It quickly proved to be impossible to keep to a rigid figure per meeting. Forecasted income was still high, good applications were being presented and there was no method of controlling them. The RAB priority lists were still creeping through the system and would not have any general acceptance until later in the year. At the June 1997 Panel meeting 67 recommendations went forward to Council for a total of £72.423 million. This did include the two large projects in Gateshead: the Regional Music Centre was allocated £1.303 million for development work and the Baltic Flour Mill £33.405 million for the building and £15 million towards its revenue costs for ten years. This was the only case of a project getting simultaneous revenue as well as capital funding from the lottery that I can remember. The Northern Arts people were good at the game!

*

Peter Hewitt feels that the Sage Gateshead (as the Regional Music Centre became) was a particular triumph for Gateshead Council. Following *Case for Capital* Northern Arts invited all interested local authorities across the northern region to bid for a new concert hall on the understanding that Northern Arts would back the strongest proposal to go forward to the National Lottery. Gateshead's was by far the most convincing bid in terms of ambition, partnership funding and overall commitment. As Peter says:

> We had no hesitation in backing Gateshead. This was a very big moment for the cultural regeneration of central Tyneside and shifted the axis to the south side of the river.

The resulting building, designed by architect Norman Foster, now crouches on the river bank like a huge glass cocoon. Peter cites it as a perfect example of good capital planning: organisations from all branches of the music world came together to create a non-hierarchical place where people could celebrate and participate. They brought their audiences with them and, as he says, 'You build this thing around them as opposed to building this thing and then saying, "Where's the audience?"' It's the project that Peter is proudest of realising during his time at Northern Arts. Christopher Frayling, who was Arts Council chair 2004–09, remembers opening the Sage in 2004 and echoes Peter:

> Here was this multi-purpose space, there was the big auditorium, there was folk music, there was jazz, there was Caribbean music, and there was this large foyer where all the music mixed. I thought, 'This is the future,' I loved it actually . . . And I sat in the coffee shop in the Baltic and I looked at the Sage, the Millennium Bridge and the Baltic and I thought it's like one of the Seven Wonders of the World what's happened up here. Not necessarily, not entirely due to the lottery – they had politicians, particularly in Gateshead, who were great at getting Euro money and matching, but the lottery enabled them to do it.

*

I have a particularly soft spot for the Baltic, which I was invited to launch with the announcement of its funding in June 1997. This involved an unnerving journey in the company of Gateshead councillors George Gill and Sid Henderson up in an outside lift which had been attached to the walls of the former flour mill. Summer had not yet arrived and the winds were icy as we ascended. At the top a flag was unfurled in the presence of a small group of shivering press. It was hard at that time to envisage the centre for contemporary art that would eventually emerge, or the rest of the wonders described by Christopher, but the enthusiasm of the Gateshead councillors was always a delight.

The Baltic's first art display was *Tarantara*, sculptor Anish Kapoor's bright scarlet PVC membrane, gloriously stretched over the empty shell of the gutted mill. Over 50m long and 25m wide, the work was installed for eight weeks during 1999 and seen by over 16,000 people; I was lucky enough to catch it on a family visit to Scotland with Brian. By some curious trick, Kapoor had ensured that when you looked up through the semi-transparent material the sky seemed miraculously close: a great moment of art even before the building began its transformation into art gallery.

*

In July, suddenly, the need for clarity about income figures became urgent. A paper on lottery cash forecasts for the preparation of business committee meeting held on 2 July suddenly showed a substantial drop. Because of Grey Gowrie's preoccupation with the SBC bid, discussion on this was delayed to another preparation of business meeting on 8 July which noted that 'the lottery cash position doesn't look good'. David Reid hinted that it might not be possible to agree on the Panel's July recommendations. This was the first real warning that I and the rest of the Panel had had. None the less Jeremy Newton was hopeful that the situation was not quite as serious as was being suggested.

A telephone call from Graham Devlin a couple of days later outlined the stark reality. He had received revised figures from the DCMS which removed up to £300 million from their ACE forecasts over the next three years. In January 1997 they had informed us that available lottery funds were likely to be £272–97million a year, a total of £816–91 million over three years – a substantial rise from the annual £240 million on which the Council had allocated its lottery budgets in September 1996. The figure now being issued was only £197 million a year, £591 million over three years. This was a very rude shock. At further emergency meetings with David Reid, Graham Devlin and Jeremy Newton we agreed that it was too late to halt the Panel's July recommendations which should go through to Council (any borderline cases being rejected); at a meeting with Grey Gowrie he was careful to acknowledge that the reduction of funds would have an effect on the SBC bid, which might now have to have a £50 million cap. With unfortunate timing, the Tate's director, Nicholas Serota, arrived in Grey's office while these discussions were going on, saying he wished to apply to ACE for £20 million towards Tate Modern.

At the subsequent Council meeting the drop in funds was clarified by the formal letter which Graham had received from the DCMS, indicating that the sharp reduction in lottery funds available to ACE from the following year was a result of 'a realignment of distributors'. Of David Puttnam's earlier suggestions to Virginia Bottomley, only NESTA would be set up as an independent body, not as a distributor but with a one-off endowment of £250 million from the National Lottery (David, whose Panel term of office ended that summer, subsequently became its first chair). There would be a new sixth good cause – the New Opportunities Fund (NOF) – created to make lottery grants to health, education and environment projects. Chris Smith's advisor John Newbigin describes this as a continuation of Hayden Phillips's battle with the Treasury: giving some money to these areas would safeguard the rest from government interference. 'It was kind of sacrificing half the army in order to stop losing the whole army,' says John; the 'additionality' principle (whereby lottery funds couldn't substitute for normal government expenditure) was a hard, but crucial, one to maintain. The NOF would also receive the Millennium Commission's share once those festivities ended. This was a further, if longer-term, blow to ACE as there had been a strong assumption up to that point that once the millennium had been and gone the Commission's allocation would be equally shared among the four other original distributors. In factual terms, instead of the 16.67 per cent of the good cause money that ACE received after the split with Scotland and Wales, it would now receive only 13.88%. It was hard, however, to oppose the changes: in the post-election review by New Labour's campaign team of which electoral promises had triggered the most public response, the creation of the NOF came highest.[19]

The situation was obviously going to necessitate a radical revision of the Council's planning budgets. Although the demands of the new programmes were already putting pressure on funds for capital, there had been no indication that the overall forecast would plummet to such an extent. As the 16 July 1997 Council minutes stated:

> Council expressed deep concern at the damaging consequences of the new planning figures, should they have to be adopted, and dismay at the way in which they had been conveyed.

19. The campaign literature had promised a new mid-week National Lottery draw, and listed four 'illustrative projects' which might benefit. These mirrored those of the earlier Puttnam presentation to Virginia Bottomley and outlined funds 'to support young talent in science, technology and the arts; to ensure our teachers have the skills and materials to make Britain a world leader in the use of information and communication technologies in schools; to help every child gain maximum advantage from their education and enrich their school experience by a programme of after-school learning and activities; to develop a national network of healthy living centres where people of all ages can get advice and assistance on how to keep fit and healthy.'

Furthermore

> the severely reduced figures with which the Council was now confronted were particularly difficult to understand and accept given that Ministers had actively encouraged the Council to develop individual programmes within the overall Lottery framework.

The irony was that these programmes had been developed partly with an eye to New Labour being elected; but once in power the politicians wanted their own mechanisms for delivery. In spite of some posturing about standing up to the DCMS and demanding at least partial restitution of the removed funds, the Council felt pretty impotent and would have to proceed as best it could, possibly by the deferment of programmes not yet running, such as the proposed one for publications and recordings.

There was one small benefit for me in the situation. It alerted my fellow Council members for the first time to the need to be fully informed of all capital projects in the pipeline. Up to that point the pace of getting the RAB lists, having them looked at by the artform departments and then awaiting revised versions from the RABs had been painfully slow. September was now set as a deadline. Meanwhile, those capital grants which were felt to be urgent, £14.6 million worth of them, were approved, and the interim scheme for discretionary grants for dance and drama students was given the go-ahead on a revised basis of £10 million over four years, starting in 1997/98. The meeting that decided this had started at 9 a.m. and finished at 6.20 p.m.

I then alerted the Panel to the situation, adding that a meeting was being sought with the secretary of state for clarification as there seemed to be some confusion at the DCMS.

*

While the department did indeed seem to be wavering with figures, the main confusion and uncertainty was happening at ACE after weeks of misadventure. The ground was fertile for more plotting, and on 31 July David Puttnam convened a meeting, in the grandeur of the Athenaeum Club on Pall Mall, to discuss the future of ACE. Present were myself, Ernest Hall, Sue Robertson, Graham Hitchen, consultant Adrian Ellis and advisors John Newbigin and Ben Evans (with whom I had recently crossed swords over some dismissive remarks I felt he had ignorantly made about stabilisation). By this time I was having sleepless nights and my diary records a feeling of depression at the way those present pulled ACE apart without providing any concrete suggestions as to how to improve it. However, Graham Hitchen's recollection is more positive. He says that David Puttnam and John Newbigin were extending the work they had done before the election on cultural policy by developing a wide vision for culture with Chris Smith (hence the renaming of the department) and wanted to see how they could get ACE to engage with this and align itself to what was called 'a broader communications and creative industries strategy'. Because of all the current turmoil at ACE, they wanted to identify some Council members they could trust to take matters forward. His notes on the tasks of the meeting identify the need for change, the direction of that change, the options for a future structure and work needing to be done now. Distracted by events and tiredness, I didn't particularly register these then, but continuing discussions would lead to the setting up of the Council's strategy group later that year. By that time I had come to appreciate the various elements more fully and happily accepted the invitation to chair the group.

*

In late July Edward Walker-Arnott delivered his draft report on the ROH. His brief had been to examine the status and supervision of its development scheme; its relationship to ACE, including systems of accountability; and the management systems, structures and procedures to be operated during its closure period.

The management of the development project was praised, and no grounds for concern about either its status or its supervision were found. It was on time and on budget, to the considerable credit of the ROH's project director John Seekings. ACE's conditions were being met, although it was also pointed out that the company's overall financial position had deteriorated since March 1997 and that the very unfamiliarity of its activities during closure carried risks. On the governance of the ROH during closure, Walker-Arnott found himself satisfied that the new regime (chairman, chief executive and finance director) which had recently been put in place – although not to be fully active until Mary Allen completed her 'gardening leave' – should bring good financial planning and financial rigour. The report referred to the criticism that under the previous regime artistic standards were high but programming was divorced from resources: financial considerations were now to be addressed at the same time as artistic ones, not afterwards. On the relationship with ACE, it was suggested that while

> the Arts Council should state clearly and succinctly what it wants and see that it gets it . . . the Royal Opera House should be allowed to get on and manage its own business.

Walker-Arnott also recommended that ACE observers should no longer attend ROH board meetings and that the ROH/ACE monitoring committee should develop a much lighter touch. Two things about this riled Council members: the intense difficulty we had had in getting information from the ROH because of their apparent reluctance to engage with us, and Walker-Arnott's adamant assertion that he had been unable to find any evidence of collusion and backroom dealings despite the fact that several Council members had spoken to him from personal experience of it.

Added to our discomfort with its contents was the information that Grey Gowrie had sent a copy of the draft to Peter Chadlington before the Council had had an opportunity to discuss it. Grey's reason was that the two of them were about to appear before a select committee and he felt that Peter should be aware of the report's contents in advance of this. This may have been reasonable but it caused Council members to make another rush to their telephones, outraged that the ROH had once again apparently had the upper hand. A tempestuous Council meeting followed. It was agreed that four Council members – Christopher Frayling, Deborah MacMillan, David Reid and me – would meet Walker-Arnott to discuss his draft so that a final version could be presented at the September Council meeting. At that meeting Walker-Arnott explained that he had written the report as a private commission for ACE and there had been no intention to unbalance it in the ROH's favour; he agreed to make four minor changes of emphasis. When he presented this revised draft at the September Council meeting he would reiterate that his report concentrated on the ACE side of the relationship and the need for it to be based on a clear expression of expectations of the ROH. Grey then sent the report to the secretary of state together with a commentary and a note on a number of contextual points.

Although the deteriorating financial position at the ROH was referred to in the report, the actuality was more extreme: when she took up her position on 1 September, Mary Allen found the organisation at the point of bankruptcy. Melanie Leech remembers that both the DCMS and ACE were having to check the ROH's solvency monthly for some time. The danger lay in the revenue grant: stopping it would have meant the ROH going into liquidation, while continuing with it in the circumstances exposed ACE to risk. At least there was general acknowledgement that, as far as the building development was concerned, lottery money was being well spent.

The ROH saga would churn on through the autumn. In November a report into its present state and prospects for survival until the re-opening was issued by Parliament's DCMS select committee, under the chairmanship of the Rt Hon. Gerald Kaufman MP. This regretted the ROH's current financial position:

> We would prefer to see the House run by a philistine with the requisite financial acumen than by the succession of opera and ballet lovers who have brought a great and valuable institution to its knees.

The Committee also accused the ROH board of 'disastrous misjudgements' in failing to find an alternative venue during the two-year closure period. Much personal viciousness was aimed at Mary Allen over her controversial change of jobs, and ACE came under fire for showing a 'serious shortcoming of financial control' in failing to insist on tighter management before it awarded the lottery grant. Within forty-eight hours Peter Chadlington had resigned as ROH chair, but Mary was persuaded by the rest of the board to fight on. She finally left the ROH some six months later, in March 1998, shortly after Sir Colin Southgate was appointed as the new chair: a full account of her time there can be found in her book *A House Divided*.

*

While this drama unfurled, the pressure on lottery funds continued. For the first round of the main A4E programme some 1,000 applications had been received, showing how much need there was from both regularly funded organisations and those new to ACE. 786 were eligible, totalling £122.6 million. In early August an all-day meeting of the A4E selection panel was held: this had been set up under the chairmanship of Stephen Phillips and comprised all artform chairs and their directors plus Jeremy Newton and me, together with some 'independents' including youth arts worker Woozy Brewster, writer Kate Mosse and dancer/choreographer Simon Vincenzi. Graham Devlin remembers 'a bunfight' of twenty-four people arguing away. We arrived at recommendations for 112 grants totalling just under £19 million, a figure which was agreed at the August Council meeting. As the original budget for the two 1997 rounds of the programme had been only £13.5 million this was a further setback to those of us trying to maintain capital budgets.

It was urgently necessary to monitor and modify future demand, but the meetings for the second, third and fourth rounds of A4E in November 1997 and April and July 1998, were no easier. The whittling down of applications into a manageable heap was hard and disputatious, and caused a heated argument about whether A4E grants were for artistic development or social regeneration. All the meetings lasted for several hours and involved two rounds of voting; the outcomes were always substantially above the amounts budgeted. When the selection panel was first set up, the RABs felt omitted from the assessment process: technically this was because their role was limited to the soliciting of applications. As the artform departments were also advising their regularly funded clients but *were* on the deciding panel, one can appreciate the RAB rage. Some mechanism was finally found to involve them but it wasn't until devolution began during 1999 and the RABs were able to devise their own Regional Arts Lottery Programme (RALP) that they were given the authority and control they desired. Meanwhile some small alleviation was offered by the Cameron Mackintosh Foundation, which contributed £500,000 to the scheme over five years, and the Henry Moore Foundation, which agreed £60,000 a year for three years for visual arts applications.

Although the lack of proper processes and application criteria gave rise to this massive over-demand, the A4E programme did begin to address some of the under-funding from which regular clients were suffering and continued to broaden ACE's constituency. In its turn it led via the RALP to the popular and regulated Grants for the Arts which exist today and have led to huge expansion in arts activity in this country. It wasn't only in the capital manifestation that those early years of lottery money provoked a sea-change in what ACE could support.

Once the directions had been changed in 1996 to allow revenue programmes to be introduced, those who grasped the opportunity opened up a whole new ball-game. If the process of getting the programmes launched was fraught with problems, the way they changed public funding of the arts can now be seen as fundamental. In the early 1990s discussions at both Panel and Council level were concentrated on the RFOs, with Projects and Schemes helping smaller companies step on to the funding ladder; individual artists were never directly funded as their commissioning was considered to be the job of the clients. Nowadays – in spite of funding cuts to the Treasury grant but bolstered by lottery money – there is much more activity, incorporating individual artists, new festivals, new site-specific work and many more participatory and celebratory events. Just one example was The Big Dance, a biennial celebration which initially started as an initiative of Ken Livingstone when Mayor of London in 2006 and had its final year in 2016. It spread UK-wide and offered hundreds of opportunities for people from all walks of life to participate in or watch marvellous dance in a wide range of settings from shopping malls to town squares to seafronts.

There was a lot of grumbling when all lottery distributors had money taken away from them to mount the 2012 Olympic and Paralympic Games in London, but no one could begrudge the part of this that was recycled into the Cultural Olympiad that accompanied them. Over four years leading up to the Games, Ruth Mackenzie as director led a team that encouraged over 177,000 events to take place in over 1,000 venues throughout the UK; over 25,000 artists took part and it is reckoned that 43 million people had some kind of cultural experience, either watching or participating. My particular memories include Martin Creed's *Work no. 1197* which demanded as many bells as possible being rung throughout the country for three minutes on the opening day of the Olympics; and the staging of all Shakespeare's plays by different companies from around the world at Shakespeare's Globe, giving British audiences the opportunity to experience their great national playwright's work in a multitude of tongues. A commissioning fund was set up for disabled and deaf artists and special emphasis was put on reaching as diverse an audience was possible. The strapline of the Cultural Olympiad was 'Once in a lifetime' but similar, if smaller, festivities accompanied the 2014 Commonwealth Games in Glasgow and look set to form part of all future Olympics (even if the 2016 Rio Games had their own challenges and didn't match up to the commitment of the London cultural organisers). When the Tour de France took a detour through Britain in the summer of 2014 it had its own cultural programme attached.

We are now also able to recognise historical events in a major way, even if the subject matter isn't necessarily celebratory. The centenary of the First World War is being marked by 14–18 NOW with a series of artists' commissions boldly planned by director Jenny Waldman. One of the largest of these was by artist Paul Cummins and designer Tom Piper who filled the moat at the Tower of London with ceramic poppies representing soldiers' lives lost. Another was the initiative by director Neil Bartlett to ask people to write to the Unknown Soldier whose statue commemorates the dead at Paddington station: 21,400 letters were received. Everyone could play their part without moving from their home or by joining the rest of the community at a nearby event: on the hundredth anniversary of the announcement of the war we were invited to turn off our lights for an hour from 10 p.m., leaving a single candle of remembrance alight. Although the resulting darkness wasn't as pitch as one would have hoped, the response was none the less remarkable. Perhaps the most evocative of all took place on 1 July 2016, the hundredth anniversary of the Battle of the Somme, when 1,400 volunteers took part in *We're Here Because We're Here*, devised by Jeremy Deller. Each one dressed in First World War uniform and representing a soldier killed at the Somme, they appeared throughout the UK, wandering alone or in groups among the population, the eerie ghosts of that terrible day.

None of this benefit, pleasure and fulfilment would have been possible without lottery funding.

SOME EXAMPLES OF PUBLIC ART

A13 Artscape – Leeds Infirmary – The *Koan* – figurative art

One element of this new spread of art is literally now before our eyes. Walsall New Art Gallery formed part of a network of new and refurbished contemporary art galleries that also included the Serpentine and Camden Arts Centre in London, the Ikon in Birmingham and the Arnolfini in Bristol. In the next phase of the capital programme they were joined by Turner Contemporary in Margate, the Hepworth in Wakefield, Nottingham Contemporary and, also in that city, New Art Exchange. These well thought-out and delivered projects, funded with ACE's lottery money, have contributed to arts-led regeneration in their respective towns and cities and raised considerable awareness of contemporary art.

Not to be forgotten either was the impact of the lottery on public art.

*

One of the largest public art grants was given to another visionary local authority. Barking and Dagenham Borough Council had submitted an application for £3.895 million during 1996 for an ambitious plan to regenerate stretches of the A13 with pieces of art combined with some community arts involvement: it came to be known as the A13 Artscape project. The grant was awarded in May 1997. The officer behind the scheme was Jeremy Grint, then head of regeneration, who worked with the Public Art Commissions Agency and a lead artist, architect Tom de Paor. Grint pays tribute to the support given by an inspirational Leader, George Brooker, who persuaded the Council not only to back the capital bid but also to provide the ongoing maintenance that the various art projects required. The idea had come to Grint through the work that the community arts group FreeForm was doing in the borough: there was general agreement that the long stretch of the A13 through Barking needed visual improvement and the lottery provided the opportunity. Having got the backing of his council, Grint speaks of the complexity of juggling the rest of those involved:

> We had bits of the community saying, 'What on earth are you doing spending money on this? You should be spending money on doing up our homes or that sort of thing, this is completely the wrong thing to be doing.' We had the local arts community wanting their slice of the pie in some of this. And then because of the matched funding we had to fit in with two

different regimes, so you had the Highways Agency in one instance, whom we were trying to get matched funding from, and then also the Single Regeneration Budget programme which was run by another bit of government, predecessors of Communities and Local Government, so you had to comply with their restrictions around that particular piece of money and try to utilise that bit of money . . . Then you've got the Arts Council, whatever they wanted, these various conditions, and then people coming down to monitor and to look at some of the designs coming forward and then trying to fit what they were saying with what some of these other agencies were saying.

In spite of the tensions, the disagreements and the egos that had to be soothed, and although eventually not all the works planned were achieved, Grint is proud of the many that were. Most are still standing and have been accepted as community landmarks. A further effect of the project was to galvanise councillors into continuing the idea of the Artscape by commissioning the art and architecture practice muf to create a new public space outside Barking town hall. This Grint describes as 'bold, brash and youthful': although it was opposed by some of the older councillors, he feels that the whole experience of the original project led to a new kind of thinking and overall openness to new high quality dense development. However, one of the works that did not please its creator were the twin cones at the Goresbrook interchange designed by Thomas Heatherwick who disliked the final shade of the tarmac in which they were delivered (although this was said to match the surrounding area, as originally stipulated). Grint could not find £200,000 to replace them, and says that initially Heatherwick disowned the pieces, although now does apparently acknowledge them as part of his work.

*

Although the excellent Paintings in Hospitals scheme had started in 1959 and since then some NHS trusts such as the Chelsea and Westminster hospital in London's Fulham Road had launched exemplary arts programmes, arts in healthcare had not taken off in a big way because of the problems of paying for it. There wasn't at the time enough empirical evidence to show its direct benefits to the healing process and therefore to put any NHS funding towards it. The coming of the lottery was thus a boon in offering another source of funding in this area, and many NHS trusts started to work with commissioning agencies to seek lottery grants not only for individual art works but also for elements of design. One such project was at Leeds General Infirmary, which received a lottery grant in November 1996 for a design by artists Tess Jaray and Tom Lomax of the entrance to the new wing of the hospital, Jubilee Square (the main building had been designed by Gilbert Scott). For artists these projects were not always easy: Tess, pointing out that each one relies on human relationships, remembers that she

> wanted to make somewhere rather special although there were tremen-
> dous limitations and there was a lot of quite special brickwork involved. I
> would say that we had a lot of difficulties . . . There was not a very good
> relationship between the architects and myself, we simply didn't see things
> from the same point of view. They didn't quite grasp that the aesthetic
> aspect was of any real importance.

The number of various bodies involved and concerns over Health and Safety also meant that 'art gets further and further away the longer you discuss it'. Nonetheless Tess feels that a good job was done. I went to see the result after it was completed in the autumn of 1998. It was beautiful, and worth all of the £700,000 invested in it by ACE's lottery money as well as the contributions from other funders. But here again there was a problem in getting the Infirmary to acknowledge both the artists' work and its lottery funding. Much correspondence went to and fro between ACE and the NHS trust before the receptionist's blank stare at being asked about the design was replaced by proper signage and an information sheet. Sadly, Tess now thinks that the hospital has broken up the Square and built over it: in spite of several enquiries to the Leeds General Infirmary no one there seems prepared or able to confirm this.

A further example, on a smaller scale, was the sculpture *Land Sea Light Koan* by Liliane Lijn, commissioned by the Isle of Wight NHS Trust as a landmark for St Mary's Hospital in Newport with the help of a June 1995 lottery grant of £31,550. The initial reception in the local media was largely hostile, because of the use of lottery money by ACE to support the commissioning of public art and also among some members of the public who did not appreciate that charitable and ACE monies were being used to fund the commission and not NHS revenue funding. A further annoyance was the fact that the sculpture was supposed to revolve but after six months – and without the regular maintenance checks that were initially promised – the contractor's design and placement of the rotating wheels of the internal motor enabling this operated only intermittently before breaking down altogether. A letter from the NHS trust chair sent to me in February 1998 pointed out that

> Whilst the Trust Board would be happy to continue to defend the Koan as a Work of Art, we cannot do so unless it is operating in the way it was originally intended.

Although we attempted to encourage the artist to remedy the situation, through legal means if necessary, she pleaded that it was the contractors' fault and she could not afford to pursue them through the warranty. She says now:

> I was unfortunate to have worked with a dishonest contractor and I was advised that I would not obtain satisfaction through legally pursuing the company or the individual. I recall that I did, however, offer to re-engineer the sculpture at my own cost. At the time, I had numerous offers of help from engineers living on the Isle of Wight, who thought the sculpture had brought something of value to their community. Unfortunately, it appeared that, due to the continuing public controversy, the NHS trust preferred to draw a line under the matter. They, therefore, asked me to make the cone stable and make good the lights, which I did, sadly, because I would have liked to have seen the work in motion as I had intended it to be.

The *Koan* however did remain and was refurbished in 2007 – Guy Eades of Healing Arts (the commissioning agency) says that it is

> now an icon for the hospital and is featured regularly on its promotional material and as a backdrop for filmed TV broadcasts and press photographs. It therefore occupies a prominent and positive profile. It remains the largest piece of public artwork that the Island has on display and has a reputation and acknowledgement beyond the Island.

Additional renovation works on the *Koan*'s motor commenced in 2016 and will continue into 2017 with the donated services of engineering firm TSTD Ltd, to see if the sculpture can be made to revolve again.

Since those examples, there has been a lot of research into the positive benefits of introducing art into a healthcare environment. One of the most recent is the establishment of the Aesop 1 Framework, which takes health professionals through all the aspects of developing and researching an arts in health programme. It's really necessary to have the research figures as it remains an area where qualitative appreciation is so much easier to find than quantitative – but it's the latter that funders need.

*

In the early days of ACE lottery funding there were several applications for memorial statues such as the Wallenberg one at London's Marble Arch (see page 89), but I think it was probably a request from the town of Morecambe to honour comedian Eric Morecambe in a similarly figurative way that finally proved too much for the modernists in ACE's visual arts department. In a presentation to the April 1998 Panel meeting, a representative from that department suggested an embargo on lottery grants for 'memorial works which were made as likenesses rather than following contemporary arts practice'. It seemed to most of us on the Panel that figurative statues, as long as they were well designed and presented, were in line with ACE's desire to widen access, but none the less RAB public arts officers were given the unenviable task of working out 'a policy for successful intervention'. I'm not sure this ever had a resolution.

9

IN SEARCH OF A STRATEGY

*The problems of devising a strategy – the Panel changes – formation of
the Council strategy group – a stressful autumn – Birmingham Hippodrome
bid – betrayal by the drama panel – December Council and the SBC –
the problems of cutting regular clients – a strategy for opera and ballet –
back to the SBC*

In early August 1997 details were circulated of the White Paper on the revisions to the National Lottery (entitled, in what was to become a recurring refrain of New Labour, *The People's Lottery*). Along with proposals for the creation of NESTA and the NOF came directions for the improvement of distribution – the need for clear funding strategies from all distributors, the power to solicit applications, more delegation, better processes for applicants. These were gratefully received by the Panel in our bid to bring more certainty into the situation. But how to go about creating a capital strategy was anything but easy.

The capital programme had been running for over two and a half years and had built up huge expectations. In spite of recent attempts to lower these, many organisations were in the middle of planning, and raising partnership funding for, substantial projects. It would have been relatively simple at the beginning, as Northern Arts's *Case for Capital* had shown, when one could draw on a blank sheet. But the inability to have a strategy and the open application system that had been demanded in the past had prevented any process for prioritising the number of applications in the pipeline, let alone those to be submitted in the future. The lack of mutual trust and openness between ACE and the RABs didn't help. Another factor which was in our minds – as future ACE Chair, Gerry Robinson, now articulates – was the fact that

> it was genuinely difficult to do because if you think about trying to define, you can very easily get into excluding things. By a series of structural definitions as to what will meet the right kind of project, very quickly you get a group of people who know precisely how to play that, they know what to say, how to write it, and almost by having a policy over-defined you can eliminate really good, from the heart, but poorly argued projects.

Christopher Frayling also argues against having too rigorous a strategy:

> The energetic ones who had commitment and vision broke through the cordon and got there and maybe in the arts that's the best way to do things.

The huge range of projects that had put in successful applications through the efforts of project champions and their other funders was certainly transforming the landscape in a way that a formal ACE strategy from the beginning would have been unlikely to do. The scattergun approach had uncovered demand that couldn't have been foreseen.

None the less something had to be done. We needed a strategy for the future and had to address the current imbalance of demand over available resources. We had to deal with expectations that had been raised and now could probably not be realised, along with the reaction of organisations which had been encouraged to delay their bids in all good faith, only to find that there was no longer the money to fulfil them.

Those of us connected with the capital programme felt that the other programmes were in their infancy and lacked the same longterm commitment. There had been a desultory discussion about deferring these when the figures dropped, but the majority of Council members was against it. Furthermore, politicians were making clear that they covered areas that met some of New Labour's prime objectives on access and participation: Chris Smith himself had stated his desire to shift lottery funding from capital to revenue. Not that the capital programme itself was bereft of political interest. Within a few months of New Labour's arrival, a rather caustic comment in the monitoring section of the March 1998 Panel minutes stated: 'Many of the more troublesome projects were of the type the government supported most and which the minister was visiting all over the country.' No further details were given, although my diary for the time notes my exasperation with Mark Fisher, who as arts minister did not always seem to be very supportive of ACE's dilemmas. Mark had been a figure in the arts world before becoming an MP (he'd been principal of the Tattenhall Arts and Education Centre in Cheshire and written a couple of stage plays); his friendships with many in the sector seemed to prevent him from being as dispassionate as the job sometimes demanded. He was none the less a supporter of the arm's length principle and now says:

> In opposition I'd been stalwart in saying, 'The government's got to take more of a lead, government policy etc., rather than the arm's length principle.' But, you know, the closer we got to being in government the more one saw what a wonderful thing it was – what a very convenient thing it was!

Within ACE, artform departments' and the RABs' revenue needs were seen as more pressing. The lottery department had never been fully integrated with artform departments and had become even more disconnected when it moved out of Great Peter Street. While individual Council members supported capital projects within their areas, their main allegiance was to their revenue clients and the development needs of their sector. I was the only person at the Council table fighting to maintain capital budgets, only too aware of the demand and the need. At the same July Council meeting at which the lottery forecasts were so dramatically lowered, Graham Devlin and Jeremy Newton, reacting to heavy political hints, recommended the extension of the stabilisation programme. This was accepted. Stabilisation awards for the majority of organisations in the pilot programme were agreed at the Council meeting on 17 September: they totalled nearly £17 million (as against the £5 million originally budgeted the year before). Applications for another round of A4E were already in the pipeline, and the publications and recordings programme was about to be launched as a two-year pilot.

Graham Devlin was in and out of the DCMS trying to negotiate but to no avail. His efforts were not helped by a new failure of communication over the forecasting of lottery income. In a conversation I had with the DCMS's Melanie Leech at around this time, she said that ACE had always been given planning figures based on a total amount of £9 billion for good causes to be raised by 2001 – a figure which John Major had stated in his launch of the National Lottery. Mark Fisher confirmed this when he accused ACE of profligacy in its allocations. He said that he and Chris Smith were under the impression that from the start ACE and other good cause distributors had been promised £1.8 billion each up until 2001 and ACE had committed more than this. He was adamant that our current situation was our own fault. But the correspondence between Stuart Macdonald, then head of the National Lottery division at the DNH, and Jeremy Newton in July 1995 had clearly based the ACE forecast on Camelot's income in any given year and its assessment of that for the year ahead. This had continued to be the practice and signalled more advantageous figures to ACE than a block forecast. In the end it was agreed to differ rather than to squabble.

In this hiatus it would have been helpful to the Panel to have some definite figures with which to work. But forward planning and budget figures for lottery operations continued to be subject to constant change for many months, indeed years, to come. In September 1997 the figure proposed by Graham Devlin for the capital programme was £76.6 million for the remainder of 1997/98 and £121.5 million for each of the following three years (the contingency for covering project overruns now reduced to 7.5 per cent from the 10 per cent agreed months earlier). To put this into context, the amount committed to capital grants in 1996/97 had been £363.551 million[20] (within five-year forecasts given to ACE at the time) and there were 628 applications, totalling £720.303 million, being assessed.

*

What was actually needed was less a strategy than some kind of rationale on how the 'A' priorities on the RAB lists might best be accommodated;

20. ACE Annual Report 1996/97.

decisions would also have to be taken about the 'national' projects that were not included. On what basis should future distributions be made? By region? By artform? If regional, should the ten Arts Boards receive equal amounts or should it be done per capita? Before any decisive action could be taken, everyone seemed to agree the need for maps, charts, text and presentations. The squeeze was definitely on, but a paper for the Panel's September meeting outlining the steps that needed to be taken to develop a capital strategy set out a timetable for its final agreement in May/June 1998. Without more direction from the executive this seems to have been accepted – in spite of my scribbling on my papers that the 'timetable is far too long. This is URGENT.' The minutes agreed that the development of rigorous strategies was indeed an important priority.

It was an intensely difficult problem to grapple with and many of us Council members felt bruised by the summer's events. But at least I felt supported by the Panel, which had undergone its own changes. As well as David Puttnam, that summer Ruth Mackenzie, Cleo Laine and Nima Poovaya-Smith had ended their terms of office and were replaced by Tish Francis, joint director of Oxford Playhouse, the Faber publisher Matthew Evans, music promoter Keith Harris and Virginia Tandy, whose background was museums and galleries. I also brought on public relations expert Lynette Royle to advise on a more positive feel about the good being done by ACE's lottery grants. Like those they replaced, these were all people with considerable jobs of their own, but attendance at the monthly meetings (10 a.m. to about 3.30 p.m.) continued to be high. Discussions remained well-informed in spite of the huge amount of paperwork often being circulated, as was the case with Council papers, only days beforehand. There was not only a huge range of applications to go through in some detail, but also monitoring reports, policy reviews and public relations matters, to say nothing of the capital strategy papers beginning to arrive. Throughout my time chairing the Panel the meetings were (almost!) always pleasant and much more focused than the Council meetings, with all their factional interests, could be. Whatever the outside pressures, one of the great pleasures of my time at ACE was always in leading such a tolerant and dedicated group.

*

In October Grey Gowrie announced that he would be standing down in the spring of 1998. He felt that ACE would benefit from a new chair and secretary-general to follow through the proposed new lottery legislation; he was also experiencing pressure from the amount of time that the (unpaid) position demanded. This meant further uncertainty and delay; both the Council and the DCMS felt that the appointment of a permanent secretary-general should be the responsibility of the incoming chair.

The high frustration of Council members at this time was matched by that of the executive. Graham Devlin declares:

> It was an absolute nightmare . . . the construction of a board as structurally divided as Council at that point was completely disempowering for me and also I think incredibly enervating for the whole organisation. You couldn't do anything: you had to spend a huge amount of time cajoling or stroking individual Council members . . . and the stand-off between the artform departments and the regions was at one of the worst levels. It did make things very difficult indeed.

*

One result of this void of leadership was the formation of a new Council strategy group which, as noted above, I was asked to chair. The Athenaeum Club discussion in July had been its genesis: now my distaste at being lectured to by outsiders had developed into a desire to do something more concrete. Other Council members agreed that ACE was dragging its heels and lacked engagement with the political debate. The DCMS was about to undertake a review of its activities and we felt that the Council had to have its own input in deciding how to reposition itself politically. The slow pace towards forming a capital strategy convinced us that this was unlikely to be delivered unless Council members got involved. So a small group of us – initially Christopher Frayling, Gavin Henderson and me – was given formal authority by the Council to develop strategies for decentralisation, Treasury/lottery funding co-ordination, education, the creative economy, national companies and the national touring perspective.

These were all issues central to ACE's work and it now seems extraordinary that responsibility for them should have been grasped by a small group of non-executives, assisted by a member of staff, Graham Hitchen, who was not even on the senior management team. Meanwhile, the DCMS was being kept abreast of the executives' thinking through fortnightly breakfast meetings between Graham Devlin and advisor John Newbigin; at David Puttnam's suggestion John was also being briefed in monthly meetings with Nicole Penn-Symons on the progress of lottery-funded projects. It's hard to think of a more dysfunctional way for any organisation, especially a governmentally supported quango, to go about its business.

The strategy group first met on 4 November. We didn't have much time to cover the huge agenda before being required to present our proposals to the spending review team at the DCMS, led by Andrew Ramsay, in December. We stressed the need for the Council to have a more focused national strategic function without sectional interests; rather surprisingly, after all the battles, we urged near-total devolution of clients and funding schemes to the regions. Our 'big idea' was a longer-term amalgamation with other bodies, such as the Museum and Galleries Commission and the Design Council, into a Council for Creativity which would work across the cultural sector and advise the government on many matters. The importance of a strong relationship between the department and the strategy group (rather than the Council itself!) over the coming months was highlighted. We agreed that a plan for the development of the necessary work should be drawn up. This would be taken forward by the executives steered by the strategy group and in liaison with the communications sub-group of Council that had also been set up. How all this time was found for detail and meetings when Council members also had their own professional employment is a matter of some wonder.

*

The general malaise was not helped by an announcement by Chris Smith in October 1997 that he had asked Richard Eyre (who had recently stepped down from his directorship of the National Theatre) to carry out an independent report on the possibility of the Royal Opera, Royal Ballet and ENO all sharing the ROH. Because of the tensions between ACE, the ROH and ENO, this caused much anxiety. The artform chairs and I drafted a letter to the secretary of state saying that since Mary Allen's departure and Grey Gowrie's announced retirement we lacked leadership: we requested a meeting. This elicited an immediate response from Melanie Leech to whom the draft had been sent. She called me to say that the letter was a 'suicide note': the secretary of state would think that ACE was in turmoil. I replied that things were not working well and we were being baulked in our determination to put things right by a department that blocked access to ministers. She said that a letter would be sent to the Council from the secretary of state promising to appoint a new chair by mid-December, who would then appoint the new secretary-general. She obviously felt that Council members were interfering too much; she said that if we wanted a meeting we should send a paper setting out some of the key issues and how we thought they should be addressed. We agreed that we would first await the promised letter. This duly arrived during a two-day Council meeting on 11 and 12 November.

The first day of this Council meeting was like a gathering of the clans, with all the RAB chief executives and artform directors present. Because of the huge attendance we broke the usual Council practice of going to the country for two-day meetings and congregated instead over the public rooms at the Royal Academy of Engineering which at the time neighboured ACE in Great Peter Street. The purpose of the first day was to explore all aspects of the current capital programme in the hope of reaching a clear forward strategy. There was a lot of sensible talk about the necessity of melding national strategy with regional development needs, how prioritising would be greatly assisted by the setting of reliable budgets, and the importance of longterm financial stability in the assessment of projects. The next day the Council got down to some detail: it was agreed that planning should take place over an eight-year period from April 1998; that £1 billion should be committed to capital over that time; and that from this sum a pot of £200 million would be put by for a handful of projects of national significance with a cap of £50 million on any individual application. Otherwise the maximum any project could receive would be £15 million. RABs would be asked to reprioritise their capital bids yet again, this (third!) time into tranches of £50 million; artform departments at ACE would then make recommendations on their lists and would work with the lottery department to map out the national provision. Although the Council reserved the right to alter the balance of its budgets in the future, RABs had made a strong case for such variations to be made well in advance so that plans could be secure for three to five years ahead.

Some other lottery budgets were set at this meeting, including £7 million over two years for publications and recordings. This was much against the Panel's advice – we all regarded the programme as one that should be delayed, if not dropped entirely, in view of the financial pressures. It never actually got off the ground: as lottery funding for one-off revenue purposes became more accepted, responsibility for those areas was quietly removed from capital budgets. The imbalance between lottery and Treasury funding remained and we were grappling with the fact that many of ACE's regular clients were still suffering through lack of proper funds. Even money that should have helped the revenue position was coming under fire. It was reported that confusion around the A4E programme was causing considerable dismay in the arts community: at a recent Theatrical Management Association conference ACE had been severely criticised. Participants had objected to the promotion of such schemes as A4E while the needs of the regular clients were being neglected. ACE was perceived to lack clarity in its decision-making and communication, and had failed to control and manage expectations generated by lottery schemes. Bureaucracy had grown and the use of consultants had increased. There was also concern at the leadership vacuum caused by Grey Gowrie's early departure and the continued delay in appointing a new secretary-general.

Much of this criticism was valid even if it showed little understanding of the restrictions of lottery rules. It reflected what many of us on Council were feeling. All the lottery programmes had been launched under heavy political persuasion without proper time for research or any real idea of likely demand, and they were putting huge pressure on the structure of the whole organisation. The sums were so big and the applications so many that to grapple them into some kind of order seemed a task that even Hercules might have baulked at. But something had to be done. I was getting very short of sleep and so, I am sure, were those involved with the projects awaiting decisions.

There were also personal conflicts, such as one over a bid from Birmingham Hippodrome. This had come in at £24 million and would be affected by the £15 million cap imposed by the Council at its November meeting. In spite of a private assurance to me by Bob Southgate, chair of West Midlands Arts, that they could do it for less, the team responsible were adamant that any reduction would seriously compromise the viability of the whole project. Crispin Raymond, who was the project manager, was a close friend and neighbour of mine in Bath: at such times separating the professional from the personal was genuinely hard. We had several difficult meetings at which I had to be careful to maintain ACE's position in spite of the pressure Crispin was experiencing. In the end, through Jeremy Newton's negotiation, it was agreed that the bid had national implications and could thus come from the reserved pot. The award was £20 million – not the £24 million requested and I know the considerable strains that this imposed. Nonetheless the project successfully delivered a completely refurbished Hippodrome, a substantial new home for the dance agency, DanceXchange, and a dancers' health centre for Birmingham Royal Ballet (which inevitably bore the name of its co-funder, Jerwood). It did indeed provide a major centre for dance outside London and one of national importance.

That battle resolved there was a brief moment of calm before another upset. In early December a letter was sent to Chris Smith and Mark Fisher (as well as to all Council members) signed by all members of the drama panel, including Thelma Holt, its chair. This highlighted the effect on theatre of four years of standstill in the Treasury grant, and complained that the drama panel had not had any say in advising on the artistic quality of applications for any of the lottery programmes. It felt that a positive arts policy had been replaced by bureaucracy and short-term schemes. That was all fine and probably justified but the letter went on to criticise the lottery which had 'created a culture of greed, envy and fantastical expectations'. I was incensed by the hypocrisy – the majority of the signatories had been associated with or been major beneficiaries of lottery projects. Thelma and I had been good and close colleagues on the Council and, I thought, had enjoyed working together. At a moment when solidarity was needed, I felt betrayed – an overreaction caused by the stress I was feeling at the time.

*

The SBC still had to be dealt with. During the autumn, chair Brian Corby and chief executive Nicholas Snowman had continued to be baffled by its inadequacy while Richard Rogers was reported at being 'incandescent' over the delay. At a meeting held at the DCMS in early September, Chris Smith urged a phasing and a capping of the bid but when it again came before the Panel there remained the problems of poor management, poor value for money, lack of artistic vision, an inadequate business plan and unresolved financial viability.

Board members Martin Smith and Elliott Bernerd then took over responsibility for negotiating the bid but the presentation they made to the Panel that October was unconvincing. Although they asked for 'the benefit of the doubt' the Panel was adamant that major concerns remained. In spite of some improvements it was noted at the November Panel meeting that the SBC had not been able to reduce its latest bid (which had come in at £113.260 million) to under £75 million as had been suggested, although a letter from Brian Corby a month later stated that they could not maintain the integrity of the SBC project with anything less than £70 million. There was now pressure from politicians to come to a conclusion. Some Panel members were in favour of the bid continuing – a memo from Patty Hopkins, subsequently circulated to Council members, argued persuasively for the Rogers vision, feeling that the SBC's board was committed to sorting out the artistic concerns – but the majority were unconvinced. The paper presented to the Council at its meeting on 10 December proposed either outright rejection or an allocation of £50 million which could only be accessed on acceptance by the Council of a revised plan drawn up by a new chief executive. At all the lobbying meetings Grey Gowrie had been in strong support of the project. He says now

> I was worried by the relatively low aesthetic quality of many of the initial building projects we commissioned or improved. I am not an unconditional Richard Rogers fan, but I believed his design for the South Bank was a work of genius. It complemented [Charles] Barry's Parliament Buildings opposite, in my view the greatest buildings in London. As a musical bloke I was, and I remain, sharply aware that London has a great orchestral tradition but no great orchestral hall. The Royal Festival Hall is much too big and its acoustic is much too lively.

His handling of the two-and-a-half-hour Council discussion was a master-class in chairing, although I was by now thoroughly fed up with any mention of the bid and outspoken about my wish that as much work had gone into getting it right as had gone into the lobbying for it. Grey delicately got those against the bid to speak first then turned to those he knew to be in favour. Gradually a sense of glowing support grew, for the concept if not for the bid itself. When it came to the vote – as already noted above, itself a rare occurrence at Council meetings – there was a majority in favour of going ahead with a commitment of £70 million from ACE to be paid over the following three years – thus breaking the Council's own recently-imposed cap of £50million for any one project. At this stage Graham Devlin pointed out that if this sum were to be awarded it would represent a large proportion of the amount available for all capital grants over the next three years on current forecasts. I then suggested that as political pressure had been responsible for our not rejecting the bid earlier the only way around the problem was to inform the DCMS that ACE wanted to give the grant but could only go ahead with a special allocation from them. This was agreed and Grey went off to deliver the message to Chris Smith, who apparently said that for ACE even to ask for such a thing lowered it in his estimation. Meanwhile, Graham made his own way to the DCMS to tell Hayden Phillips that, although his Council had decided thus, he as accounting officer could not support it. Everyone then calmed down a bit and at the Panel meeting on 16 December it was reported that the department wanted the case for support to be put more fully. My final ACE telephone call of 1997 came as I was enjoying a quiet dinner on a post-Christmas Sunday evening. It was Elliott Bernerd, calling from a Caribbean island: he wanted to know what the position on the SBC bid was. I brusquely said it was in the hands of the DCMS.

*

1998 began with my joining Jeremy Newton and Moss Cooper to give a capital strategies presentation to Chris Smith. As there was no capital strategy at this time, I can only think that we went through the statistics that Jeremy and Moss had been presenting through the autumn. My diary records that while the secretary of state seemed interested he was more insistent that lottery funding should be diverted to revenue, in particular to regional theatres and music in schools.

Perhaps he was influenced by the fact that the 1998/99 Treasury grant, announced in early January, was £184.6 million, £1.5 million less than that for 1997/98, and came with a warning of a future reduction in 1999/2000. In view of New Labour's apparent interest in arts and culture, this was highly disappointing; Chris had been keen to raise it but was hampered by New Labour's pre-election commitment to stick to Tory spending plans for at least the first year.

When the Council came to discuss allocating these diminishing funds to regular clients there was no enthusiasm for a policy of 'equal misery for all', but with some minor adjustments that's how it ended up. A similar feeling had permeated the artistic review discussion in May 1993 following the publication of *A Creative Future*. At this the Council had determined to reconsider its funding portfolio, weeding out organisations who had passed their best-by date and introducing some new ones, but in the end the status quo was more or less maintained.

Whatever the intentions, it has always proved hard to make such difficult choices: a more recent example is ACE's bungled attempt at doing the same thing in 2008, leading to chief executive Peter Hewitt having to face an angry crowd of actors at London's Young Vic. The system introduced in 2010 whereby arts organisations apply to become part of the National Portfolio on a three- (now four-) yearly basis certainly appears fairer, although such are the demands of the application form that arts organisations can concentrate on little else other than its completion for some three months before submission. In some cases help is sought from consultants to assist in what should surely be a straightforward planning exercise. One queries if such a scale of disruption is necessary in view of the regular information sent to ACE's relationship managers (whatever happened to the term arts officers?) even if the cuts regularly demanded to the Council's workforce have reduced some of the more personal contact. To its credit, ACE seems to have acknowledged this and adjusted its system accordingly: it has now launched a four-year application cycle for the arts, museums and libraries, with three levels of funding in which the lowest have less demanded of them, the highest more, with emphasis on their need to display how they fulfil their leadership role. Successful applicants receive NPO status, while individual artists and creatives ('individuals engaged in creative work within our remit to support art and culture'[21]) can apply to Grants for the Arts, along with non-NPO arts organisations and those 'who use the arts in their work'.[22] This may make life easier for the majority of organisations, and perhaps it's right that the sixty-nine currently receiving in excess of £1 million grant a year should sing louder for their public supper.

Nine of these organisations are the five national opera companies (Royal Opera, ENO, Opera North, Welsh National Opera, Glyndebourne Touring Opera) and the four classical ballet companies (Royal Ballet, Birmingham Royal Ballet, English National Ballet and Northern Ballet Theatre) which between them take some £79 million of the Treasury grant. An attempt by ACE to plan strategically in future for these large spending areas has proved to be elusive. In 2011 I was asked to act as a special advisor for an analysis of the future of funding for these two expensive artforms. The job was supposed to take six months but the change of personnel during yet another restructuring and the apparent lack of any inhouse financial data to back up the discussions meant that eighteen months later little progress had been made. Just at the point when outside help had been recruited to provide the figures we had long been requesting, a new senior arts team decided that special advisors' advice was not needed and that was the end of that. The final analysis maintained all companies (it was announced in June 2017 that ENO would be readmitted to the NPO fold from 2018) and mainly concentrated on the importance of building new relationships with theatres visited and of audience development – hardly new themes in a touring company's life. It was a worthy piece of work that needed to be done but perhaps one that could have had a more strategic outcome and cost a lot less money if data had been readily available.

*

21. ACE 2016 proposal for public investment in art and culture from 2018 onwards.
22. http://www.artscouncil.org.uk/funding/applying-grants-arts#section-1.

Back to 1998 and the message that we were in quite a serious situation with the capital programme was beginning to sink in. In early January Graham Devlin rang me to say that he had just looked at the bids going to that week's Council meeting, had compared them with the money available and was very worried. It was a relief to know that the penny, so to speak, was finally dropping. It continued to drop at a meeting with the SBC quartet – Brian Corby, Elliott Bernerd, Martin Smith and Nicholas Snowman – who at last seemed to appreciate the reality about lottery forecast figures. They had, however, picked up that there was a £200 million pot for major projects and saw that as their salvation. It had to be pointed out that that was a planning figure for several large national projects over an eight-year period. At the same time Chris Smith wrote to Grey Gowrie saying that he had considered the proposal that he should vary the draw-down of lottery funds to allow for the SBC bid but on reflection he felt that ACE had sufficient funds to make an award to the SBC of £70–£75 million if it chose to do so; he couldn't see any justification for adjusting the flow of lottery funds which would have the effect of reducing the funds going to the other good causes.

His formal assent was, however, required to any proposals for redeveloping the SBC, and he sought ACE's assurance on various artistic, value for money and management questions. This reflected his department's uncertainty about the bid, mirrored in a comment made to Christopher Frayling and myself a few days before by Melanie Leech. She wondered how ACE could think of giving its strong support and an award of this size to a bid which still needed a mass of basic conditions attached. Melanie confirms that by this time Chris Smith and his officials at the DCMS were becoming more hardened: while applauding Richard Rogers's articulation of his vision during his presentations, after he had departed they began to query some of the financial detail and projected visitor numbers. She feels that their more negative attitude finally kicked in when one of them raised the question of pigeons crapping on the glass roof and the cleaning problems that would ensue.

10

A NEW BROOM

*Gerry Robinson appointed as chair – the end of the strategy group –
formation of a new Council – resolution of the SBC bid – Jeremy Newton
resigns – travel notes – the new Council meets – the Eyre review
and the ROH*

Chris Smith's letter about the SBC was discussed at the January Council
meeting. Grey Gowrie now feels that the then chancellor of the exchequer
had also vetoed the proposal:

> Our South Bank lottery project was completely feasible if Gordon Brown
> had let us pay for it over six or seven years, based on a conservative lottery
> revenue projection well below the returns we were getting at the time.
> Objective city accountants bore witness to this. But Gordon was in his
> (otherwise, to my mind, admirable) fiscally conservative phase and using a
> tight squeeze on public spending to build up the reserves he blew much too
> quickly (again in my view) on the NHS later. The whole thing is a sad story.
> All these years later (2017), the South Bank is still in a mess: a rebuke to a
> great cultural capital. And London still has no great orchestral hall.

It was clearly going to be necessary to brief the incoming chair on the
subject: that afternoon it was announced that businessman Gerry
Robinson would take over from Grey Gowrie in the spring. As part of the

selection process run by the DCMS, Gerry, a Labour supporter, had been approached by Tony Blair and Chris Smith, but he says that he genuinely did not want to take on the job. Memory now plays its tricks: Gerry recalls that Chris Smith suggested he attend one of the Council's all-day meetings, which he did in December. He says that this was a clever move on Chris Smith's part: he sat through all the hours of talk about the SBC before it was revealed that the money was not there to do it, and thought, 'Ah no, this has to be improved upon, there are better ways of running this.' I was surprised to hear this: I'm sure I would have remembered his presence and he's not listed in those attending the meeting. But I was delighted at the appointment. I knew Gerry slightly because we attended the same Pilates studio and I knew that behind the Irish charm lurked a formidable business acumen: exactly what ACE needed at the time.

Meanwhile, deep frustration at the management vacuum continued. Although many Council members, including myself, were very hands-on we didn't have the day-to-day capability to produce detailed strategies for either ACE itself or the capital programme and to force them through. Nor, as non-executives, would it have been right for us to do so – the strategy group itself was operating on pretty dodgy ground in terms of governance. Melanie Leech remembers many conversations with individual Council members at this time, all expressing their concern and often threatening resignation; while urging them to remain and help to sort it out, she says that she relied on Christopher Frayling and myself to give a reasonably honest view and assessment of what was going on. However, some thought I wasn't up to it: Chris Price, who had succeeded Ernest Hall as chair of Yorkshire & Humberside Arts Board, told me that his chief executive, Roger Lancaster (one of the angry brigade in the ACE/RAB squabblings), didn't rate me at all and didn't think I knew anything about strategy. But at least I knew that one was badly needed, and that no one within the system was supplying it. From attending a meeting of the English Regional Arts Boards group in early February I found out that the RABs were working on their own strategy and structure for the funding system but were refusing to liaise with ACE about them. I was glad to hear several of the RAB chairs on the Council agreeing that ERAB was not only a waste of money but highly divisive and needed to be dumped.

The strategy group (which by this stage numbered most of the Council) did what it could but it wasn't the answer. At an early meeting with Gerry Robinson we outlined its roots and recommendations. Gerry responded that he couldn't think of any system more likely to be dysfunctional. He wanted a slimmed-down Council to operate on key principles: all present – myself, Christopher Frayling, Gavin Henderson, Thelma Holt, Deborah MacMillan, Stephen Phillips, Chris Price and John Spearman (who had joined the Council as an 'independent' member in December 1996) – agreed that this required the resignation of the current Council. I was deputed to gauge the reaction of absent Council members to this. The strategy group, it was agreed, had served its purpose and should be disbanded. My telephone conversations with the other Council members showed that most of them favoured change and a smaller Council, although all were concerned that their sectors did not lose representation.

On 11 February Gerry attended his first Council meeting. He announced that Peter Hewitt had been appointed secretary-general and, to bring it up to date, the title would be changed to that of chief executive. Peter would join ACE on 9 March. Gerry swiftly disposed of the SBC question, saying that ACE could not fund all of it and should work with the DCMS to find other supporters – above all, it was important to ensure that the arts spaces would be satisfactory. The bid was finally rejected in March, after which Gerry met the new chair of the SBC (Elliott Bernerd having succeeded Brian Corby) and intimated that a sum of £20–£25 million might be available for the project.

The latter figure would remain in future forecast lists, nothing purposefully happening there until the Australian Michael Lynch arrived as chief executive in 2002. He immediately got to work with the fifty-seven organisations he said he had to consult before plans for the complete refurbishment of the Royal Festival Hall could commence in 2005. The building reopened in June 2007. Because of the requirements of working on the Grade 1 listed building the auditorium was left looking very much as it had always done, regardless of the fact that almost every item had been renovated and replaced. The acoustics, front of house and backstage areas, however, were hugely improved. Plans for a £120 million scheme to address the regeneration of an area in and around the Queen Elizabeth Hall,

Purcell Room and Hayward Gallery were finalised in 2013 but thwarted by the skateboarders who refused to move from their pitch in the (commercially useful) undercroft. Once more, SBC plans proved controversial, especially the support for the skateboarders given by the London mayor, Boris Johnson. A scaled-down project to undertake repairs in those three venues and to improve environmental and access issues was launched a year later; to this ACE awarded £16.675 million, nearly 70 per cent of its (much reduced) £24 million cost. The refurbished buildings are due to open in 2018.

*

Even if Gerry was still only chair-designate his influence was already being felt. A discussion of the ACE business plan promised that 1998/9 would be a year of transition during which business would continue as at present while plans were laid for fundamental change from April 1999. As far as the capital programme was concerned, the minutes of that February Council meeting refer to

> the uncertainties caused by the current position in which consideration of [capital] applications was having to be delayed for a short time [sic!] pending completion of the strategy. Members recognised the importance of retaining the interest of funding partners, without whose contributions many important projects would be unable to proceed, and urged that ACE and Regional colleagues should do all they could to maintain confidence in the capital programme.

Not, in the circumstances, any easy ask.

The tranquil environment of Dartington Hall in Devon was the setting for a two-day Council meeting on 18 and 19 March, Gerry's second as chair-designate. He describes the ACE he inherited as

> An absolute shambles in my view, it was a complete shambles . . . I remember making the mistake of saying the most animated voice was the voice in the lift saying 'Fourth Floor' – didn't go down all that well!

He argued that executive power should be returned to the management team and that a smaller Council, without sectional interest, should be appointed, with clarification of its roles and responsibilities. Council members should include those closely involved in the arts but they should not chair panels; although sound advice was vital, he felt responsibility for each artform should rest with the artform director who should decide whether or not to have a formal panel. He confirmed his suggestion that all existing Council members should be prepared to stand down. This seems to have been agreed, although over the next few days there were a lot of telephone calls among artform chairs now querying the pace and indeed necessity of change: the consensus suggested by the Council minutes was not the reality. Peter Hewitt thinks that most of the RAB chairs saw that a Council made up of non-representative interests would probably favour regional funding and support in the longer term. He says that some of the artform panels were viewed as metrocentric power blocks which did not really consider the interests of arts and culture beyond London. As a former chair of the dance panel with wide regional representation I would dispute this, but certainly the RAB chairs seemed more amenable to the proposed changes.

Peter echoes Gerry's view of a shambolic organisation:

> It was deeply dysfunctional . . . not just in terms of the non-executive, it was also deeply dysfunctional as an executive. When I arrived at the Arts Council there was no real sense of corporate leadership whatsoever . . . there was lottery and Jeremy, who had sort of established his own empire, and the rest and even among the rest it was riven with differences and there was no sense of corporate executive thinking or rationale or strategy whatsoever and that took a long time to solve . . . I expected some of it but it went well beyond what I had expected.

He had been part of the Puttnam group which forged New Labour's cultural policy before the 1997 election, and confirms that there had been some discussion about abolishing ACE altogether; the appointment of Gerry Robinson as chair was the political way of giving it a further chance. Another member of the group, John Newbigin, disagrees. He can't remember any discussions about abolition although giving the national companies direct funding from the DCMS and leaving ACE to focus on artists and lobbying and the promotion of the arts all over the country had been mooted.

Gerry moved swiftly, following the Council meeting with a letter to all Council members setting out how he would like to proceed over the coming weeks. Advertisements would be placed for new Council members and the existing Council would step down at the end of May. To obliterate any doubt he referred to the March Council minute agreeing to appoint a Council of ten without sectional interests, although he stressed that authoritative artistic expertise and a regional perspective were essential.

Peter Hewitt was also working on an April paper, *Towards a new Arts Council of England,* in which he outlined the need for ACE to be policy-led, to adopt a genuinely national role and to exercise leadership on behalf of the arts in the whole of England. He urged the Council to agree to re-structure: he had come away from Dartington 'well-seized of the deep concerns . . . about the advisory systems' while acknowledging the need to ensure a high level of artform expertise throughout the system. A clear understanding of the future relationship between ACE and the RABs – to whom as much funding as possible would be delegated – was needed. The Council minutes of 29 April state that while some of the artform chairs

> recorded dissent from some elements of the proposals, the majority of Council members welcomed and supported [them].

Indeed, few of the artform chairs were signing up quietly to the new order, in spite of now conciliatory noises from Gerry Robinson about continuing the panels even if their chairs were no longer on the Council. In their resignation letters to the secretary of state, several of them complained about Gerry's and Peter's attitude and registered their concern about the future of Panels. So un-reassured were the drama panel that they resigned *en bloc,* alongside their chair, Thelma Holt.

One panel that would be kept was the Lottery Panel, as this was dealing with more specific and practical issues. But we would now have to continue without a director: on 3 March 1998 Jeremy Newton was announced as the first chief executive of NESTA. While the Panel was reassured to learn that Moss Cooper, as operations director, would be working with Peter Hewitt to finalise a national strategy for the capital programme, he was not appointed to the senior management team, so lacked the influence Jeremy had had. For the present, the Panel was urged to be cautious and to commit as little as possible. The urgent need for planning figures was noted and Peter promised that a framework for planning would be in place soon.

Things began to settle down and the telephone calls with my artform chair colleagues ceased. As a presumed supporter of the Robinson plan, I had a distinct feeling that I was *persona non grata* for consorting with the enemy. It probably didn't help that I was one of the existing Council members to be invited to apply for the new Council. My letter from the DCMS, with the salutation Dear Sir/Madam, had obviously been through the spell-checker and was addressed to 'Prune' Skene.

*

The application process didn't take long and on 13 June I had confirmation that I was to be invited to join the new Council. The others transferring from the previous Council were David Brierley (who had joined it in November 1997 as chair of South West Arts), Andrew Motion and Christopher Frayling. The news wasn't greeted with unanimous glee from those close to us: at a lunch party in Bath that weekend Helen Frayling and my husband Brian declared themselves founder members of a Partners of Unpaid Public Servants Society, weary of the phone calls and of being abandoned for continual meetings. Brian was on the whole sympathetic, rarely showing frustration at what could have seemed like my adulterous love affair with ACE as I whispered into the telephone and made incessant trips to London. He was semi-retired by then and wanted to travel: my diary had to be juggled between my job at the Arts Foundation, my ACE 'affair' and regular trips abroad. Having celebrated the new year of 1998 in Moscow, we also managed to fit in trips to Greece, Egypt, Iran, France, Malta and Libya during that year alone. It was good for me as these were the days before instant communication through mobile and email, and I could genuinely put thoughts of ACE behind me. Until, that is, a great pile of paperwork was expressed out to some remote spot, all to be read and digested before a Panel meeting shortly after my return.

Less welcome travel were the train journeys between Bath and London. ACE and other meetings demanded these several times a week. Although they provided good reading time for the vast amount of material each meeting generated, the irregularity of the First Great Western service added hugely to my stress at the time. I became accustomed to hearing the running-down of the engine as we came to yet another halt, and I still can't hear a story of stranded or delayed commuters without a flash of panic. To this day when entering Paddington station I'm haunted by memories of the harassed run to the Tube or taxi rank, late yet again – and, in those days before everyone had a mobile phone, unable to alert anyone – and the heart-sinking 'Delayed boarding' notice in the evening when all you want is to get home.

*

The new Council numbered eleven and included dancer Deborah Bull, the pianist Joanna MacGregor and sculptors Antony Gormley and Anish Kapoor.[23] That there were two eminent sculptors was allegedly the result of one of them being slow in responding to the invitation; by the time he did so the other already been approached and confirmed.

We all met in mid-June for an informal lunch at Gerry's Granada head-quarters near London's Green Park. There was refreshing talk about the need to be genuinely strategic even if it meant taking unpleasant decisions, to stop the 'report/consultant' culture, to be upbeat with the press. This was more like it!

Our first formal meeting in July showed one immediate change: it began at 2 p.m. and finished at 4.30 p.m. And there was good news: the outcome of the recent government spending review was to give the DCMS an additional £290 million over the period 1999–2002, which would mean a substantially increased grant-in-aid figure for ACE. A new structure was proposed to allow genuine delegation of responsibility to the RABs; it was recognised that this would depend to a considerable extent on a new and much stronger relationship between ACE and its regional partners. Graham Marchant (who had handed over the general management of The Place to Sue Hoyle in April of that year) was welcomed to his first meeting as the new director of policy and arts.

23. For the full list please see Appendix 1.

*

Gerry and the rest of the new Council hadn't long to wait before they got their first taste of ROH matters. On 30 June Richard Eyre's review had been published. In an accompanying letter to Gerry Robinson, the secretary of state confirmed that he was going to accept Richard's recommendations that the ROH and ENO companies stay in their respective houses and a liaison body be established to coordinate the activities of the three lyric theatres (the Opera House, the Coliseum and Sadler's Wells). He supported Richard's arguments that the continuation of public subsidy to both the ROH and ENO should be closely aligned with improved access and that education was the only way to create a society that valued the arts. The review criticised ACE for failing to hold its clients fully to account and the secretary of state stressed that while recognising that the new Council was beginning to address those concerns, there was no case for complacency. Attached to the secretary of state's press release announcing the findings of the review were copies of firm letters he had written to the chairs of both the ROH and ENO, insisting on the accountability, good management and financial viability which the review had raised and which he expected the companies to address. Overall the review was welcomed by the Council as a realistic and sensible analysis of the problems and opportunities of the two major lyric companies. ENO was being dealt with through its stabilisation process (and was now saying that it needed £20 million as part of this for capital refurbishment); meetings were set up for senior ACE staff and ROH management to analyse the forty-five ROH-specific recommendations in the report and a timetable for addressing them. Sir Colin Southgate, the new ROH chair, had recently demanded a doubling of its revenue grant, which the secretary of state had found surprising in advance of consideration of Richard Eyre's recommendations on financial stability and planning, efficient management structures and value for public money.

I had not been impressed by Southgate's first attendance at an ROH/ACE liaison group meeting that February (as it turned out, it was also his last, as he refused to go to any more). Complaining that he would have more time to sort things out if he didn't have to attend so many committee meetings, he made it clear that he was unable to produce a budget and business plan for at least six months. He was also dismissive about some suggestions we made to widen his board's expertise. Mary Allen subsequently confirmed that he considered all at ACE to be interfering busybodies – an unhelpful attitude, we felt, when the ROH depended so much on public funding. But it was to the corporate sector that Southgate held allegiance: at a press conference shortly after his appointment he was quoted as saying, 'We have to take care of the corporate sector because they are the people paying for this.' At the same event, our attempts to widen access to the ROH were dashed by his comment that he didn't 'want to sit next to somebody in a singlet, a pair of shorts and a smelly pair of trainers'.

By September the ROH was announcing a shut-down of all programmes until the re-opening and then a reduced programme – this meant a restructuring of their closure grant as well as of their grant-in-aid but, in the circumstances, ACE had to pay out. The ROH would otherwise have gone bust and the lottery investment in the development would have been wasted. No one was prepared to see either happen.

The mood of the Council was none the less hardening and we gave full support to Gerry's much tougher stand with the organisation. We unanimously backed a letter he wrote to the ROH which made it clear that ACE was no longer prepared to be kept in the dark about their private donations and no longer able to accept a case for additional support without proper business plans. A row then erupted over the Council's refusal to guarantee substantial revenue funding in the future which the ROH claimed (yet again) would mean withdrawal of funds from some major donors. The secretary of state and the DCMS became involved and tried to insist that some of the extra Treasury money which was being promised to ACE had to be ring-fenced for the ROH. Gerry threatened to resign and so did the majority of the Council. Finally it was agreed that, in addition to the anticipated funding, the department should give ACE a further £4 million which would be granted to the ROH. In the circumstances, the Council had little choice but to agree. Chris Smith feels that as he had just negotiated a £100+ million increase in the Treasury grant to ACE this 'outrageous flouting of the arm's length principle' was allowable.

The relationship didn't improve until the appointment of the American Michael Kaiser as executive director, and his confirmation, in early April 1999, that the ROH would re-open on time and on budget. Which indeed it did, on 1 December 1999, with a gala performance in which Darcey Bussell as Aurora danced the Rose Adagio from *The Sleeping Beauty*, re-awakening the House as she had put it to sleep in the same role two and a half years before. In spite of all the rows and tensions, the ROH remains one of the world's great opera houses. The Floral (Paul Hamlyn) Hall, rebuilt with the lottery grant and now one of London's most impressive sites, hosted (until disruption to the building caused by the Open Up project, see below) not only opera and ballet goers but also tea dances, Big Sing Fridays, Family Sundays and free lunchtime recitals. The second auditorium became the Linbury Studio Theatre and offered a mixed programme of dance and some opera from smaller, more diverse companies, although this didn't include as much experimental work by the two Royal residents as we had originally hoped. In early 2016 the Linbury closed for substantial refurbishment to allow a more flexible space for a range of stagings: this was part of a major project, Open Up, which also includes improvements to foyer and entrance spaces, all to be funded by private donations (the present ACE capital team must be mightily relieved).

Real efforts have been – and are being – made to widen access to both the Opera House itself and to its programming, but there remains an aura of privilege in the way that people working there talk about 'the House'; one can easily feel patronised. If the seats in the main auditorium still seem inordinately expensive (although not uncompetitive with other world-class opera houses) – £250 for a top-price seat for a performance starring tenor Jonas Kaufmann – the ROH boasts that 40 per cent of tickets are under £40. You just have to be quick off the mark to obtain them and be pre-pared to suffer some discomfort: seats can be hard, views vertiginous and sightlines leave a lot to be desired.

THE PLACE, LONDON

If the relationship with the ROH was marred by ill feeling, The Place provided a better example of how things should be done. General manager Graham Marchant had achieved much since the granting of the feasibility study as one of the first lottery awards in March 1995. An architectural competition had been held; Allies & Morrison had been appointed and the design was well ahead at RIBA Stage D; other planning was sufficiently advanced for a full grant of £5.081 million to be awarded in July 1997. However, just before he left to take up his new position at ACE, Graham received a major blow: the King's Cross Partnership, which had been expected to supply most of the partnership funding, had told him that the most that he could expect was £100,000. Sue Hoyle therefore inherited a situation of general staff demoralisation. Few other partnership funding approaches had been made and the board lacked both leadership (the longterm chair wanted to stand down) and any capital project experience. But her attitude was positive:

> I believed that the building project would happen and because I believed it would and told everybody it was going to happen it was much of 'can-do', and I think as much as anything else when you're running a building project you have to be optimistic, and pragmatic at the same time.

Her first task was to revitalise the board. She recruited a new chair, Ian Fisher, an energetic businessman in his 40s who loved contemporary dance. Other new members were a top construction lawyer, Ann Minogue, who gave an enormous amount of pro bono legal advice, and a property developer, Fergus Low, who provided invaluable experience in property deals. Once the board had been taken through the model by Bob Allies and had signed up to the design, these three, together with the longstanding treasurer Graham Reddish, formed a steering group with authority to work with Sue Hoyle on running the capital project. The fact that the group was expert and could be convened quickly made the arrangement a 'joy' for Sue. They swiftly agreed that, because of the partnership funding problems, the plans should be delayed for a year and split into two, the new studios taking priority because of the income stream they would release, and the refurbishment of the drill hall being delayed if funds proved inadequate. This also allowed the London School of Contemporary Dance to be re-housed in the drill hall during the rebuild of the studios. Manoeuvring the space like this meant that Sue had four different offices during the project which for her was a positive:

> [The staff] didn't feel I was sitting in an ivory tower running a really horrible building project.

A difficult decision was also taken to remove two of the studios from planning for cost reasons, although the building was designed in such a way that these could be reinstated later.

With all this in place the partnership funding could be addressed. Sue felt that the story should be about helping the next generation of dancers:

> We needed to have appropriate conditions for kids to experience dance for the first time, for teenagers to come to classes after school – or in school – and for young people to train as dancers . . . Once we had the narrative and you could tell it convincingly the money could follow.

Young dancers would provide role models for the King's Cross district (which at that time was a hotbed of drug dealers and prostitution) and the building would contain community benefits such as a cheap café. By highlighting these bonuses, the King's Cross Partnership was persuaded to overturn its previous decision and award the project £750,000, to which a further grant of some £80,000 would subsequently be added. Grants from other trusts, foundations and individuals followed. Because of the delays and design changes, Sue did have to go back twice to ACE for supplementary grants of £293,710 and £296,518 before completion.

Building work finally got going in the summer of 1999. There were many difficulties: the listed status of the building, the protracted negotiations with the site's seven neighbours, the health problems of the project manager and the lead architect, both perhaps related to stress. In overcoming these Sue pays tribute to the steering group and to her staff, particularly David Burnie, director of administration and finance, and John Ashford, director of The Place Theatre – he had been a journalist and was very helpful in the writing of applications. The fact that both he and Richard Alston had high public profiles helped fundraising and public relations. This support and no doubt her own capability resulted in very few sleepless nights for her.

She had also realised that the building project would necessitate changing the whole organisation. It needed to become more forward-looking and more outward-facing. She successfully applied for a stabilisation grant to help achieve this. This involved far more supervision than the capital side and Sue remembers that one of the most stressful things about managing the whole project was keeping the lead technical advisor for stabilisation entertained while the organisation itself delivered the necessary outcomes. Two bits of advice from Fergus Low also helped her through: the first was to make all the mistakes on the drawing board and not on the site (in other words, make a meticulous forward plan and then stick to it); the second related to the business plan, where she had made huge efforts to be collaborative and inclusive. While Low accepted that this was good practice, he underlined that the final version had to be hers alone, a lesson in leadership that she has never forgotten.

The project finally opened during the week of 10 September 2001, just after the 9/11 terrorist attacks in the USA. The public relations specialists Bolton & Quinn none the less did manage to get some publicity for it. The Place continues to thrive: Gerry Robinson quotes it as an exemplary project that was enabled by the lottery. The story has an aftermath, to do with the early decision to remove two studios from the plans. Their later reinstatement meant that another fundraising drive had to be undertaken after Sue Hoyle had moved on to run the Clore Leadership Programme, and she felt that those she left behind must have hated her for that. On a subsequent visit she was delighted when they unanimously told her that although there had been a lowering of spirits about six months after the opening, once the adrenalin caused by what had been achieved had diminished, the new project had helped to reinvigorate it.

11

STILL SEARCHING...

*The strategy search goes on . . . – London's problems –
and on . . . – some contrasting openings*

During all the time of Council upheaval, creating a capital strategy was shifted to the sidelines. So, too, was any decision about the applications that were already in the system, including those that had been given development funds and were about to submit their main bid. With Gerry's background in business and and Peter's in capital planning, I had high hopes that these urgent matters would be quickly tackled, but the energy being brought to general policy matters seemed to ebb away as soon as the subject came up. It was some eighteen months before a final list was delivered and two years before a strategy for the future was achieved. Why did it take so long?

Returning to the last days of the Gowrie regime, the immediate priority had been the RABs' 'tranches'. By the end of January 1998 the post delivered the hefty documents, heavily stamped 'confidential', for the lottery department to pore over in time for the Panel's March meeting.

Meanwhile tempers were starting to fray. The Panel meetings were usually collegiate and businesslike, but an eruption occurred that January when Tony Pender said that dictating to the RABs and asking them for more 'tranching' when ACE had not prepared its own strategy had led to much regional bad feeling. He was supported by Paddy Masefield who talked about 'blood on the walls' in the regions over A4E. Tony asked for a moratorium to be placed on all applications until a new chair and secretary-general had revolutionised the whole system. The rest of the Panel looked bemused at this outburst, which then abated, and we carried on with our discussions. Tony's request did not go unheeded, however, highlighting as it did our general anxiety over the squeeze on funds. When looking at the applications before us, only those with top priority and in need of immediate decisions were recommended; those over which there was any doubt were rejected and all others were deferred pending the new regime. I later queried in my diary why a moratorium on the whole programme had not been called at the time of the drastic drop in forecast figures the previous July. It was a good question to ask. I noted that at the time we had a new acting secretary-general who wanted to show his negotiating skills with the DCMS, but the answer really lies elsewhere: in the pressure to get the money out; the immensity of the problem; the lack of clarity about the income figures; the incessant squabbling between ACE artform departments and the RABs. There was also the absence of any strategic directive as a result of the leadership gap caused by Mary Allen's sudden departure. Since the drop in income we had tried to be responsible and reject those applications that did not score highly on all criteria; now we tightened up even more.

In March the Panel looked at the RAB tranches. Each RAB had been asked to prioritise future capital bids in their region within an overall figure of £50 million but this amount had been disregarded by most of the ten. Their priorities totalled £618.19 million, not including many of the 'national' projects which they felt should be accounted for separately. Moss Cooper presented their priorities and those of the artform directors (where they met as well as where they didn't), together with lists of projects that had already had feasibility and development investment from ACE. Once more the discussion was hampered by confusion over the figures. The Panel was informed that a total of £176 million cash was available up to

2001 but that a potential £340 million could be committed during that time. This Alice-in-Wonderland approach to figures continued to be a *motif* over the next few months.

We did our best to make some sense of the lists but in view of the general muddle it was impossible to come to any conclusion other than that an eight-year plan was needed. It was not a pleasant situation to be in but Peter had just become chief executive, an incoming chair was professing his desire to tackle renovation with urgency and there was the prospect of a new Council with fresh impetus. It didn't seem too long to wait for some certainty.

At Grey Gowrie's last Council meeting on 29 April there were grim forebodings about the future of the capital programme, once more to the refreshing (for me) sounds of pennies dropping. There was general recognition at last that the capital progamme funds were likely to be heavily oversubscribed and that applicants' expectations had to be curbed.

It was clear by now that existing bids could not be dealt with through any imposed strategy but would have to be agreed through the priority lists compiled by the RABs and commented on by the artform departments. This was a delicate business, involving millions of pounds' worth of projects. On the human side, suffering was inflicted on those leading the projects (and their other funding partners) by, in several cases, multiple deferments. Confidentiality was essential although this attracted criticisms from the clients of lack of communication and openness. The Panel was continuing to do its best to suppress demand: although we rejected all feasibility studies, we were sometimes thwarted by the Council who perversely agreed that some of them should go through.

It was a relief to hear from Moss Cooper that Gerry Robinson and Peter Hewitt were taking a very draconian view of the capital programme and wanted to reduce it down to a shortish list of projects. While I was aware that this would mean a lot of disappointment, it would at least bring some certainty and stop the deferments. In late April Gerry, Peter, Jeremy Newton and I met to look at budgets – this seems to be the first time that concrete evidence was produced and properly considered. The balance of funds available for the capital programme up to September 2001 was now said to be £297 million, perhaps a tactical figure reached by Peter since the

Top left: Graham Devlin. Top right: Nicole Penn-Symons.
Above: Moss Cooper and Prue Skene during a trip to Yorkshire
in March 2000 to visit various lottery-funded projects.

Top: Sir Gerry Robinson. Above: Peter Hewitt.

Gerry Robinson

Derrick Anderson

David Brierley

Deborah Bull

Christopher Frayling

Antony Gormley

Anish Kapoor

Joanna MacGregor

Andrew Motion

Prudence Skene

Hilary Strong

The members of the new Arts Council of England, 1998.

Opposite: Darcey Bussell as Princess Aurora in *The Sleeping Beauty* at the re-opening of the Royal Opera House, 1 December 1999.
Above: the dance studios at The Place.

Opposite, top: Bob Allies and Sue Hoyle at the re-opening of The Place in September 2001.

Opposite, below: project manager Ian Maxey and Sir Richard Stilgoe on the Orpheus Centre building site.

Top: Sadler's Wells Theatre, London, in the process of being re-built.

Right: portrait of Ian Albery by Adam Birtwistle which hangs at the stage door of Sadler's Wells Theatre.

Above: at the opening of the Lowry in 2000. From left to right: Councillor Bill Hinds (then Leader of Salford City Council), Michael Wilford (architect) and Felicity Goodey (chair) show the model of the building to H.M. The Queen.

Left: at the opening of RADA in November 2000. From left to right in the lower part of the picture: Nick Barter (principal), Bryan Avery and H.M. The Queen.

top RAB/artform priorities had been dramatically squeezed to £297.514 million over that period. This list included the Regional Music Centre Gateshead (£41 million) and Bristol Harbourside Centre (£58 million) but not the planning figure of £25 million that had been given to the SBC nor that of £50 million which had been indicated to the Royal Shakespeare Company (RSC). The Public in West Bromwich was also in at £19 million, although, in spite of their having already received three awards totalling £1.8 million, the Panel were adamant that there were still too many uncertainties in the bid to allow for recommendation on a final figure. The list could be justified by the organisations on it having both RAB and artform support and, in many cases, having already received development money. However, this very sensible and seemingly definitive outcome wasn't taken any further. The relationship between ACE and the RABs was so fractured that it was impossible to take a firm decision without sending it back to all the component parts for yet more discussion.

We also needed a strategy for the future under the new policy directions. These suggested that priorities for all lottery programmes should be broad geographical spread, reduction of economic and social deprivation, help for children/young people and sustainable development. However, the Panel was not prepared completely to roll over at the politicians' demand as its 2 June 1998 minutes indicate:

> It was felt that while many of the new policy directions being discussed were noted in the Directions and Guidance documents issued by the DCMS and could be seen as government priorities, ACE must determine how it would be best able to support these initiatives through the Arts Sector.

Accordingly, future ACE discussion would add cultural diversity, new technology/multimedia and artists' work spaces.

As already noted, Peter Hewitt and Moss Cooper were asked to finalise a national strategy to be agreed by the Panel and Council. Peter had been dismayed, on joining ACE, to find that no such strategy was in place; he had argued with senior ACE executives during the early days of the lottery that there must be ways of injecting a degree of prioritisation and planning into the process without actually calling it a national strategy. He was also surprised that no other region had followed the example of Northern Arts and produced a regional strategy. It was now very difficult to find any mechanism for making hugely important choices between projects which would withstand scrutiny. It says something about the immensity of the task that someone so instrumental in bringing early order to a region should have found it so difficult to take the lead in creating a national strategy.

Nearly a year had passed since ACE had been warned of a drop in the forecast figures – it seemed shameful that little had happened other than a lot of discussion, paperwork and deferrals. On 20 May, at the first Council meeting with Gerry as chair, the warnings were stark: total demand amounted to four times as much as the funds that were likely to be available up to 2006. Further discussions were to take place with the RABs to determine which projects should be recommended for delay or rejection: the definitive list discussed at the end of April does not seem to have been mentioned. As a result, the minutes summed it up pretty well:

> Serious concern was expressed at the position in which the Council found itself which had been brought about by a combination of: expectations generated at the outset of the capital programme; earlier public statements that all projects which passed the Council's assessment criteria would receive awards; the Council's inability to operate strategically; the reduction in funds available to the Council following the sixth good cause [the establishment of the NOF]; the outcomes of the first overall review of all projects known to be in the pipeline; and the need now to provide also for a number of revenue programmes.

Officers were urged to communicate the position as positively as possible – hard to see how that could be accomplished.

In spite of Peter Hewitt promising a more hands-on role and the Panel being told that a new policy would be forthcoming within a matter of days, the dithering, as we shall see, went on for the next few months, not helped by continuing tensions within the lottery department itself between the operations and monitoring divisions. When Jeremy had been around, the in-fighting had been more contained; now it often seemed to erupt over relatively petty quarrels, mainly caused by pressure and uncertainty.

*

A national capital framework was promised for discussion by the Panel at its June meeting, with a priority project list to be formally agreed at the July Council. Neither was forthcoming. During his appearance at the 30 June Panel meeting, Peter was keen to point out that the framework was not a national capital strategy but a rationalisation of what was possible, based on regional priorities with some national implications. It would detail the projects selected for inclusion in the planning period to 2006. Although some would be delayed within a queuing system, at least they could be certain that, if on the list, they would receive funding. A communications strategy would be completed to deal with the announcements and to handle the disappointment of those applicants whose projects were removed from the lists. It was agreed that no applications should be discussed until the appearance of the national capital framework at the Panel's next meeting on 20 July.

Meanwhile, the figures were changing yet again: in June the Panel was told that the total amount available for the capital programme was being set at £630 million over the eight-year period from 1998/99 to 2005/06. Moss Cooper was continuing to meet the RABs in an attempt to reduce demand even further. Each RAB was now asked to prioritise over a longer period within a £60 million envelope, to identify time frames for each project and to investigate whether they could be 'engineered' into simpler, more cost-effective solutions.

*

The needs of each RAB naturally varied but London's problems were the greatest. It was a world city, a national capital, a region and a group of communities where the number of arts organisations was at its most dense. In a letter of 26 June 1998 to Peter Hewitt, Sue Robertson, now chief executive of London Arts, outlined both the general and the particular issues that made it impossible for her to prioritise bids. ACE was requesting a national strategy within which the RABs could work, but it was unrealistic to overlay a strategic framework on a volume and range of applications which had not been generated strategically. Huge over-expectation had been created, and the lack of a clearly agreed approach to the national companies and national projects caused a particular problem for London where so many were based. Many bids now facing rejection had initially been encouraged; now they would lose partnership funding, and those that depended on capital investment to create new revenue streams would face closure. Finally, she pointed out, a notional allocation of £60 million to London, the same as that indicated for each of the other regions, simply could not be justified.

The tone of the letter was relatively measured and well argued but the result was London Arts deciding to opt out of the current capital strategy process. This was certainly not helpful – particularly as they suggested no alternative. Sue now says that she was worried that the tranching exercise would turn the RABs into decision-makers and this would expose them to litigation because this was all new territory; but as the lists also went through ACE's artform departments and then the Panel and the Council, the responsibility was, at the very least, shared. At the time Sue was also working with all the other funding agencies for London (including museums, galleries, libraries and heritage bodies) on a cultural strategy for the proposed new mayor of London (Ken Livingstone would be elected in 2000). This she found exciting because it could focus on London alone and lacked the ACE/RAB tensions; moreover, it could be done with a fresh start and longterm view, luxuries denied to ACE in its current predicament.

The balance of ACE lottery expenditure between London and the regions was contentious from the start. London bids were often the largest (London housed the majority of national institutions), had most political backing and could raise partnership funding more easily. Distribution was subject to demand and in the early days when no strategy nor solicitation was allowed by ACE it was difficult to address any imbalance. The problem was regularly discussed and remains a big issue. In a 2013 report, *Rebalancing our Cultural Capital*, the authors David Powell, Christopher Gordon and Peter Stark caused a considerable stir when they showed that all good cause lottery distributors gave at least twice as much to London as to the regions and, in the case of ACE, three times as much. The authors argued that this could not be, and never should have been, justified. Even in the late 1990s parliamentary questions were often raised on the matter. ACE's position then (and to some extent now) is that many of the London grants have national impact. It is clearly an important matter and one that, in lottery terms, would have been easier dealt with had there been a strategy from the beginning.

In spite of all the problems, it's nice to hear Sue Robertson speak for all of us who were working within the system at the time:

> At the end of the day, despite structural issues and lines in the sand about who did decision-making, the Arts Council and the RABs were driven by people who really cared about the arts. Some knew more about one bit than another but actually everybody knew it was serious, important and an unprecedented opportunity for arts and culture. I think people, across the board, tried very hard to address everything seriously, I don't think anyone was ever casual about it, everyone realised [the lottery] changed the mould of arts funding and the way people did things and that it was all really a huge opportunity and we mustn't mess it up, although things took time and there were problems . . . We should have said that more to ourselves, really, at the time.

*

The promised framework and confirmation of a definitive list once more failed to materialise at the Panel's meeting in July, when we were told that the work had again been delayed: the RAB chief executives and the artform directors were asking for more time. In spite of their having been asked to do this work for months, it would now not be ready until September. The discrepancy between demand and available funds for the capital programme was starkly demonstrated: there was £2.5 billion worth of capital expectation within the arts system but only £27.5 million was now available for the rest of the financial year, of which £6.5 million would be needed for applications of less than £100,000. The July Council meeting would address the requirement of the new Lottery Act of 1998 (which had come into being on 2 July) to develop a strategic plan and a process for prioritisation; the priority project list would then be confirmed and published.

A capital planning procedure paper duly introduced the new Council to lottery matters on 29 July. It had been the subject of intensive discussions with lawyers and with the National Audit Office (NAO) and its prime purpose was to dampen expectations and to introduce a more orderly and strategic approach to the Council's lottery capital programme. Quite understandably, the new members were incredulous that bids that had been encouraged by ACE and the RABs were now having to be turned away. Only applications that could not await the delivery in September of a full strategic plan were considered: on these the Council accepted the Panel's advice. The exception was the Panel's recommended rejection (mainly because of lack of funds) of the Tate Modern bid of £16.687 million. Council members felt that this was a visual arts development of major national and international importance with which ACE should be involved – I resented being the lonely voice of the bureaucrat arguing about process, lack of money and the problems of giving another large bid to London. None the less Nicholas Serota had done his lobbying well and the bid was transferred from the rejection pile to the deferment list, although with a request to reduce its level. I had recently paid a visit to the building site and seen how the former power station was being transformed into something inspiring. I noted in my diary, however, that they had already had substantial amounts of money from both the Millennium and HLF distributors: 'It's huge, it's London and we just don't have the money.'

Graham Marchant, the new director of arts and policy, had been given the task of devising a national strategy. This was required by September but he rang me in August to say that he could not do it in the time available. He had thought he could draw up a list of about £66 million worth of projects up to March 2001 and by later that year he could devise a strategy for capital and revenue combined. However, he had now been given the figure of £55 million up until 2000 with which to work. He felt that there was a general reluctance to draw up lists and commit to figures: as I noted in my diary, without lists, 'It just means more waste and more disappointment and more anger.' The RABs were pressing for equal amounts to be distributed among them but Graham was adamant that this was not going to happen; projects should be selected on their merits and on their national, as well as regional, relevance.

A public statement from Peter Hewitt on capital planning followed: ACE was considering what would be the best way forward to plan strategically for capital development and advised caution for anyone considering a bid. He confirmed that ACE had only £55 million available for commitment to new capital awards up until March 2000 and very few large projects in the future were likely to receive substantial lottery awards – hardly a statement to assuage the festering anger among those who had been serially deferred.

Even though the executive was having problems with the strategy and budgeting, they none the less saw fit to rap the Panel's knuckles. The minutes for the 15 September Panel meeting state:

> Executive Team intervention was seen as necessary following the 20 July Lottery Panel meeting owing to the very large amounts of money being recommended for commitments in relation to the amounts available for the commitment for the year.

I'm surprised they got away with such a comment – or indeed that I, as chair, allowed it to be minuted without a suitable retort. In spite of a mound of paperwork, hours of discussion and many requests from the Panel for finalisation, the executive team, struggling to develop a truly national strategy for arts funding, was not delivering capital strategy, nor framework, nor viable lists of agreed projects. Meanwhile Graham Marchant was complaining that any proposed process for drawing up a priority list would result in a list which had no degree of consensus.

In the current climate of indecision the only option in most cases was to defer yet again, in some cases for the seventh time. We were also upset by the return of the Tate's bid after our recommendation to reject it, especially as the promised new paperwork on it had not yet been prepared. Several Panel members, including myself, sent angry letters to Gerry Robinson expressing forceful views about this breaking with the process. He agreed that he would veto any further recommendation of the Council to fund the current bid and said so at the Council meeting on 22 September. None the less, Tate was invited to submit a considerably improved application with the proviso that lobbying of Lottery Panel and Council members was likely to be counter-productive. Not entirely so: a reduced bid was submitted and £6.2 million awarded in January 1999. Like so many projects that had involved a good deal of argument and stress, Tate Modern turned out to be a huge success when it opened in May 2000. I think now most would agree that it was right that ACE should have contributed to this: we funded the conversion of level four of the gallery into a temporary exhibitions space. One of my last engagements on behalf of ACE was a grand dinner overlooking the Turbine Hall when Nicholas Serota rattled off a long list of thanks to about twenty or more supporters without notes – he included the tribute to John Major already mentioned by Virginia Bottomley. He was also gracious in his thanks to ACE, something that did not always happen at such events.

*

Lottery-funded projects were continuing to open, with contrasting experiences. On 10 October at the Arc Theatre in Trowbridge (which had received £836,008 in July 1997 for its refurbishment) I was named on the credit plaque and cut the opening ribbon among much general rejoicing.

At the Jerwood Space, however, on 21 September, the chair, Alan Grieve, announced that he was handing back the £1.42 million grant which had been awarded by ACE in July 1997, implying, I thought, that this was because of the demands of the monitoring department. Alan had conceived the idea of the Jerwood Space after listening to theatre directors Stephen Daldry and Katie Mitchell bemoaning the lack of good, reasonable rehearsal space in London. He had found a neglected building in Union Street in the London Borough of Southwark and purchased it from the Council. He commissioned Paxton Locher to draw up architectural plans to turn it into a rehearsal and gallery space. The total budget was around £3 million and he was advised to submit a lottery application. He admits that he found the application and monitoring processes

> wearisome . . . we weren't very good at [them], it didn't come naturally to us, we were an adventurous, new, proactive, private foundation.

His dislike of bureaucracy was sharpened by the acrimonious time he had with the Charity Commission when he tried to register Jerwood Space with them. At the time he particularly resented the implication that artists who had been nurtured in the Space would possibly go on to earn money by selling their work. He later said that his main reason for returning the ACE lottery grant was that he had become acutely aware that the pressure to find partnership funding was causing good projects to fail. As a result, the Jerwood Foundation had changed its former policy of not awarding capital grants (an early beneficiary of this had been the Royal Court Theatre, see pages 87–88). The upshot of this change was that Grieve felt that, as a donor, he was compromised by also being an awardee – and so the grant was returned, much to the amazement of Gerry Robinson and all at ACE. The Jerwood Space has turned out to be probably the most sought-after rehearsal space in London, set up by Richard Lee on behalf of the Jerwood Foundation and run on a Robin Hood basis of charging commercial rents to some in order to subsidise those less able to pay. Richard explains:

> The idea of a place where people would interact has come about here – I'm very proud of that part of it because it's the idea of excellent facilities for the work of art and it's about trying to raise the status in society's mind of the fact that the people we pride as artists are people who are working, they're not just having fun, they're not just indulging, it is a working place and they have business to commit.

*

That autumn the Panel agreed a divide between the past and present from the future, recommending for the latter the creation of a new capital programme, to be known as CP2, for introduction in 2000. That at least was a decision, but it still left the question as to what should be done about the existing applications. A two-day Council meeting in October would decide priorities and policies and, with some grumbling about the further delay, the Panel acknowledged that it would have to await its outcome and be ruled by its judgements.

A paper from Peter Hewitt was awaiting the Council in September. Entitled *A New National Role for the Arts Council*, it mainly consisted of arguments for a substantial amount of delegation of clients to the RABs, together with recommendations for the improvement of communications throughout the system and definitions of what should be considered 'national'. In spite of ACE's own problems with its lottery budgets, it had been strong-armed by the DCMS into contributing £12.5 million of lottery money towards a number of events to be shared with other lottery distributors to celebrate the Millennium. It was never clear why other distributors had to contribute to something that had its own Commission. (A similar situation arose in January 1999 when the Council was pressurised into putting £10 million of lottery funds into the formation of a Youth Music Trust: an excellent project, but one very much promoted by politicians at a time when other budgets were being severely squeezed.)

The Council was informed about the October strategic debate and, as the relevant minute states,

> members recognised the need for Council to consider with particular urgency the capital programme and the large number of current and anticipated bids which the Council would not be able to support. For the October meeting, the Council would have to be sufficiently informed about these bids in order to prioritise between projects and to apply a national perspective and overview.

The word 'urgency' seems ironic in the circumstances.

SADLER'S WELLS THEATRE, LONDON

On 13 October I went to the opening ceremony of Sadler's Wells. It was quite an event. This project had experienced considerable difficulties but the buccaneering spirit (in their own words) of Ian Albery and his theatre administrator, Nadia Stern, had got them through. A nice story from Nadia concerns the moment she went out to look at the wrecking ball about to take its first hit at the old building and saw Ian frantically signalling from across the road. He had just heard from the lottery department that they were not to destroy even one brick until — the condition was lost as the noise of the wreckers' ball deafened her. She also now confirms that the theatre was on the verge of bankruptcy at the time, and any delay to the cash flowing into the building programme would have pushed them over the edge.

The whole project was riddled with problems, more than justifying David Hall's initial reservations on its business planning and his criticism of the technical assessors who had not foreseen what it would actually cost to build a 1,500-seat auditorium. On the expenditure side the Wells had battled with its contractors, and on the income side its partnership funding had been hard to achieve. In December 1997 an application for a further £6 million had been made to ACE because of the failure of some complicated leasing deal that had been suggested by the Sadler's Wells chair, Ian Hay Davison. Additional costs had also been incurred, partly by the funding conditions of ACE and the local authority – what exactly these were it is hard to say, but Ian Albery was clearly continuing to use every trick in the book. What to do about substantial supplementary bids was always a real dilemma for ACE. We were aware of the bad public relations that could surround a 'bailing out', particularly of a large London project, but the fact remained that if extra money was not granted the building work would stop, leaving a large hole in the ground and no dance house. So the money went through . . .

Although far from finished, the theatre was now about to open, with a starry guest list including Prime Minister Tony Blair and his wife, Cherie Booth. The performance was by Rambert Dance Company to whom Ian had long since promised the occasion: Christopher Bruce, Rambert's artistic director at the time, had been the first company director of stature to support him when the bid was originally mooted. The honour came with definite drawbacks: stage rehearsals had had to take place with the dancers wearing face masks against the dust. The immediate problem on the night was that there was no entertainment licence and the performance couldn't start without one; nor could the bars open, which hurt Ian more as he was losing vital income from alcohol sales. Nadia remembers Islington Council's Building Control turning up in hard hats among the celebrity audience: when they asked what her solution was to any perceived problem, her answer was always that extra staff would be on duty. But 'extra' staff were few in number: 'and we ran out of "extra" staff after very few minutes so there was a recycling of staff'. Building Control didn't seem to notice that the same faces were appearing at different problem spots throughout the theatre. At a quarter to eight, just as Ian was deciding to open the performance anyway and take the consequences, the licence was faxed through.

The building work continued for several months, builders leaving as audience arrived. Nadia remembers

> at 4 p.m. each day it stopped being a building site and the foreman would hand over to me and at 11 p.m. each night I handed back to them . . . And we'd have 100 people on site every night . .

While acknowledging that for the two of them it was 'a big rollicking adventure', both Ian and Nadia express sympathy for those members of their staff who found the whole experience extremely stressful.

The funding saga wasn't over. By December it was becoming clear that ACE had to address a further demand for £5 million from Sadler's Wells. Although the building had opened there was still a partnership funding gap of some £6 million and an overspend of £5 million on the project. Before agreeing to any amount, the Council proposed that Bill Wilkinson, a former financial controller of the RSC, should test the viability and stability of the organisation. Wilkinson concluded that although there had been construction problems and overspends (on which Sadler's Wells were taking legal advice against the construction company, Bovis), the capital project had not been badly managed and had not run out of control. Without a further grant of £6 million the organisation would cease to trade. Rather than have such a high-profile lottery project go into liquidation after so much investment, the Panel had little alternative but to agree. After considerable discussion the bid was recommended, but with very strict conditions. I saw Ian Albery that evening and told him of the Panel's recommendation, saying how hard it had been to achieve consensus and begging him not to put in any more supplementary bids. This he brushed quickly aside with the comment, 'Now we must work on the revenue grant!' It was through such one-minded persistence that things were accomplished. The Council confirmed the grant at its March 1999 meeting, making its total investment in the building £42 million.

Whatever the problems and the questions about value for money, it's hard now to think of cultural life in London, particularly that of dance, without Sadler's Wells Theatre. It remains a tribute to Ian Albery's championship as much as to Alastair Spalding's subsequent artistic direction. Contemporary dance in particular has benefited enormously from its programming, commissioning and the work of the associate artists based there; it is rare to attend a performance that isn't packed with a predominantly young and enthusiastic audience. As well as the main house, both the Peacock Theatre and the Lilian Baylis Studio present varied and stimulating programmes of dance, and the community and learning programmes are exemplary. Half a million people a year visit one of the theatres, and there are now plans to develop another 500-seater on the Olympic site in east London. It feels good to have persevered through the car wash of the early Ian Albery presentations.

12

FINAL RESOLUTION

*Some seeds of discord and losing of tempers – more Panel changes –
creeping towards some decisions – more talk and paper – the end of CP1*

In spite of initial promises of fast progress towards change, the two-day
Council meeting at the Monkey Island Hotel at Bray-on-Thames on 27 and
28 October 1998 didn't get very far. The euphoria that surrounded the re-
formed Council's first meetings was disappearing: the gathering was
preceded by a letter from Antony Gormley and Anish Kapoor to Gerry
Robinson and Peter Hewitt, circulated to all Council members. This
protested about the lack of consultation with Council members regarding
strategy and outlined the two sculptors' perception that the 'New' Arts
Council had become an instrument of 'New' Labour:

> Art is not a tool in regeneration nor can it be seen as an opportunity to get
> people off benefit. Art fought a long battle for its autonomy and we do not
> want to be part of a government initiative to harness it to a monetarist
> agenda.

The main item for discussion was the delegation of ACE clients to the
RABs. As for a future capital strategy, little advice was forthcoming. The
Council looked at a list of projects taken from RAB priorities which the

Panel had drawn up in some desperation and awarded development grants for the Laban Centre of Movement and Dance in Deptford, the Almeida Theatre in north London and the De La Warr Pavilion in Bexhill–on-Sea, together with a handful of smaller grants for instruments, vans, staging and public art commissions. The Panel had recommended rejection of all other applications: it was the only way we knew of stopping the demand. The list of deferrals was already long and it seemed crazy to add to it. But it was upsetting to see good applications turned down and terribly frustrating that no one at senior level seemed prepared to tackle the problem.

The good news was that the DCMS had confirmed an additional £120 million grant-in-aid over the three years from 1999 to 2002, plus a further £5 million for a 'New Audiences' programme. The secretary of state had also undertaken to maintain the arts share of lottery proceeds beyond 2001. It had always been Chris Smith's intention to raise the arts budget as soon as spending plans allowed. Considerable pressure had also been applied by Gerry Robinson: in spite of initial scepticism, he had quickly become aware of the social and economic benefits of the arts as well as their own intrinsic value. He had had what he describes as a kind of conversion: he was finding the company of artists more enjoyable than that of the business people he had formerly spent time with. He also came to admire many of the arts managers he had met who were

> doing very smart things and surviving on shoestrings and managing in a phenomenal way and I very quickly came to the conclusion that we weren't giving enough money to the arts.

In spite of this Damascene moment, he admits that he found those working in the arts to be dramatically less honest, more two-faced and 'more mobile in their views' than those in business.

The despair felt at the continuing delay was again turning the mood of the Panel fractious. When discussing an evaluation of the monitoring process at about this time, members of the Panel became irritated with what we saw as bland and brief recommendations. We also felt that more feedback should have been sought from organisations being monitored. Tony Pender, in particular, was incensed by the way the evaluation had been handled and let off quite a bit of steam. In addition to the strategy vacuum, the Panel was increasingly frustrated that conditions they had wanted to attach to certain grants were still not being met before further monies were paid out. (This was also to be a criticism in the forthcoming National Audit Office report.) We asked that all applicants be warned that this would no longer happen: all criteria and conditions had to be fully met before further funds were released. This request seems not to have made much difference: shortly afterwards I was querying the commitment to the Regional Music Centre in Gateshead of a further £2.95 million of development money without having the requested assurance that governance, revenue and fundraising issues had been resolved.

Criticism from outside ACE also continued. In early November I attended a Theatres' Trust/Royal Court conference about theatres and architecture. I had been assured that this was not going to be about lottery bashing but, in a fifteen-minute attack, theatre consultant Iain Mackintosh did just that. In a weak attempt to fight back, my diary refers to the insularity of the speakers and the lack of reference to new technology, community use or the sort of spaces that theatres might want to use in the future. This was perhaps unfair because the role of the Theatres' Trust is to preserve theatre buildings rather than consider future spaces, but I was becoming bored by the endless carping. The present ACE situation was an unpleasant one but I wanted more acknowledgement given to those projects that were being successfully completed. In 1993 the Trust had published a report on the condition of theatre buildings in England which had originally been commissioned by the government in 1991. It had not been published then because the results were too embarrassing, painting as they did a nationwide picture of theatres in terrible states of repair. It would have been good if ACE could have worked with the Trust to remedy this through lottery funding but, as we know, that would have required a strategy . . .

Under the new regime there was much less hands-on involvement by us Council members – deeply frustrating when nothing seemed to be happening. I felt myself to be a particular victim of this as there was still no sign of a decision about the future of the capital programme, to say nothing of the current and regularly deferred bids. Council members were actively discouraged from getting too involved personally: Gerry was highly supportive of Peter and clearly did not want to listen to any grumbling. Even specialist advice wasn't always welcomed: a terse minute from the October 1999 Council meeting reports a comment which Antony Gormley had made on the design of the annual review:

> Accepting the validity of the concerns voiced by Antony Gormley, which had now been resolved, members recognised the difficult balance to be achieved in upholding the non-executive status of their role and agreed the need to guard against too close an involvement in work properly delegated to and the responsibility of senior staff.

Which was all very well if the executive delivered.

In November 1998 a new organisational framework was put before the Council: a director of arts strategy would assist the director of arts and policy, Graham Marchant. Advisory panels were to continue to advise artform departments on playing a truly national role.

The new framework collapsed almost immediately when Graham Marchant was fired. He had been having problems, when trying to devise a national strategy, in reconciling national and regional demands and, as it seemed to him, dealing with the intractability of the RABs. He had also been appalled when Peter Hewitt had given encouragement to The Public project without consulting any of his senior colleagues, the Panel or the Council. The main cause of his going, however, was his failure to establish a good relationship with either Gerry Robinson or Peter Hewitt. His exit came as a relief to him:

> By that stage I was just deeply grateful, I've never been more grateful about anything in my life. I'd never been fired and I can't say it was an enjoyable experience but . . . it cost the Arts Council not a small sum of money to have fired me like that.

I was sad because I respected Graham's intelligence and knowledge. We shared an arts management background, both of us having run performing companies, and I could relate to him more than to any other member of the senior management team. With him went any hopes of a paper on the formation of a national strategy. In its absence the Panel meeting scheduled for 1 December had to be cancelled.

The only good news at this time was the announcement of the 1999–2000 Treasury grant: at £213.8 million it was larger than forecast, even with the inclusion of the extra money that had been forced upon us for the ROH.

*

More paperwork awaited in the new year, this time another huge presentation to the Panel's January 1999 meeting by Moss Cooper. This consisted of financial context, RAB and artform prioritisation and the state of projects that had received development grants. There were also guidelines for additional prioritising factors such as the contribution to national/regional strategy, areas which had had comparatively low awards so far, and projects which would make a significant contribution to helping with problems of social exclusion or deprivation. We were now promised a detailed capital strategy paper, to be drawn up by an external consultant, for the March Panel meeting.

This idea then seems to have been dropped. Although it was a relief that this was not going to be another exercise by an outsider, there was a problem in that no alternative was being suggested. In its place Moss Cooper provided a paper on CP2 for the March Panel meeting, setting out the lessons that had been learned from the first capital programme, now known as CP1. There had been a substantial improvement in accessible facilities and the three-stage process introduced after Adrian Ellis's review had reduced risk. On the downside were the difficulties experienced by organisations due to inadequate planning, revenue problems and a lack of success in integrating artworks into building projects. There was also the fact that ACE had not funded many buildings which could be considered architecturally 'landmark'. The paper hoped that CP2 would address some of the areas that CP1 had somewhat neglected, such as cultural diversity, and noted that any capital strategy would have to reflect the Council's priorities, on which work was still continuing. After a long Panel discussion it was noted that a revised capital strategy paper would be put to the Council at its April meeting. It says much for the goodwill and patience of the Panel that it went on accepting the procrastinations, but it had little option to do otherwise.

Around April there was some tidying up to be done. The stabilisation committee was promoted to being a Panel in its own right and plans were being laid for the delegation of smaller capital and revenue lottery grants to RABs. In the meantime, the executive team would take responsibility for deciding grants of under £100,000. The Lottery Panel was renamed the Capital Advisory Panel with a renewed membership: Paddy Masefield, Tony Pender, Neil Cross and Tish Francis left us, their skills being replaced respectively by Jo Verrent (director of East Midlands Shape), Jonathan Blackie (who worked in regeneration in the north-east), Ian Armitage (from Mercury Asset Management) and Rosemary Squire (executive director of Ambassadors Theatre Group). Deirdre Figueiredo of Craftspace Touring was recruited to represent the craft sector – in spite of the low level of applications submitted to date we hoped this would rise. A day-long Panel meeting was planned to take place in Manchester in May for a policy discussion on the capital strategy, doubtless to give the new members an opportunity to revitalise the process.

The slogan under which the Council met for another two days in late April was 'making a difference'. Reports were given from a series of task groups: arts content in new technologies, generating new resources for the arts, putting the arts in context, publishing, recording and distribution initiatives, lifelong learning and public engagement/audience development. There were also papers on support for the individual artist, innovation in production, funding for excellence, a cultural diversity development programme, and 'beyond barriers', a strategic national initiative to promote access and participation. Apart from a decision that for CP2 there was a need to introduce an orderly queue and to work within a strategic, geographical, operational plan and budget across a period of years, there was still no actual decision among all this other activity on how this was to be achieved. Nor was there any decision on how to deal with the huge demand still pressing from CP1.

So when the Panel met in Manchester on 5 May it had little to guide it. This was in spite of another huge pile of paperwork on matters such as 'Defining a National Capital Strategy', 'Private and Public Partnerships' and 'Towards a Capital Strategy'. There was little concrete outcome because of the need to await a national ACE plan: my diary reflects bewilderment about how to take the whole thing forward after so many months of delay, broken deadlines and overwhelming amounts of paperwork.

*

We began to get to grips with things at a meeting on 13 May when David Brierley, Graham Long (appointed executive director of planning and resources in September 1998), Moss Cooper and I tried to propose, from a list of current capital projects, those we could fund and those we couldn't. It was something that should have been done months before but I noted that we had been waiting, since Graham Marchant's departure, for a senior executive to listen, which Graham Long now seemed to be doing. Moss remembers that

> I used to sit at my kitchen table at night trying to work out how this should pan out; there was no one within the senior management who was prepared to say 'We must find a better strategic process.'

He also highlights the difficulties in having strategic discussions with some of the regional and artform executives: some were pushing their own priorities and were disinclined to query the robustness and sustainability of their favourites.

Our meeting resulted in a paper from Graham Long that set out financial planning figures. This was a start, although there was still confusion about whether these provided for supplementary bids. At the May Council meeting strategic priorities and overall budgets were agreed which meant that detailed planning work could go ahead. The plethora of task group topics discussed in April had been narrowed down to five new ACE priorities, none of which was succinctly expressed:

- support for new work, experimentation and risk and the centrality of the individual artist;
- new artforms and collaborative ways of working, often in and with new technology;
- diversity and public inclusion;
- children, young people and lifelong learning; and
- touring and distribution including through broadcasting, recording and electronic publishing.

The proposed allocation for the completion of CP1 was now set at £73 million, with £280 million allocated for CP2 up to 2005/6. This would mean some very difficult decisions, including the removal of certain projects which had already received development funding. In order to arrive at a final list, further data was being prepared and further discussions with RAB chief executives and artform directors would take place – one wonders now how they could have found anything new to talk about. One project that would remain on the books was West Bromwich's The Public: against the Panel's advice for rejection, the Council agreed a further development grant of £942,405, to be drawn down in stages with strict conditions. The future commitment for the project continued to be as much as £19 million, a figure that remained on all the prioritised lists.

The Council's strategic priorities were at last setting a path for the future. From among them the Panel in June agreed four key priorities for CP2: the needs of the existing built environment; support for 'soft' infrastructure (i.e. technology and equipment); support for new art/audiences, and the desire to remedy the failings of CP1 regarding the lack of applications from black and Asian groups. More urgently, it was agreed that an indicative list of priorities for the ending of CP1 be drawn up by the executive team with input from Moss Cooper and discussion with me: special meetings of the Panel and then Council would take place in early July to agree this.

A flurry of meetings followed, including, amazingly, yet more with RABs and artform departments, as a result of which Peter Hewitt realised how little could be achieved with the £73 million agreed in May. With Gerry Robinson's agreement, he raised the amount available to £160 million; by the time the Panel met on 1 July this had been stretched to a total of £269 million to be spent on CP1 projects over the period 1999 to 2006. While this would have the effect of proportionally reducing the amounts available for CP2 to a mere £84 million, it would enable a larger number of projects on the priority lists to be green-lighted, although in many cases over a longer period of time than many would have thought desirable. The Panel gave its approval to the proposed list of projects, which then went to a specially convened Council meeting five days later.

Because of the short notice, only four Council members, including

Gerry Robinson and myself, were present at the Council meeting on 5 July but the others had been asked for their prior input on the circulated list. There was some concern about the predominance of performing over visual arts (particularly from the two eminent sculptors on the Council), and the fact that insufficient attention was paid to the new strategic priorities; overall, however, there was an understanding that the Council had to deal with a state of affairs that had lasted far too long and that a list finally had to be agreed. The Council discussion highlighted the need for particular care to be applied to communications with the projects both on and not on the list; the necessity of ensuring a much more integrated approach to projects in terms of core, stabilisation and capital funding; and the securing of satisfactory assurances on future revenue needs from the projects included in the plan. The recommended list was then agreed and Council members present were requested to sign a written resolution, drawn up in accordance with Council bye-law 3 and setting out

> That the recommendations of the Capital Advisory Panel at its meeting on 1 July 1999 to accept the projects identified by the Panel to be included in the current Capital programme; and to note those projects not included in the current capital programme by the Panel be and are hereby agreed.

The purpose of this piece of formality seems to have been that the meeting was officially inquorate; all non-present members had signed it in advance.

An immediate result was some confusion as to what to do when a project on the CP1 list did not meet the assessment criteria. In such cases it was agreed that the applicant should have one opportunity to reapply.

Awards were then swiftly made to certain approved organisations, some of whom had suffered months of deferment. The Almeida Theatre, Hampstead Theatre and Laban in London, Gateshead's Regional Music Centre, FACT in Liverpool and Theatre Royal, Plymouth all received multi-million pound awards – though some of the attached conditions were stringent. As some projects had been languishing within the system for many months, I insisted that their offer letters should contain an apology. The SBC was awarded an £898,690 grant towards a master-planning exercise from the £25 million which it had been allocated under CP1.

*

In August 1999 I had a small operation for breast cancer. Many of the people who feature in this book were also experiencing health problems: Mary Allen's operation for breast cancer had preceded mine by three months, Grey Gowrie was in hospital awaiting a heart transplant, Graham Devlin had been diagnosed with a brain tumour (the reason for his deafness in one ear, but subsequently and happily found to be benign) and David Brierley had had a recent heart bypass. Although I've mentioned stress quite a lot and there is no doubt that on occasions the levels were high, I think it would be fanciful to blame my cancer on this. Medical opinion was that it had taken some time to grow and life wasn't by any means all bad. Both my job and my life outside ACE were fulfilling and happy; in spite of the many obstructions to getting things done there were also benefits to being a Council member. I was closely involved at a time when both the capital and the new revenue programmes were beginning to make a real difference to people's lives, and I enjoyed the companionship of my colleagues. The more lottery projects that opened, the higher was the sense of pride of being chair of the Panel which had invested so much time and wisdom in the whole process. However painful it had been to deal with the finalisation of CP1, decisions had now been taken and some of the pressure was off.

THE ORPHEUS CENTRE, GODSTONE

While all the capital planning shenanigans were going on at ACE's offices, wonderful things were continuing to blossom elsewhere. The demand for disabled access throughout all projects was paying off: organisations were gradually wakening up to the possibilities of offering hugely improved facilities to people of all abilities. If the Panel had regretted an absence of projects directly connected with disability the previous autumn, the Orpheus Centre in Godstone, Surrey, which opened at this time with great celebration, was exemplary. This was the brainchild of the musician and lyricist Richard Stilgoe who formed the idea after some weeks he had spent annually with twenty young disabled people and twenty music students working together to create a concert:

> If you take a group of people who have got to do a show on Friday they ignore the differences between themselves quite quickly and start getting on with that . . . The diversity of story that the disabled people brought to their invention meant that we got some astonishing stuff out of it; the feeling of this group euphoria at the end of the week was unbelievable, everybody had felt useful and united and different from the way the rest of their lives were, particularly the music students . . . Any organisation needs everybody to get something from it and everybody to feel they've contributed and I didn't know that would be the case to begin with and I didn't know it was necessary . . .The frustration of these music weeks was that at the end of the week everybody went away and waited fifty-one weeks for the next one to happen and for a lot of them it was the defining week of the year, and so I wanted to do thirty-eight weeks, three terms, and add in life skills, shopping, budgeting, all that stuff. So we were doing a proper working towards independent living, working towards fulfilment for people and that's why the residential Orpheus Centre was necessary.

Fortunately it was at about this time that the lottery came into being. Richard's first application was rejected because, he feels, the disability assessor was unrealistically adamant that a disability project should be entirely run by the disabled. But he re-approached ACE and persuaded officers that, having given vast amounts of money to the ROH and its like, this was a project 'that might actually get a bit of approval from people'. The bid was improved and in June 1996 the Orpheus Centre was awarded the £2.0136 million for which it had re-applied. Richard admits that in preparing for such a vision

> Ignorance is very important – if you go into a project like this you mustn't know how difficult it's going to be; you must go into it with a lot of passion and a lot of zeal and not too much knowledge. Too much knowledge and you say, 'The hell with it, this is going to be far too hard to do.'

In his ignorance he relied on consultants' advice, some of which he says was appalling (mostly around the cost of running the care side). This was not picked up by the ACE assessors, but

> we were starting something that the Arts Council didn't know about, because the whole area of disability art was quite new in, when are we talking, 1998, 1996/7 . . . And we were intending to do something that nobody had any experience of, really, which is one of the reasons it was quite tricky.

For Richard it was a total personal commitment. Many of the arts people responsible for a lottery bid found it changed the way they operated, and Richard is a good example of this:

> I suppose the big change for me in the whole organisation was changing from a starter-upper to being a completer-finisher. I've always been quite good at having an idea and saying, 'Gosh, this is exciting,' and then losing interest in it. Very much Mr Toad and in this there had to be a lot of Eeyore, a lot of Rat and a lot of Owl . . . just Toad, no, it wouldn't have got done.

The Orpheus Centre opened in May 1998 and Richard is still very much involved, both as a trustee and active participant in the work, which is now extended into prisons:

> We are training people to be good at presenting themselves in public, at interviews with social services and all of that and we are doing what I think all young people should do which is to have lots of performing arts experiences at school so that you create your own stuff, you create what's inside you, you will often act and sing about stuff which is worrying you which you wouldn't dream of talking about because you're doing it at one remove. You are being asked your opinion by your teachers instead of being told what to do, you're working with lots of different age groups, you are – heavens above, you just know who you are, fantastically valuable for every pupil, particularly valuable for a bullied and ignored group of people in wheelchairs.

He says his involvement with the Centre stops him feeling guilty about the enormous amounts of money he has earned from writing musicals with Andrew Lloyd Webber. Again, it seems a terrible pity that his words about the importance of creativity are not being listened to by the present government, which is intent on closing down arts departments in schools and banishing arts subjects from the national curriculum.

13

A QUESTION OF MONITORING

Problems with supplementaries – National Audit Office report –
Milton Keynes theatre and gallery – the English Stage Company –
the Royal Shakespeare Company – RADA – the Lowry

While the operations side of the lottery department was searching for a strategy, the monitoring department was overseeing those projects that had already been awarded grants and (within the limits of the directions) was helping them to completion. Nicole Penn-Symons feels that this assistance often acted as mini-stabilisation. Alan Grieve was not the only one to moan about the monitoring process but hundreds of thousands, often millions, of pounds were involved and both ACE itself and the lottery directions demanded regular reports and reviews, concise breakdowns of expenditure before any claims against the grant, and the completion of many forms. More importantly, for arts managers inexperienced in handling capital projects, it provided a discipline that might otherwise have been lacking.

And then there were the 'supplementaries'. Several projects came back for more money: as with any building project there were overspends and difficulties in raising partnership funding which caused cash flow problems. The question of how these supplementary bids should be dealt with and where they should figure within the tightening budgets was regularly discussed.

The Panel's view was set out in a letter Nicole Penn-Symons wrote to Peter Hewitt in June 1998. She argued the principle that all lottery-funded buildings should be well designed, fit for purpose and of high quality. While extra funding should only be given when all other avenues had been exhausted, under-funding could badly destabilise a project and weaken that principle. Whatever criticisms there might have been about bailing out projects, to abandon them would not only waste the original investment but in many cases would kill off important arts organisations.

During 1997/98 the monitoring department had the extra task of providing evidence to the National Audit Office. The NAO had been on the case from early days and since 1996 had been looking into the risk factor of fifteen major projects,[24] each of which had received a lottery grant of over £5 million and had already made significant progress in terms of building work being completed and grant paid out. During the course of writing the report, the investigators from the NAO – whom Nicole Penn-Symons felt were inexperienced and overawed by such an enormous capital programme for the arts – looked into the workings of the monitoring department with assiduity, in some cases accusing ACE of handing extra money over to projects without proper investigation. Nicole vigorously rebutted this, pointing out that supplementary grants were awarded only when all other alternatives had failed; furthermore, to close projects would be much more expensive and less value for money than keeping them afloat. In the autumn of 1998 ACE had been given an opportunity by the NAO to comment on a draft of its report, and Peter Hewitt responded to this with some gusto. He felt that many of the conclusions could not be sustained after any reasonable, fair and balanced interpretation of the facts. There was virtually no acknowledgement that ACE was already carrying out many of the recommendations contained in the report, and he objected to the style and tone of some of the language. Amendments were also sought by Robin Young, who had succeeded Hayden Phillips as permanent secretary at the DCMS in April 1998. Writing to Sir John Bourn at the NAO in March 1999, he reiterated that ACE had already introduced

24. For the full list of projects please see Appendix II.

measures that the report recommended and argued that some of the supplementary grants castigated in the report were justified.

The Council minutes for January 1999 state that the report was intended to be published that March 'following clearance by the Chairman of Council and Chair of the Lottery Panel'. However, the next thing we saw was a press statement on 13 May issued by David Davis MP, then chair of the Public Affairs Committee, asserting that ACE had been proved to be 'a soft touch'. These words, gleefully seized on by the press, never appeared in the report itself. In putting out his own statement, Davis outrageously pre-empted both the NAO's official press release and his own committee's discussion of the report – as well as taking a very partisan approach to its contents.

The immediate response from all of us at ACE was anger that the amendments we had sought had not been fully recognised. Re-reading the report now, however, it seems to me remarkably balanced. There is criticism of ACE: there was inadequate supervision of some of the building monitors attached to each project; ACE's business assessment and planning team had shown some serious inadequacies (I don't remember anything about their role); conditions were not always met before further grants were paid; and the Panel was not always presented with options in cases of failing projects. But there was also a recognition that the projects were complex, that many of the reasons for nearly all of them being over-time and over-budget had been unforeseeable when work commenced, and that ACE had already taken action to remedy its own deficiencies.

Peter Hewitt was summoned to appear before the Public Affairs Committee on 21 June 1999 to answer the report. The terror that such grillings inspire caused much preparation, with rehearsal after rehearsal. Once before the Committee, Peter outlined the many changes that ACE had made to its processes and highlighted the benefits that the finished projects were already producing. The Council congratulated him on his presentation but none the less he says that

> I was still dismayed by the press release that was put out at the end of the Public Affairs Committee, because I'd imagined rather naively that I'd get a good write-up. That's not how it works, they don't work like that.

Perhaps the fact that he had made 'mischievous references' to the considerable overspends in the building of Portcullis House (the office block for MPs where the committee hearing was taking place) did not recommend him to his inquisitors. The effect of David Davis's 'soft touch' remark would remain, although the forecast in his press statement that

> there is a real risk that ultimately lottery funds may have been used to no long term effect at all . . .

was proved spectacularly inaccurate. All the projects listed in the NAO report, with the exception of the National Centre for Popular Music, have subsequently thrived. In the early 2000s Peter Hewitt commissioned a comparison of a selection of private-sector building developments with some funded by the lottery. This revealed that the private sector cost overruns were very considerably higher, by about 18 per cent.

*

In contrast to the NAO's assertions, all requests for supplementary grants were carefully scrutinised by the Panel. One example was a bid by Milton Keynes Borough Council (MKBC). This was an important local authority bid which reflected a longterm desire to give its 'new town' image a cultural edge by building an arts complex comprising a 1,330-seat theatre and art gallery in the centre of the town, to be designed by architect Andrzej Blonski. A grant of £19.67 million was awarded in January 1996. Because of escalating costs, MKBC then asked to postpone the gallery for a later application but the Panel, feeling that the scheme should not go ahead without the gallery, requested that they look again at the bid, and, if necessary, re-apply for a larger amount (there was still enough money about then to make such suggestions). No re-application was made and the work went ahead, with the gallery reinstated, on the original grant. However, in June 1998, they needed a further £750,000 to complete the work. It was too late to complain about not heeding the Panel's original advice, but we did think that MKBC itself could pick up more of the overspend. Eventually ACE granted a further £500,000 on the condition, in another *volte face*, that it went only towards the theatre's fit-out costs with not a penny going towards the gallery. The complex was given a fine opening in October 1999 and the gallery welcomed over 4,600 visitors during its first weekend. It is now one of the UK's leading public galleries, presenting a programme of international contemporary visual art. Such has been its success that it is now undergoing a further building project to double its existing gallery space, add a learning centre and improve access throughout, due to open in 2017. The theatre has established itself as a major receiving house on the UK touring circuit. Both organisations have more than fulfilled MKBC's vision in establishing Milton Keynes as a high-quality place to live.

*

There were follow-up stories to three other major bids that have already been mentioned. A second supplementary request from the English Stage Company (ESC) – this time for £1.869 million to cover increases in construction and closure costs – came to the March 1998 Panel meeting. Deferment was recommended: while acknowledging that the project was making progress, the Panel now questioned the provision of a restaurant and suggested that the project could be scaled down. This would have been hard for the ESC to undertake: by now the building contract for the refurbishment of the Royal Court theatre had been secured and two West End theatres contracted for the closure period. It was perhaps the furore over the ROH closure plans that led us to query the ESC's risk in this regard, but the ESC were adamant about the need to keep open. At the time there were fewer new writing theatres in London than there are now, and the ESC wanted to safeguard its commitment to this form. Closure costs did reveal problems, however; one being the need to ensure that British Actors' Equity would agree to ESC's continuing to pay subsidised rather than West End commercial rates during its stay in the West End. Vikki Heywood remembers constant negotiations with ACE assessors over what was capital expenditure and what was revenue. By April 1998 there were major concerns about partnership funding (the Jerwood donation had not yet been committed), and the Panel had to suggest that serious consideration be given to aborting the project. This was, in my recollection, the first and only time that such a suggestion was aired and it was quickly rejected. Such action would have cost ACE the £10 million already spent plus the costs of liquidation for the ESC, to say nothing of leaving a substantial hole in the ground and the loss of an organisation that was artistically important. It was only in July 1998, when intimation of the Jerwood negotiations was given to us in the strictest confidence, that a supplementary grant of £2.545 million was finally agreed by the Council. This was more than the supplementary originally discussed that March, but perhaps extra costs had been incurred during all the deferment. A further supplementary of £1.325 million was paid out in September 2000.

The ESC was one of the most difficult projects to deal with out of more than five hundred grants over £100,000 that we awarded between 1995 and the end of March 2000. The risks were enormous, and failure would have been catastrophic for everyone concerned. ACE was under an obligation to consider every alternative, but while it did so the months of delay caused considerable problems. As Vikki Heywood points out, the longer it took to investigate the danger, the more dangerous it became. The 1996 *Omnibus* film made by Stephen Daldry and David Lan ended with the slogan 'The Royal Court will reopen Autumn 1998' but it was still unfinished in the autumn of 1999. By then, in a final twist of obstruction, it was competing with *grands projets* such as the Millennium Dome that had to be finished by 31 December. Electricians and other workmen suddenly vanished from the Royal Court, allegedly to be seen on the millennium sites with banknotes falling out of their pockets. The theatre did not finally reopen its doors in Sloane Square until February 2000, and did so with a considerable deficit on the capital project in spite of ACE's supplementary payments. Its saviour was *The Weir* by Conor McPherson. This had opened at the Ambassadors Theatre during the ESC's stay there and had subsequently transferred to the Duke of York's for a long commercial run. Its director, Ian Rickson, subsequently took over the artistic direction of the ESC and, Vikki says, was somewhat displeased to find that what should have been a healthy reserve generated by the success of his own work had been severely depleted to cover the extra costs of the capital project. The theatre has continued to run successfully as a centre for new writing, regularly filling its two auditoriums. Its website carries a quotation from *Harpers & Queen* declaring it to be 'London's coolest theatre'. While its restaurant and bar have captured a lively post-show clientele, it has never achieved planning permission to open up the entrance from the restaurant on to Sloane

Square which would provide much greater public access. Vikki Heywood's vision of waiters nipping up and down with trays of coffee and people having a lovely time sitting out in the square remains unfulfilled.

One of the major problems for the ESC was its poor relationship with its building contractors, Schal (whom they nicknamed 'Shan't'). That company had not done its initial homework on the problems of the site; once work started, it had overseen considerable delays. Many projects experienced similar difficulties in their relationships with contractors. I remember pushing for ACE, together with other good cause distributors, to get to grips with what seemed to me to be cartels within the construction industry. This initiative unfortunately fizzled out on lawyers' advice. But arts managers were horrified with practices that seemed barely legal, such as a contractor gaining a tender on a competitive price and almost immediately saying they could not complete the project for that amount. Project manager Simon Harper says:

> What I found when I first got involved with capital projects was actually that the theatre side was infinitely more disciplined about programme than the construction side because we had absolute deadlines – that show will open at that time, we've sold all the tickets and there will be a thousand people outside the door – whereas in the construction industry they're quite happy to go, 'Yeah, we'll get it there, you might need three or four months longer . . .'

In terms of managing projects, Vikki Heywood stresses the importance of having board members with experience of and interests in the construction industry. On the Royal Court project, she not only lacked an expert voice at her ear but had no bargaining power: it was a one-off project without future contracts to offer. Vikki is about the only arts manager I know who repeated her experience of running a capital project when she moved on to the RSC – although she says this was by default. Having only taken on the appointment of executive director there for a six-month period, she was inveigled into staying and master-minding the huge reconstruction of the Royal Shakespeare theatre that finally opened in November 2010. For this she had the invaluable advice of board member Paul Morrell, then a senior partner at the quantity surveyors Davis Langdon. I too benefited from his expertise, given with real generosity, when I became chair of Rambert in

2000 and got involved with the construction of its new headquarters on the south bank of the Thames.

The RSC bid itself had been problematic. In August 1995 the company had raised, with both Grey Gowrie and Jeremy Newton, their need for a major redevelopment of the Stratford-upon-Avon site. They promised that all the capital and revenue implications would be carefully thought through – in contrast, they were keen to point out, with some other major bids, such as the ROH and the SBC. A planning study award of £100,000 was made to them in April 1996 but, before a further bid could be considered, the three-stage process was introduced in early 1997 and they had to re-write their second application. This was for £3.252 million to cover development and some equipment. Perhaps because of the confusion, but in spite of their earlier promises, the second bid was rejected by the Panel in March 1998 on the grounds that the project had not been properly thought through and a 'fundamental review' of the whole thing was needed. Shortly afterwards, the RSC was informed by lottery officers of the £50 million cap being imposed on major national projects – a further shock, as the scope of their plans demanded much more. An award of £832,498 was made in September 1998 for equipment but otherwise the RSC was advised that all future major projects were being postponed pending the delivery of a national strategy.

This was a good example of how the changes in ACE processes caused frustration and fury. But ACE had genuine concerns about the scale of the proposals. I remember seeing the plans of one particularly grandiose scheme designed by Dutch architect Erick van Egeraat which involved pulling down not only the 1932 Shakespeare Memorial Theatre but the Arden Hotel opposite and many of the surrounding cottages. And during this time the RSC was carrying one of the biggest deficits of all ACE's funded organisations. None the less we realised that something had to be done about one of the country's most historic theatres. A planning figure of £50 million was confirmed to the RSC and this remained allocated for the long time that the redevelopment took to resolve itself.

The van Egeraat scheme collapsed and the capital needs of the organisation became entangled with more general upset: the RSC, under Adrian Noble's direction, substantially changed its pattern of work, withdrawing from its London home at the Barbican. It wasn't until 2007, after Michael Boyd had succeeded Adrian Noble, that a plan by Bennetts Associates, incorporating some of the Art Deco features of the original building at Stratford with a new thrust stage auditorium, was adopted and work started. Vikki Heywood also pays tribute to the then RSC chair Christopher Bland for his part in accomplishing the project and to Susie Sainsbury, who chaired the project committee, whose help and support she heavily relied on. The building opened to a mostly favourable reception in November 2010; the full story of its chequered development can be read in *Transformation* by David Ward.

*

Another project always on the monitoring agenda was RADA. The cost of its building work was going up by 1999 (because of such matters as the rising water, see page 79); partnership funding was slow to come in, in spite of the valiant efforts of chairman Richard Attenborough. Although RADA was uniquely lucky in receiving royalties from the Bernard Shaw estate, its financial position was dire. This had not been helped by their taking out a loan to acquire another building in nearby Chenies Street, to which the Academy decamped during construction work. Assessor David Hall again:

> I was absolutely flabbergasted, because this is not our definition of partnership funding, which they thought it was, and secondly it explained why, when I looked at their initial draft financial results, their interest payments had rocketed and their operating deficit had considerably worsened.

Chenies Street remained a problem. RADA was keen to keep this additional space after the Gower/Malet Street building opened and resisted considerable ACE pressure to sell it in order to complete the partnership funding and to ease their cash flow. This was another project that took many meetings, putting considerable pressure both on their senior management (who were also continuing to run the Academy) and the ACE officers and monitors who had to deal with them. For me, it meant some agreeable lunches with Richard Attenborough which always left me full of optimism that all would be well. David Hall, who says Attenborough should have been canonised for what he did for RADA alone, nevertheless remembers a crisis meeting at ACE when Attenborough uncharacteristically thumped the table and said that he was going to have to mortgage his house and did ACE want to bankrupt him? Tension was diffused when David inadvertently called him Lord RADA, to laughter all round.

Finally all was resolved and the finished building was re-opened by H.M. The Queen in November 2000; it provided five theatres as well as the studios and workshops needed by a drama school of world renown. The Chenies Street site was subsequently redeveloped to create more spaces and in 2012 RADA obtained the lease of the adjacent drill hall, which they renamed RADA Studios.

As a final piece of the lottery jigsaw, the dance and drama grants scheme was indeed taken on in full by the Department for Education in 2001, where it was split between the Further and Higher Education Funding Councils for England. Also at this time a number of dance and drama schools (including RADA) formed themselves into a new higher education institution called the Conservatoire for Dance and Drama, in order to access mainstream higher education funding as distributed by the Higher Education Funding Council for England (HEFCE), as an alternative to the Dance and Drama Award route. The other schools forming the Conservatoire are Bristol Old Vic School, Central School of Ballet, the National Centre for Circus Arts, London Academy of Music and Dramatic Art, London Contemporary Dance School, Northern School of Contemporary Dance and Rambert School of Ballet and Contemporary Dance.

*

The relationship between the Lowry and ACE remained poor. In early January 1999 I chaired a meeting attended by Felicity Goodey and the chief executives of Salford Council, ACE, the Millennium Commission and the HLF (all co-funders). Although the meeting was called at the Lowry's request, Stephen Hetherington, its chief executive, disdained to attend. The Lowry wanted an upfront payment of £12 million from its ACE grant, in spite of the fact that they had not supplied the requested fully integrated business plan nor had they addressed the risks about a £6 million partnership funding gap. ACE still had concerns about the viability of the proposed artistic programme, and were also perturbed by the Lowry's reluctance to admit that they had dropped a rehearsal studio for cost reasons. Rental from this had featured as a source of income in the business plan. Nicole Penn-Symons – heavily pressured by the NAO at the time to insist that clients gave full information – had to ask those working on the project six times at a meeting before its removal was finally admitted. The Lowry team adduced the furore over the incident to be an example of ACE's intractability.

The payment was finally agreed (Felicity says that she had to ask the Millennium Commission to intervene) but the peace didn't last. In June 1999, the Millennium Commission agreed an additional grant of up to £5.3 million towards building overrun costs and the gap in partnership funding. This was to be conditional on ACE and the HLF contributing a further £3.5 million and £1 million respectively. A letter from Chris Smith (wearing his chair of the Millennium Commission hat) to Gerry Robinson in December 1999 urged action on this. He pointed out that the Lowry was now planning to advertise an opening date of 28 April 2000; in order to do so

> the Trustees [of the Lowry] need to have firm assurances that additional grant from the Lottery Bodies will be forthcoming in order that they can honour the commitments they have to make.

ACE was not to be hurried; more meetings were called to go through its continuing concerns, much to Felicity Goodey's exasperation:

> You keep going because you believe in something and I passionately believed in the Lowry. Yes, I can laugh about the ups and downs now, but God it was stressful, I lost a stone in weight!

At last the further grant of £3.6 million was agreed at the Council's February 2000 meeting – £100,000 being added to the requested sum specifically for the costs of further detailed market research and subsequent audience development. Once more there really was no alternative. The formal offer letter from Peter Hewitt to Stephen Hetherington expressed ACE's anger at the way the project was being handled and their considerable concerns about its overall viability:

> I have not yet seen a business and operating plan with detailed and credible substantiation . . . Such plans as far as they exist do not yet convince me . . . I have not yet seen any considered sensitivity analysis, risk management strategy or contingency provision . . .

He advised that the letter be shown to the trustees who, he felt, were at personal risk. In his reply Hetherington referred to the detailed sensitivity analysis undertaken in the original business plan; stated that the first three months of programming were fully contracted with low-risk deals; rejected the idea that a risk analysis and detailed market research had not been undertaken; confirmed the Lowry's assets which had been gifted to them by Salford City Council and ended with bewilderment that ACE still had concerns.

The correspondence exemplifies the stand-off between the two organisations. While the Lowry team obviously felt bruised, all of us at ACE were apoplectic at its apparent reluctance to share its problems and to supply the information we requested. I spent many hours on the telephone with Felicity Goodey but it was her management team that seemed unwilling to communicate with ACE officers and assessors.

The Lowry did open on 28 April 2000 although with much the same problems as Sadler's Wells, as Felicity Goodey relates:

> With a week to go before the opening night, the flooring hadn't gone down in any of the bars . . . they hadn't painted the external curtain walls of the main theatre . . . two days before the opening they opened a tin of paint and found it was the wrong colour; it was a special paint and they had to drive all the way to Scotland to get another consignment overnight . . . On opening night I was waiting for the fire certificate at the same time as I was waiting for our guest of honour, DCMS secretary of state Chris Smith; I didn't tell him the reason I had to stay outside was because without that fire certificate, we couldn't open the theatre.

Finally the certificate came through and the opening gala took place. However, the evening had an epilogue which is burned into Felicity's memory:

> Michael Wilford, the architect, and I were kind of leaning on each other for support, utterly exhausted, at about one o'clock in the morning outside the

building . . . this was the Saturday night/Sunday morning of a Bank Holiday weekend . . . and the site manager from the construction company wandered up and, somewhat diffidently, presented me with a Sainsbury's carrier bag. 'What's this?' I asked. 'It's the keys to the building,' he said and scarpered. When I looked in the bag there were the keys to every door in the building, hundreds of them, and not one labelled. We couldn't lock any part of the building – with a multi-million pound art collection in it! So nobody went to bed that night either.

The opening wasn't the end of the problems. Moss Cooper says that there remained a £13 million capital shortfall; during the first four years of operation a £4 million deficit in revenue was accumulated. He finally brought together 'reluctant' public funders – HLF, ERDF, the North West Development Agency and Salford City Council – and got them to agree a £17 million package, thus ensuring that the Lowry was relatively debt-free in the early years of building up its business.

The opening gala was followed by a short season of the first performances ever given outside London by Paris Opéra Ballet – Felicity cites this as an example of Stephen Hetherington's vision and contacts. As far as ACE was concerned, helpful conversations about the artistic programme only began when Robert Robson was appointed theatres director in 1998. He subsequently became artistic director in 2003 and his sudden death in September 2013 shocked the arts world. Shortly afterwards, the Lowry published *Beyond the Arts: Economic and wider impacts of The Lowry and its programmes*, an independent assessment where the key findings owe much to Robert's work and highlight the success that the original lottery investment provided:

- The Lowry employs over 370 staff and its activities support the equivalent of 533 full-time jobs across the UK, the majority in the North West;
- The Lowry contributes £29m per annum in gross value added to the national economy, corresponding to a total expected contribution of £239m over the coming decade;
- The Lowry is the most popular visitor destination in Greater Man-chester and one of the most popular in the north-west, with around 820,000 visitors per year, a total of over 11 million since opening in 2000;

- Around a quarter of its shows are either world or UK premieres and/or international calibre shows available to audiences in the north-west only because of the presence of the Lowry;
- The Lowry has been a cornerstone of the £1.4 billion regeneration of Salford Quays – now the new home to the BBC – which has seen the former docks regenerated into one of Greater Manchester's strongest-growing areas in terms of employment, population and households;
- Only 11.3 per cent of the Lowry's income comes from public funding – well below the average across regularly funded arts and cultural institutions of 40 per cent – and the return on this investment is £16.27 for every £1 of public money – higher than national benchmarks for other public sector interventions.

Of the self-contained business centres originally mentioned by Felicity Goodey, Quaytickets services a number of events in the Greater Manchester area including the Manchester International Festival. Although it's a pity that all this was achieved with so much ill-feeling on both sides, it's none the less an excellent example of what lottery investment achieved on the largest scale.

*

Looking back on various lottery projects I am struck by the problems caused when those receiving grants were not open with ACE. Jeremy Newton acknowledges that his one big mistake in setting up the systems was to make the monitors too much like 'Arts Council police', which sometimes resulted in a lack of mutual trust. Often bad news was kept from them or, as with the Royal Court, they were seen as 'going native' and replaced. While Sue Hoyle does not accept that her previous employment at ACE made it any easier to obtain supplementary grants for The Place, she underlines that it had taught her to be open about the problems with ACE officers and monitors. Peter Jenkinson also speaks of the benefits of openness and mutual trust: it was in no one's interests for projects to fail. Nicole Penn-Symons endorses this and says that the projects that offered a candid relationship found that the monitoring process could actually be helpful. Not that friendly overtures were always successful. Nicole remembers inviting Nicolas Kent, then director of the Tricycle Theatre in London's Kilburn, to discuss some outstanding problems on his bid:

> The only time he could come in and see us with one of his people was lunch hour . . . In those days you gave somebody a sandwich if they came to you in the lunch hour . . . He went bananas: 'How on earth can you sit there, supplying us with sandwiches and all of this when everybody is looking for money and the arts are going bust?'

Nicolas was, in fact, one of the most appreciative recipients, even thanking me for the excellent ladies' loos at the Tricycle many years later.

*

In his report on The Public, Anthony Blackstock mentions three other 'failures': the National Centre for Popular Music, Ocean in London's Hackney (which went into receivership as a community music venue and in 2011 was taken over by the Picturehouse chain of cinemas) and the Dovecot Arts Centre in Stockton-on-Tees. Since then the Dovecot has successfully re-opened as ARC, a multi-purpose arts centre presenting hundreds of professional, community and educational events engaging with more than 110,000 visitors a year. (In December 2016 Arts Professional reported a collaboration which ARC had set up with a local Clinical Commissioning Group, leading to an investment of over £200,000 in creative arts activity for older people at risk of hospital admission or social isolation and thus proving entrepreneurism and the importance of arts in healthcare.) But these were four out of hundreds. In the concluding paragraph 90 of his report Anthony states:

> I find the Arts Council is properly chastened by its involvement in [The Public's] deeply troubled process and outcome. Its record across the whole range of 399 major capital projects totalling £1.486 million has been excellent in the main. England's stock of new and restored buildings now attests to the Arts Council's highly competent supervision.

It is a credit to all concerned – project champions and managers, advisors of all kinds and all concerned at ACE – that more didn't go wrong. Or, perhaps, that so much went so spectacularly right.

14

GETTING THERE

Getting to grips with CP2 – my final days at ACE – Pride of Place

With a final list achieved for ending CP1, the first capital programme, the way should have been clear for some proper thinking about CP2, the second phase. But any hope that something could be put together quickly was soon dashed. The September 1999 Council meeting was informed of 'a delay in the flowchart indicating linkages and integration within the system' but the general consensus was that CP2 needed to be as clear and as simple as possible and that 'it would be well worth taking a little longer to ensure this outcome'. By the end of September there was still nothing to go out to consultation as had been promised: once again the timetable was slipping badly.

Part of the problem was the lack of involvement of senior ACE executives. During the summer Peter Hewitt had been very taken up with preparation for his appearance before the Public Affairs Committee; he was also dealing with an impending theatre review, yet another orchestral review and a restructuring which would reduce ACE staff by a third. Graham Long had been on paternity leave. Nobody had replaced Jeremy Newton as lottery director and this was a serious weakness. The advertisement for the appointment of a director of capital services, promised in April 1999, had not gone out until July. It was October before interviews finally took place, and Moss Cooper, who had been acting in the role and was fully conversant with the territory, got the job. He did not, however, become a member of the senior management team and this caused delay as decision-making had to go through another layer of management. The task of synchronising all streams of ACE work – something the Panel discussions had stressed again and again – was given to the new director of arts, Kim Evans, who took up her position in October.

Throughout the autumn the discussions crawled on, not only about the strategy itself but also about the general consultation process surrounding it. Something that had been promised as short, sharp and selective now looked likely to be a massive exercise involving eight to ten national seminars, each to be attended by about eighty guests and twenty ACE/RAB staff. A meandering draft document full of 'maybe this, maybe that' was produced by way of a letter of invitation to them. Again, my frustration was enormous and I blew up at Peter Hewitt in an email about

> my extreme dissatisfaction with the whole process of the compilation of this strategy. High consultancy fees and a vast amount of staff time have been given to it and still we end up with a completely open-ended document that gives no indication of our thinking.

Drastic action was needed and at one point in early November I threatened to resign as chair of the Panel unless something was sorted out. So much had been promised by the senior management team for so long and still nothing was happening: I felt that my position as chair of the capital panel was finally becoming untenable. As a result I had a meeting with Peter Hewitt, Graham Long and Kim Evans, the outcome being that Peter would write a strategy paper by the end of November. The paper was duly delivered and discussed at the December Panel meeting. It was given general approval, although there were concerns at the suggestion that we place a higher priority on the projects with higher partnership funding – this would discourage the very ones which we hoped particularly to support. The paper was then sent out to public consultation with responses due by early February 2000. But the vital mapping exercise was delayed because ACE systems staff were working hard on an IT integration project and would not be available until March.

The CP2 consultation document received 302 responses. There was support for the strategic approach to lottery grants; for the principle of targeted funding to areas that were socially, culturally or economically deprived; and for a more inclusive approach to race, disability and social/economic class. The integration of capital and revenue funding and investment in artists' work spaces were also welcome. Lottery funding of up to 90 per cent of total costs in cases of particular need was approved, as was a simplified application process and a single point of entry into the scheme. But ACE's overall wish to be the minority funder found no favour, nor did the large number of priorities outlined, particularly the emphasis on new work, experimentation and risk, and new artforms that used new technology. The devolution of funding to the RABs for grants of under £100,000 met with 80 per cent disapproval among respondents; the low level of lottery funds allocated to CP2 was also regretted. There was criticism of ACE's self-congratulation about the successes of CP1, about the document's language and the fact that it contained no reference to literature, photography, video or crafts.

As well as the consultation, the Council had to address two areas in its thinking about CP2. The big item on its table was now the theatre review. This had first been mooted in July to address the perceived plight of regional theatre where years of under-investment were resulting in unambitious programming and audience decline. Peter Boyden had been appointed in September 1999 as the consultant responsible for its delivery. From the start both Council and Panel agreed that it was important that it was developed in tandem with CP2. This would ensure that regional theatres – which for some unidentifiable reason had not benefited in the numbers they might have done during CP1 – could be among the first to apply for its successor.

The second necessary CP2 decision was on the amount of applications ACE would be able to consider from arts organisations about to be hit by the demands of the impending Disability Discrimination Act. From 2004 this would compel anyone running a building to take reasonable steps to make physical alterations to ensure accessibility. The projects funded under CP1 had made great progress in this area and the principle of complete access insisted upon at the start had definitely changed attitudes. But compliance had proved expensive and dwindling funds would not allow the same kind of investment in the future. Access would continue to form a fundamental part of future bids but could not be applied for on its own.

In spite of the disfavour in the consultation responses, the devolution of smaller grants (including capital ones) to the RABs had already started the previous July; they were now being delivered via RALP. A row had immediately blown up when it was discovered that the RABs, having been given responsibility for grants of up to £100,000, were planning to impose a maximum of £50,000 on any one grant. A compromise was reached on this when it was mutually agreed that grants for capital sums – including equipment and the commissioning of public art – could be for up to £100,000, and those for projects and organisational development would have a cap of £30,000.

As the responses had shown, the consultation paper on CP2 was wide-ranging: so many priorities listed had little strategic value. It was now a question of producing a concrete policy. For something originally intended to be simple and unbureaucratic, the formation of CP2 seems particularly unwieldy. The first problem was who was going to do it: the senior management team's attention was focused on the theatre review and its members seemed disinclined to take the responsibility. Moss Cooper was dealing with the wrapping up of CP1. At the beginning of April a somewhat rambling document (its authorship remains anonymous) appeared. Three 'gateways' into the programme were proposed: cultural diversity, under-provision (both geographic and artform) and the new, which

> should not be defined in any great detail, but it would include: new forms of artistic expression (for example – new technologies and arts and disability), new opportunities for artists (for example, new artists' spaces and new opportunities for disabled artists), new audiences and new arts participants and new forms of access to the arts, including through education and improved disabled access.

This extract shows the style and language of the document – it seemed anything went, as long as it was NEW! The idea of the new had attracted little support in responses to the consultation paper but this was one occasion when it was felt that ACE had to assert its own priorities.

The paper proposed a single entry system for CP2 based on an expression of interest form; but on the subsequent selection process it only offered 'first thoughts'. The three gateway priorities would be scored and weighted, and the RABs and artform departments would offer an assessment which would lead to a 'balanced strategic portfolio of projects which meets [ACE's] strategic aims'. Once accepted on to the scheme, each project would have a pool of specialist technical advisors attached, in the same way as the stabilisation programme, with a 'whole life' team allocated by the monitoring department. The initial eight criteria would be retained, but for assessment rather than scoring purposes. It was proposed that the £176 million allocated to CP2 be split into two rounds of £88 million, with £20 million from the first allocation being earmarked for culturally diverse projects – in seeming ignorance of the fact that the final CP1 list had reduced the amount available to only £84 million. The maximum grant to any one project would be £5 million.

Before the Panel could see the paper, the senior management team decided it needed more work and referred it back to the capital department where two officers, Marion Doyen and Malcolm Allen, were given the job of knocking it into shape. They added ACE's overall priorities, highlighted the need for synergy with other ACE/RAB programmes and generally tightened up the language. But the senior management team was still unhappy with the result and, after more meetings with no one apparently willing to take on the job, I agreed to rewrite the paper – disregarding the admonition delivered the previous October against operational interference by Council members. I did this over the Easter weekend, keeping the main outline but sorting out anomalies and making it, I felt, more comprehensible. The result was agreed by the Council at its May meeting with the proviso that further detailed work should now be taken forward in order to launch the new programme in July.

This did happen, although I was no longer there to see it. My term as an ACE member had finally come to an end, and the June 2000 Council was my last. Shortly before that I attended the openings of Tate Modern and the Lowry, relieved to see the final – and highly successful – realisation of two projects which had involved such time and stress. The launch that April of the Film Council (the private company set up by the DCMS to distribute lottery film money) had given some journalists the opportunity to have a further go at ACE's involvement with film. Work on a new logo to acknowledge ACE lottery funding was nearly complete: the previous November the Council had decided that something really had to be done about the hideous sign that had been approved in the summer of 1996. And on 12 June 2001, nearly a year later, the list of entrants for CP2 was finally announced. In the majority of cases, ACE was no longer the majority funder but worked with partners such as the Regional Development Agencies to deliver projects that as well as art concentrated on regeneration and diversity.

A leaving party followed my last Panel meeting on 6 June. In a speech of farewell Moss Cooper declared that I had been a 'nightmare' to deal with, always questioning, complaining about the inadequacy of the paperwork and demanding progress, but I like to feel that this was said with some affection. We have remained friends and certainly I was sad to break the link with many of the lottery staff as well as Panel and Council members. Christopher Frayling and Andrew Motion also finished their terms at the same time and we were given a lunch and presented with beautiful Rupert Spira bowls. I treasured mine – until it was accidentally broken as I finished writing this book (it was subsequently miraculously mended by the ceramics restorer Amy Douglas). I am more ambivalent about the CBE I received in the Queen's Birthday Honours that summer. It was given for services to the arts, especially dance, but I feel that the Honours people were fastidious about mentioning the lottery. It was recognition, I suppose, of the amount of voluntary time I had given, but everything I accomplished – or didn't – as chair of the Panel depended on a lot of other people.

There was one piece of unfinished business. I felt that the achievements of the first capital programme had never been properly acknowledged and I persuaded Peter Hewitt to produce a celebration booklet to detail what had happened and to highlight some specific projects. I worked as editorial consultant with a firm called August to produce this; the plan was to circulate it to MPs, journalists and other opinion formers. For me an important part of the idea was to send a copy to each project champion in recognition of the success story to which they had contributed. *Pride of Place* was launched in May 2002 with a reception at RADA, but there is no evidence that it was ever circulated as planned; somewhere in the storage vaults of ACE many thousands of copies must be lying. At least it still seems to be available to order free.

I left ACE with very mixed feelings. It had been a roller-coaster and I felt particularly badly about the delays in wrapping up the first capital programme. Even reading back now over the sequence of events I can't really see what took so long or why I couldn't force a quicker outcome. On the bonus side, I feel genuine pride in all that was accomplished, the thousands of projects, both large and small, that went through during the four years I chaired the Panel and the fact that so very few failed. There will never be a time like it again and it was a privilege to have been part of it.

15

LIFE GOES ON

Rambert – the Arvon Foundation – Nesta

Having been a public servant for so long, I wanted to return to working with arts companies. In December 2000 I went back to Rambert as chair and then took up a similar position in March 2001 with the Arvon Foundation which ran two highly respected centres for creative writing in Devon and Yorkshire. I had left thinking that capital work was behind me but soon found that was not to be: both organisations were about to embark on substantial building projects.

The housing situation at Rambert was dire. For forty years the company had had its headquarters in Chiswick, west London, but by 2000 it was becoming apparent that it had to move. Its two rehearsal studios were both smaller than any stage on which the company performed, and a third even smaller studio sported the warning sign 'Don't Jump in this Studio'. Its important dance archive was kept in a cupboard underneath a water tank and had no public access; the building above ground level was inaccessible to anyone with restricted movement; and the company's ambitions both for its choreographic development and its learning and participation programme demanded more space. Various options to move had been investigated but no affordable solution had emerged. Then, out of the blue, in 2001 we were approached by Iain Tuckett, director of Coin Street Community Builders (CSCB) and a man who genuinely considers contemporary dance to be the most perfect form of human expression. He offered the company a site worth £5 million on London's South Bank in the heart of the cultural area which includes the SBC and the National Theatre. In return for a community programme Rambert would pay a peppercorn rent for the site (an immediate saving since its Chiswick rent was then £80,000 a year), but be responsible for the building costs. With the help of a grant from the London Development Agency we appointed Allies & Morrison as architects – their work at The Place was a strong recommendation – and they designed the outline for a building for which the total cost was estimated at £11.5 million.

Getting the seed money and finalising the designs took some time but an application for planning permission was finally submitted in November 2005. At the same time CSCB submitted its plans for the main part of the site which comprised a leisure centre (including a public swimming pool) and a residential tower of forty-eight storeys, the latter to provide income for the former. In August 2007, following delays caused by the height of the CSCB tower, planning permission was finally granted to both Rambert and CSCB. Conservation bodies such as English Heritage remained unhappy about the way the tower, even when reduced by three storeys, intruded in two London views. They continued to cause problems for the CSCB application with a series of ministerial referrals, rejections and appeals; although Rambert's planning permission was still in place, CSCB would understandably not sign any contract with the company until they knew that they had consent for the whole site.

While all this delay occurred, the total costs of the Rambert build rose to £14.5 million. Rambert had never had much private revenue support, raising between £60,000 and £150,000 a year from individual, foundation and (occasionally) corporate sources. Following CSCB's offer of land and the commissioning of Allies & Morrison in 2004, a development team of four was recruited to spearhead the capital campaign, to be launched on the realisation of planning permission which was originally estimated to be March 2006. The constant delays and frustrations of the planning process meant a steady deterioration of morale, and by the autumn of 2007 the head of the department and her deputy had both resigned. Little money had been raised, although a network of politicians, opinion formers and potential donors had been identified; no one was willing to make a financial commitment until all planning issues had been resolved and the project had a high degree of certainty. Two noble exceptions to this were the Foyle Foundation (to which David Hall had moved as director) and the philanthropist Ian Taylor, both of whom pledged an early £500,000 and remained steadfast through the years of delay. An early application had been submitted to the ACE capital department but by that time the guidelines were very strict and it was not considered ready for consideration.

It was a depressing time for us all but while uncertainty hung over the capital project, Rambert's artistic director, Mark Baldwin, was building up a strong company of dancers and repertoire and audiences were growing. Chief executive Nadia Stern (fresh from all her Sadlers's Wells experience) was continuing the work on rebuilding the company's reserves which had been started by her predecessor Sue Wyatt after many years of deficit. Various other building options were pursued but none had the advantages of the CSCB site, and I saw my job as keeping this proposed move to the South Bank on the drawing board. Persistence was rewarded in April 2009, when Iain Tuckett nobly said that we could go ahead even though he still hadn't got the green light for the rest of the site. A fundraising team was recruited, building contracts were signed and, by an amazing stroke of good fortune at last, ACE provided a grant of £7 million. It had ended its capital programmes in 2007, but by 2010 was considering a relaunch and wanted to back a few pilot projects that were ready to go. Rambert was in the right place at the right time. My term as chair ended in December 2009 but I remained attached to the company as an ambassador. My successor, Howard Panter, the rest of the board and, above all, the valiant Nadia Stern pushed the project through until it opened its doors in December 2013. But it was by no means an easy ride. Beverley Dawson, who now runs ACE's capital department, praises Nadia in particular:

> Nadia's drive to deliver that project was extraordinary and I do remember saying in a meeting that there are other companies that would have given up by now because of the number of legal and land issues that it faced.

Let us not forget that Nadia had learnt lessons from that master of persistence, Ian Albery.

Through the hard work of Naomi Russell and then Zoe Crick the fundraising target was met in good time, before building was completed. The design has won three architectural awards including the RIBA National Award 2014, and has been nominated for at least two others. It was officially opened by H.M. The Queen in March 2014, an occasion I sadly missed because I was in New York. But I later heard glowing accounts of her interest and knowledge as she toured the building and met board members, donors and staff. Needless to say, it was the photograph of a brief nodding of the royal head while watching a rehearsal that featured on the front pages of the tabloid press. I was touched when the chief executive's office was named the Skene Room; whenever I pass the building I do feel a pride in having kept the flame alight.

*

The Arvon project was very different. The Hurst, a Georgian manor house set in hills above the Shropshire village of Clun, was the home of the playwright John Osborne and his fifth wife, the former journalist and critic Helen Dawson. He had died in December 1994 and on his deathbed had beseeched Helen to remain at the Hurst and to keep it going. This was quite a burden for her: he had left large tax bills and the expenses of running a large house and grounds were considerable. Grey Gowrie, a friend and neighbour, had stepped in and suggested a deal whereby the Arvon Foundation would purchase the property and turn some of the outbuildings into a third writing centre, with Helen being allowed to live in the main house until her death. To finance this, an ACE lottery grant of £400,000 was successfully applied for and granted in September 1997, with Helen refunding £75,000 of the purchase price as part of the required partnership funding. She also bequeathed the royalties from Osborne's plays to Arvon on her death. At the time I came on board, Arvon's newish director, Helen Chaloner, had just received confirmation of a further grant for £522,500 towards the practical conversion of the outbuildings. Altogether £201,776 still had to be raised as partnership funding.

As an Arvon team we were relative innocents. I obviously had an overview of capital projects through chairing the Panel but had never been involved in a practical way, and Helen Chaloner's experience was limited to the time she had spent as her predecessor David Pease's deputy during the work done on the first lottery grant and her preparation of the second application. We were fortunate in having the poet John Sewell, who was also a surveyor, on the council of management and prepared to chair a property committee. A project manager had been appointed but he lived a three-hour drive away from the Hurst, which made the necessary regular supervision of the building site a problem.

We set about tendering for contractors and immediately hit a stumbling block when the cheapest came in substantially over the budgeted figure. This, together with a decision on VAT that went against us, necessitated applying once more to ACE for a supplementary grant of £251,449, granted in March 2002. We finally started the work on site in April 2002, with practical completion being granted that December. I knew something about building projects from the paperwork and site visits I had read and experienced when chairing the Panel, but I quickly learnt that it was quite another thing to be involved with a project on the ground. We had monthly meetings on site when Helen Chaloner, John Sewell and I grilled the project manager about progress and likely over-spends; decisions had to be taken about balancing additional costs with possible savings; funding from trusts, foundations and individuals had to be doggedly pursued. The amount of work was enormous and tribute must to paid to my predecessor Sir Robin Chichester-Clark who continued to raise funds and to Helen Chaloner, who not only had to do all the necessary administrative work but also concurrently run the Arvon Foundation on a tiny staff.

And then there was Helen Osborne. She was splendid in her welcome of Arvon and her acceptance of the project, but it was obvious that having the builders around was a huge strain. The purchase of the house had not been accompanied by a proper survey and it was obvious that such things as rewiring were urgently needed. But having builders on site was one thing, within the house itself was another and she refused to have any but her own local workmen involved there. As these on the whole lacked the professional certificates that ACE demanded, the work remained undone and it was this that caused such problems in the future.

Although she put a brave face on it, I knew that she dreaded the intrusion of new faces that the writing centre would bring, and it was by a wonderful chance that we appointed as the first centre directors two young men, Ed Collier and Paul Warwick, with whom she immediately bonded. As they established the centre they closely involved her in its decoration; she delighted in letting them squire her around the area, introducing neighbours and attending events such as race meetings, thus giving local credence to the whole idea. The Osborne Centre at The Hurst was officially opened by Dame Maggie Smith in March 2003. It was a shock for all of us when suddenly, in January 2004, Helen died of cancer. Not only did she leave to Arvon a house that was literally falling down but also three huge dogs: for some months these lived on in her kitchen causing terrible smell. After much discussion about their future they were all found other homes.

The house was indeed in a terrible state: the front walls were being held up by the ivy that encased them and I remember seeing the main staircase sway badly when someone put a hand on it. It was a terrible, expensive bequest to the Arvon Foundation and to my successor as chair, Nigel Pantling: for years the organisation struggled to find the funds to deal with it. Relief came at the same time as Rambert got its capital grant: ACE was impressed by Arvon's emphasis on sustainability and also put them on to the pilot programme. Finally, the money was forthcoming to give the main house a complete makeover and transfer to it the writing centre, leaving the outbuildings for writers' residencies. I found the re-opening, in May 2014, a splendid affair but one tinged with nostalgia. Memories flooded back of Helen Osborne knocking up delicious omelettes on her Aga as she downed copious amounts of whisky. Any pride I might have felt in the original refurbishment was somewhat deflated when speaking to Beverley Dawson, ACE's capital director: she says that she was amazed on visiting the Hurst for the first time after the re-opening that ACE had ever awarded its earlier grants. All the activity was tucked away around the back, the access arrangements were pretty token and the main house was a huge liability that strained the resources of the organisation. It was only when she learnt the back story of how it had all come about that she seemed reconciled.

*

I became involved with one other organisation that had its roots in those lottery years. The National Endowment for Science, Technology and the Arts (NESTA, which now likes to be known as Nesta) ran a fellowship programme for some years but none of its awardees generated any of the copyright income that would have swelled its endowment and it never achieved its position of a National Trust of intellectual capital that its founders had envisaged. I became a trustee in 2006 when Jeremy Newton's successor, Jonathan Kestenbaum, has just been appointed. When interviewed at the DCMS for the position, I had highlighted my Arts Foundation experience of running a fellowship programme; it was therefore disconcerting to discover, some three months after becoming a trustee, that the fellowship programme had been abandoned and half the staff were about to be sacked. The chair, Chris Powell, did later admit that perhaps it was something he should have mentioned at the interview, but I also blame myself for not demanding a better induction. It was a good example of Donald Rumsfeld's 'things we don't know we don't know'. The emphasis had changed from an organisation supporting individuals into something that was more of an investment arm, often contributing minor amounts to larger organisations' initiatives. It was also a struggle to see any real engagement with the arts – it had become NEST.

I felt the forces were against me and resigned after a year, still somewhat bemused by what it was all about and loathing the jargon in which, I felt, everything was becoming couched. Perhaps the powers that be felt the same because in 2007 departmental responsibility for Nesta passed from the DCMS to the Department of Innovation, Universities and Skills. Nick Starr, then executive director of the National Theatre, replaced me as the 'arts' trustee and used his own innovation and skills to obtain a substantial grant for the National's Live screening programme. In 2010, as Robert Hewison points out his excellent *Cultural Capital: The Rise and Fall of Creative Britain*, Nesta escaped the coalition government's 'bonfire of the quangos' and became an independent charity. I'm still not sure exactly what it does, but its website specifically states that it does not support individuals. It does, however, state that it is 'an innovation Foundation. We back new ideas to tackle the big challenges of our time . . . Making the case for collaborative problem-solving'. Its arts activity concentrates on the digital but includes an investment fund which gives loans to arts organisations to 'achieve sustainable growth and increase their social impact'. I view it with unreasonable scepticism because of it being one of the causes for the ACE drop in lottery income and of my unhappy time there. However John Newbigin tells me that

> it commands almost universal admiration and several countries have set up intentional imitations, partly because it's seen as much more than just another 'think tank' but as a quite unique research and action research resource.

AN AFTERMATH . . .

At the beginning of this book I spoke of the success of the capital programme. Sadly, I do not think it has always been seen as such because so much journalistic comment has fastened on its very few failures. But there seems to me little doubt that artists, audiences and participants now enjoy a network of new and refurbished buildings that offer a degree of facilities and comfort that barely existed before and certainly were not taken for granted. Those years of capital plenty provided a huge investment in the cultural infrastructure which was both much needed and set higher standards for the future; the strains it imposed on those responsible for delivering the thousands of projects were, I hope, somewhat ameliorated by pride in their accomplishment.

On the down side, there was of course the inevitable aftermath of increased revenue needed to run the new buildings: this is when the early optimistically high scoring for the financial stability criterion came home to roost in many cases, causing headaches for ACE and other funders. Arguably and ironically, it was not until the cuts to Treasury funding by the Tory/Liberal Democrat coalition government from 2010 began to bite that a more entrepreneurial attitude entered the arts world, which included deeper investigation into the use of spaces. In a speech to the Creative Industries Federation in November 2016, ACE chair Sir Peter Bazalgette, who made himself very much responsible for promoting a more commercial attitude, referred not only to increased income from capital assets such as catering facilities, office space, car parks and shops, but also alluded to Salford's Islington Mill which offers bed and breakfast and to the hostel run by New Brewery Arts in Cirencester.

ACE itself is a different beast from what it was in the late 1990s. In the seventeen years since I left the Council the 'arm's length' principle has been amputated further. In the early years of the New Labour government more Treasury funding did indeed pour in but, as Robert Hewison describes in *Cultural Capital*, this came at the expense of signing up to the government agenda of targets and objectives:

> In future, Creative Britain would have to carry a clipboard, and submit to the managerialism that contradicted the very idea of creativity.

Even this, however, was not seen to be enough when the coalition government started to wield its scythe around public funding. Rumours abounded at each spending round that ACE was to be abolished, but so far it has survived. However, the hope expressed by secretary of state Peter Brooke back in 1993 that it would no longer have to suffer reviews into its work and staffing remains hollow. It is not dead but has certainly suffered deep cuts: its national and London offices share one floor of a Bloomsbury office block into which are also squeezed six other 'government agencies', including Sport England, UK Sport and the Horserace Betting Levy Board. No doubt their proximity helps the DCMS keep a beady eye on them all. The DCMS itself has survived (also contrary to speculation), although removed from its smart offices in Cockspur Street from which Peter Palumbo found it so difficult to escape; it is now in some back rooms at the Treasury.

Some consistency in the regular roundabout of secretaries of state and ministers was granted by Ed Vaizey's term as the longest-serving arts minister – he was appointed in 2010 and remained until the summer of 2016, when he was ousted as part of Theresa May's post-Brexit turnaround of government ministers. Before he went, and after some delays, he produced a *Culture White Paper* in March 2016. It was the first since that published by Jennie Lee, *A Policy for the Arts*, in 1965 and was welcomed for its commitment to the arts and heritage, its emphasis on cultural access for all, particularly disadvantaged youth, and its desire to ensure diversity throughout cultural organisations. It contains a plethora of schemes and initiatives (some new, some already announced, some already in action, some to be the particular responsibility of one of DCMS's quangos, others to be delivered through a series of partnerships – a favoured word) as well as, hey ho, another review of ACE (this time the 'tailored' one already mentioned). While speaking of the importance of cultural communities, however, it fails to address the devastation that is being wreaked on arts organisations by government cuts to local authorities, but where its hypocrisy is breathtaking is in its attitude to education. Containing as it does a quotation from the then secretary of state for education, Nicky Morgan – 'I want every single young person to have the opportunity to discover how the arts can enrich their lives. Access to cultural education is a matter of social justice' – and much about the need for all young people to have access to the arts and culture generally, it is silent on the fact that under the present Conservative government arts education in schools is diminishing rapidly.

The tailored review was issued by the DCMS in April 2017 and overall gave ACE a good report, saying it seemed to be an effective and well-governed organisation – in spite of darkly hinting that efficiencies can always be made. While re-endorsing the arm's length principle it stresses that ACE should be seen as a development agency and its tone relies heavily on investment rather than grant-giving (it urges that ACE 'should build the financial skills capability of the sectors, supporting them to diversify further their revenue streams, embed commercial skills and commercial leadership, and become "investment ready"'[25]); there's much about the need for diversity and access, evaluation and risk management but sadly nothing about the importance of ACE promoting the arts sector as vital to the cultural life and well-being of the nation.

Cultural commentary has increased since the 1999s into an industry, much of it centred on cultural value. As Robert Hewison describes, attempts to define this began in the mid 2000s; more recently the Warwick

25. https://www.gov.uk/government/uploads/attachment_data/file/610

Commission issued a 2015 report on the subject entitled *Enriching Britain: Culture, Creativity and Growth*, only to have its findings subsequently questioned in early 2016 by *Understanding the value of arts & culture* by Geoffrey Crossick and Patrycja Kaszynska, commissioned by the Arts and Humanities Research Council, which argues that previous enquiries have been based on inadequate research. The *White Paper* also joins in the debate, particularly in terms of culture's intrinsic, social and economic value. Skipping quickly over the intrinsic, in three sentences suggesting that culture enhances wellbeing and 'life satisfaction', it recognises more fully the social, mostly in terms of the contribution it can make to mental and physical health and 'community cohesion'; in terms of the economic, a table shows the 'value of culture' (assessed by gross value added, nominal terms – make of that what you will) rising from £3.75 billion in 2008 to £5.4 billion in 2014. The national cultural policy debate has also included ACE's own strategic framework for 2010–20 entitled *Great Art and Culture for Everyone*; Robert Hewison's informative book; and regular calls from GPS Consulting to rebalance the funding between London and the regions, including the already mentioned *Rebalancing our Cultural Capital*. ACE has listened and committed itself to spending at least 75 per cent of its lottery income outside London in the future.

The Council itself now consists of a (relatively) manageable membership of fourteen, a reasonable mix of arts practitioners and those from philanthropic and finance backgrounds, with the five regions each represented by the chair of its area council, which provide local information and advocacy and take decisions on revenue applications up to £800,000. There was some controversy when Sir Peter Bazalgette replaced the Labour-appointed Dame Liz Forgan as the Council's chair in 2013, but mutterings that he was a Tory placeman were swiftly smothered by his obvious interest in the arts and his indefatigable touring around the country. Political allegiance did not stop some immediate cuts to ACE under his watch, but to him and to Darren Henley, who took over as chief executive in 2015, must go much of the credit for the surprise announcement of a brief blast of oxygen being pumped into the system by chancellor George Osborne's 2015 autumn statement. Recognising the economic benefits that the cultural industries contribute to national life, he marginally raised the Treasury grant instead of clubbing it still further. The Council still seems to meet more than is perhaps normal for a board (nine times a year) and its minutes are now posted on ACE's website, albeit with substantial redactions ('withheld here in line with the requirements of section 22 of the Freedom of Information Act 2000'); the main power appears to lie with the executive team, consisting of chief executive and deputy, and national directors of arts and culture, finance and communications. They were joined in the autumn of 2016 by the chief operating officer and the executive director, enterprise and innovation, tipping even further the balance away from arts experience and knowledge. The executive team and various officers drafted in for specific items bring the attendance at Council meetings to about twenty-six, only slightly fewer than the large roomful into which I ventured at my first Council meeting. Sir Peter Bazalgette stood down in early 2017 and the arts world reacted positively to the news that Sir Nicholas Serota succeeds him. Having experienced his lobbying skills I have every hope that he will be able to keep the profile of the arts high among politicians; it is certainly good to know that such a senior and successful figure will be fighting for the sector.

*

As noted above, all the good cause distributors had a substantial amount taken from them by the 2012 London Olympics, but once these were over the coalition government fulfilled a promise they had made on coming to power in 2010 to bring the arts, sports and heritage sectors back to the 20 per cent of the good cause money they had received before the 1997 election, with the Big Lottery Fund (the successor to the NOF which now covers health, education, environment and charitable causes) receiving 40 per cent. The lottery remains a considerable feature of British life and, perhaps curiously given the extremely small odds in favour of winning, its takings were holding up remarkably well in this time of austerity. Perhaps it offered a pinprick of hope in an otherwise desolate life. But having announced a record year in 2015/16, Camelot had to report a sudden and dramatic drop when ticket sales fell by £226 million in April–September 2016 compared with the same period the previous year; the £156.6 million that ACE received for that period compared with £175 million the year before.[26] Camelot cited economic uncertainty for the fall (a side effect of Brexit perhaps?), together with competition from rival lotteries. It would be worrying if it started a downward trend. A table in the 2016 *White Paper* showed that while the Treasury grant dropped from £451,964 million in 2009/10 to £447,871 million in 2014/15, ACE's lottery income rose over that period from £175,111 million to £235,306 million. While the overall increase in ACE's funding is to be welcomed, the growing imbalance in growth levels between Treasury and lottery income increases the pressure on the organisation to breach the 'additionality' rule and sneak lottery funding to its regular revenue clients.

Meanwhile, what has happened to the capital programme that is the main subject of this book? Following the CP2 programme, a third round of capital bidding was launched as Grants for the Arts – Capital in 2003/4 which selected a handful of projects that were ready to go. In March 2007 the capital department was wound up, which seemed to me a great pity. Some of the earlier buildings were beginning to need refurbishment, and I could never understand the decision not to allocate at least a few million pounds of lottery income annually which could have supported a few new projects and renovated some older ones. It would also have meant maintaining a department which by that time could offer exemplary knowledge: the staff had gained real expertise and their practical advice to those embarking on capital projects was invaluable. In justification, Christopher Frayling (who became chair in 2005) says that the days of the *grands projets* were over and with the Olympics looming there seemed to be more pressing calls on the diminishing income which would result. Peter Hewitt agrees, and adds that more emphasis was being put on local delivery and on local authorities to maintain infrastructure – the whole strategy of local government engagement was crucial to that. This only goes to highlight the

26. The total drop in ACE income for the year 2016/17 was announced in *Arts Professional* on 20 June 2017 as being £55million (https://www.artsprofessional.co.uk/ news/lottery-arts-funding-plummets-ps55m?utm_source=Weekly-News&utm_medium= email&utm_content=Lottery-arts-funding-plummets-by-£55m&utm_campaign=20th-June-2017).

drastic cuts that have been applied to local authority budgets since 2010, imperilling both capital investment and revenue support.

It proved unrealistic to ignore capital needs for long. Beverley Dawson, who had worked in operations and monitoring during CPs1 and 2, had been retained to mentor and advise the ACE regional officers who oversaw the finalisation of projects after the closure of the capital department. She was asked to recruit a team of four and in June 2010 a budget of £26 million was allocated to nine pilot projects that were deemed in a sufficient state of preparedness: both the Rambert and Arvon projects were beneficiaries (see pages 241–44 and 244–46). This led to the introduction of two programmes: £219.6 million of lottery money was put aside for grants over £500,000 in 2012–15, and £24 million for smaller grants of £100,000–£499,000 (amounts below £100,000 can be applied for under Grants for the Arts). For the 2015–18 period, these amounts are respectively £88 million and £32.5 million.

The new capital programmes are very different from the early days described in this book, with emphasis being put on the necessity that they will improve the resilience (that word again!) of an organisation. Leadership, governance, a strong artistic programme and sustainable business plan are all boxes that have to be ticked before any construction grant is agreed, and it is very unlikely that ACE will be the major funder of any project. For such large amounts of money this now seems self-evident, but in the early days, with pressure to set systems up and get money out, it didn't happen in quite that way.

Capital grants are now also part of the battleground over our old friend, the 'arm's length' principle. The DCMS's departmental plan 2015–20 highlighted support for The Factory in Manchester; a Great Exhibition in the north, and help for the Manchester Museum to establish a new India Gallery. The Factory, a new arts and culture project on the former Granada studios site in Manchester (close to the then chancellor's own con-stituency), was promised £75 million, with a further £9 million a year to run it; the Treasury was also committed to handing out £5 million to a Birmingham 'dance hub'. Neither project seemed to be a burning priority for the arts community; more welcome were the direct grants announced in the March 2016 budget including £2 million to refurbish the Hall for

Cornwall in Truro, £13 million for Hull's City of Culture, a new Shakespeare North theatre in Knowsley and £14 million for the STEAMhouse in Digbeth, Birmingham. Any extra money for the arts can only be welcomed, but it is a pity that such disbursement bypassed the body designed to distribute it with knowledge, experience and skill. Such reliance on political whim and expediency raises questions about what will happen to such projects in the future. Brexit and its consequent reshuffling of the Cabinet table makes for considerable uncertainty.

The STEAMhouse is interesting because its purpose, outlined in a Department for Business, Innovation & Skills press release, is to convert a former tea factory into 'a creative innovation centre . . . to bring together arts and culture with science, technology, engineering and maths, and drive innovation within the former factory walls'. This is a good recognition of the need to bring science and the arts together, a need that is woefully unrecognised by the government when it comes to the education sector. As mentioned in the White Paper, there is ample evidence to show that exposure to cultural activity enhances children's lives and builds knowledge, creativity and self-confidence. And yet the current Conservative government is, as already stated, introducing an English Baccalaureate that does not include one compulsory arts subject: STEM (Science, Technology, Engineering and Mathematics) and not STEAM. Since the financial crash of 2008 youth participation in all artforms has reduced dramatically: the only exception being film and video. While it is good to see modern technologies being used, this cannot make up for the loss of the motivation and self-worth that physical involvement provides.[27] As the Warwick Commission recommends in *Enriching Britain: Culture, Creativity and Growth*:

27. In a debate in the House of Lords on 3 July 2017 the Conservative peer Lord Nash said that the sharp decline in GSCE students taking arts subjects was 'more than made up for' by an increase in pupils taking IT and computing, also implying that many took arts subjects because they were deemed to be 'easier' (https://www.thestage.co.uk/news/2017/arts-gcse-decline-compensated-rise-claims-tory-education-minister/?utm_source=newsletter1&utm_medium=email&utm_campaign=newsletter1). Many in the arts world questioned the relevance of the comparison and deplored the latter sentiment.

policymakers and educators should do their utmost to give young people at all stages of the education system exposure to the multi-disciplinary mix of science, technology, arts, humanities and enterprise that underpins creative success.

To all in the arts world this undermining of the importance of the arts is an extremely dangerous and short-term policy, as are the cuts to benefits that have disadvantaged disabled artists, against which Jenny Sealey, artistic director of Graeae, and others are so valiantly campaigning.

*

This book won't probably teach many lessons. It is extremely unlikely that such a wash of money will ever again appear at such a level and have to be distributed so quickly within such tight strictures. It is written to be a record – albeit a subjective one – of a highly unusual time in the funding of the arts. If it dwells on many of the dramas and problems of my time on the Arts Council that is because it is those moments that one mostly remembers and, if keeping a diary only intermittently, propels into print. Overall I hope the book shows how fortunate I was to be so involved at a time when funding for the arts was undergoing such a tremendous change and to work with so many talented, committed and passionate people.

APPENDIX I
Council and Panel Members 1992–2000

COUNCIL MEMBERS 1992–94

Lord Palumbo of Walbrook, chair, property developer and patron of architecture

Denys Hodson CBE, vice-chair and chair of education committee, former director of arts and recreation for Thamesdown Borough Council

Beverly Anderson, chair of advisory board on touring, education consultant and broadcaster

William Brown CBE, chair of the Scottish Arts Council, background in independent television

Professor Christopher Frayling, chair of advisory panel on art, professor of cultural history at Royal College of Art

Peter Gummer, chair and chief executive of Shandwick public relations

Sir Ernest Hall OBE, chair of Yorkshire and Humberside Arts Board, founder of Dean Clough, the enterprise, arts and education centre in Halifax, and pianist

Michael Holroyd CBE, chair of literature panel, biographer

Bryan Magee, chair of music panel, philosopher

Clare Mulholland, chair of advisory panel on film, video and broadcasting, director of programmes at the Independent Television Commission

Mathew Prichard CBE, chair of the Welsh Arts Council, chair of Booker Entertainment and patron of the arts

Clive Priestley CB, chair of London Arts Board, freelance management consultant

Lord Rix CBE, chair of advisory panel on drama and of arts and disability monitoring committee, chair of Mencap and former actor-manager

Stella Robinson, chair of Northern Arts Board, Labour councillor in Darlington and County Durham

Sally Shaw, chair of photography advisory group, former Manchester City councillor

Prudence Skene, chair of advisory panel on dance, executive producer of English Shakespeare Company

Professor Anthony Smith CBE, chair of training committee, television producer and founder of Channel 4 and the Museum of the Moving Image

Robert Southgate, chair of West Midlands Arts Board, deputy managing
    director of Central Broadcasting Ltd
Professor Colin St John Wilson, chair of architecture advisory group, architect

COUNCIL MEMBERS 1994–98
Lord Gowrie PC, chair, director of Sotheby's Europe, Provost of the Royal
    College of Art and former Arts Minister
Sir Richard Rogers, vice chair, architect
David Astor CBE, chair of Southern Arts, farmer
Richard Cork, chair of visual arts advisory panel, writer and critic
Professor Ray Cowell, chair of East Midlands Arts Board, vice-chancellor
    of Nottingham Trent University
Professor Brian Cox CBE, chair of North West Arts Board, former professor
    of English and pro-vice-chancellor of Manchester University
Charles Denton, chair of film advisory panel, former head of television drama
    at the BBC
Professor Christopher Frayling, chair of advisory panel on film, video and
    broadcasting, rector of the Royal College of Art
Maggie Guillebaud, chair of South West Arts Board, former educationist
Peter Gummer, chair of lottery advisory panel, chair and chief executive
    of Shandwick public relations
Sir Ernest Hall OBE, chair of Yorkshire and Humberside Arts Board, founder
    of Dean Clough, the enterprise, arts and education centre in Halifax, and
    pianist
Sir David Harrison CBE, chair of Eastern Arts Board, master of Selwyn
    College Cambridge
Gavin Henderson, chair of music panel, principal of Trinity College of Music
Michael Holroyd CBE, chair of literature panel, biographer
Thelma Holt CBE, chair of drama panel, theatre producer
Deborah MacMillan, chair of dance panel, artist
Professor Andrew Motion, chair of literature panel, poet, biographer and
    professor of creative writing at the University of East Anglia
Rod Natkiel, chair of West Midlands Arts Board, television producer and
    director

Trevor Nunn CBE, theatre director

Stephen Phillips, chair of touring advisory panel, broadcaster

Trevor Phillips OBE, chair of London Arts Board, writer and broadcaster

Usha Prashar CBE, chair of combined arts advisory panel, public servant

Christopher Price, chair of Yorkshire and Humberside Arts Board, politician

Clive Priestley CB, chair of London Arts Board, former civil servant

Roger Reed, chair of South East Arts Board, chartered secretary

David Reid, chair of Southern Arts Board, chair of finance committee, former
    IBM resident director

Stella Robinson, chair of Northern Arts Board, Labour councilor in Darlington
    and County Durham

Prudence Skene, chair of dance advisory panel and then of lottery advisory
    panel, director of the Arts Foundation

Robert Southgate, chair of West Midlands Arts Board, consultant to Central
    Television

John Spearman, deputy chair (formerly chief executive) of Classic FM

Professor Stuart Timperley, chair of Eastern Arts Board, management
    consultant

COUNCIL MEMBERS 1998–2000

Gerry Robinson, chair, executive chairman and chief executive of Granada

Derrick Anderson CBE, chief executive of Wolverhampton Metropolitan
    Borough Council

David Brierley CBE, former general manager of the RSC

Deborah Bull CBE, principal dancer at the Royal Ballet

Professor Christopher Frayling, rector and professor of cultural history at the
    Royal College of Art

Antony Gormley, sculptor

Anish Kapoor, sculptor

Joanna MacGregor, concert pianist

Professor Andrew Motion, poet, biographer and professor of creative writing
    at the University of East Anglia

Prudence Skene, director of the Arts Foundation

Hilary Strong, director of Edinburgh Festival Fringe

LOTTERY/CAPITAL PANEL MEMBERS May 1994–May 2000

Peter Gummer (Lord Chadlington), May 1994–March 1996

Jon Foulds, May 1994–June 1996, chairman of the Halifax Building Society

Lady (Patty) Hopkins, May 1994–, architect

Dame Cleo Laine OBE, May 1994–September 1997, singer

Ruth Mackenzie OBE, May 1994–July 1997, executive director of the
    Nottingham Playhouse

Paddy Masefield OBE, May 1994–March 1999, member of the National
    Disability Arts Forum and vice-chair of ACE arts and disability monitoring
    committees

Tony Pender CBE, May 1994–March 1999, chartered surveyor

Dr Nima Poovaya-Smith, May 1994–December 1997, senior keeper of
    international arts at Bradford Art Galleries and Museums

Sir David Puttnam CBE, May 1994–July 1997, film producer

Prudence Skene, April 1996–May 2000, director of the Arts Foundation

Dr Neil Cross, July 1996–March 1999, executive director (international),
    3i Group plc

David Brierley CBE, September 1996–, former general manager, Royal
    Shakespeare Company

Lynette Royle, March 1997–March 1998, corporate communications director,
    United Distillers

Matthew Evans CBE, September 1997–July 1999, chairman of Faber &
    Faber, publishers

Tish Francis, September 1997–March 1999, joint director, Oxford Playhouse

Keith Harris, March 1998–, music manager and chair of the African and
    Caribbean Music Circuit

Virginia Tandy, April 1998–, director of Art Galleries and Museums Services
    at Manchester City Council

Ian Armitage, May 1999–, director, Mercury Asset Management

Jonathan Blackie, May 1999–, director of regeneration for One NorthEast

Deirdre Figueiredo, May 1999–, director of Craftspace Touring

Rosemary Squire, May 1999–, executive director, Ambassador Theatre Group

Jo Verrent, May 1999–, director, East Midlands Shape

Matthew Kennedy, October 1999–,

Ron Spinney, January 2000–, chairman, Hammerson plc

APPENDIX II
NATIONAL AUDIT OFFICE REPORT:
FULL LIST OF PROJECTS EXAMINED[28]

Total cost	Amount of lottery money received	1st grant awarded	Opening date
The Royal Opera House, London			
£214,000,000	£78,500,000 (37%)	17 Jul 1995	1 Dec 1999
Royal Albert Hall, London			
£66,317,000	£20,200,000 (30%)	24 Jan 1996	30 Apr 2004
Sadler's Wells Theatre, London			
£52,518,000	£36,000,000 (39%)	13 Nov 1996	13 Oct 1998
Royal National Theatre, London			
£42,820,000	£31,590,000 (74%)	2 Apr 1996	[29]
Royal Academy of Dramatic Art, London			
£32,428,000	£23,746,841 (73%)	15 May 1996	29 Nov 2000
Royal Exchange Theatre, Manchester			
£31,999,000	£23,057,250 (72%)	23 July 1996	30 Nov 1998
Milton Keynes Theatre & Gallery, Milton Keynes			
£30,954,000	£20,171,485 (65%)	24 Jan 1996	4 Oct 1999
Royal Court Theatre, London			
£25,832,000	£18,825,850 (73%)	13 Sep1995	23 Feb 2000
Victoria Hall & Regent Theatre, Stoke-on-Trent			
£24,587,000	£16,135,000 (66%)	2 Apr 1996	22 Sep 1999
Shakespeare Globe Theatre, London			
£16,826,000	£12,400,000 (74%)	11 Oct 1995	7 Jun 1997
National Centre for Popular Music, Sheffield			
£14,977,000	£11,085,000 (74%)	11 Dec1996	1 Mar 1999

28. The figures here are as in the NAO report. Some of the projects, including Sadler's Wells Theatre and the Royal Court Theatre, subsequently received supplementary amounts.
29. The Royal National Theatre never closed; the refurbished areas opened gradually from December 1997.

Cambridge Arts Theatre, Cambridge
    £12,674,000   £7,390,000 (58%)   17 May 1995   Dec 1996

National Glass Centre, Sunderland
    £12,562,000   £6,901,000 (55%)   15 Nov 1995   Oct 1998

Dovecot Arts Centre, Stockton-on-Tees
    £9,108,000   £6,631,750 (73%)   25 Sep 1996   11 Jan 1999

Malvern Festival Theatre, Malvern
    £6,880,000   £5,087,640 (74%)   26 Jun 1996   24 Apr 1998

SELECT BIBLIOGRAPHY

Allen, Mary, *A House Divided*, London, Simon & Schuster 1998

Beyond the Arts: Economic and wider impacts of The Lowry and its programmes, Manchester, New Economy 2013

Blackstock, Anthony, *The Public: lessons learned*, London, Arts Council England 2011

Bogdanov, Michael and Michael Pennington, *The Wars of the Roses*, London, Nick Hern Books 1992

Caterer, James, *The People's Pictures: National Lottery Funding and British Cinema*, Cambridge, Cambridge Scholars Publishing 2011

Creative Future, A: The way forward for arts, crafts and media in England, London, HMSO 1993

Crossick, Geoffrey and Patrycja Kaszynska, *Understanding the value of arts & culture*, Swindon, Arts and Humanities Research Council 2016

Culture White Paper, The, London, Department of Culture, Media & Sport 2016

Doeser, James, *Step by Step: arts policy and young people 1944–2014: a Cultural Enquiry*, London, for King's College, 2015

Enriching Britain: Culture, Creativity and Growth, Report by the Warwick Commission on the future of cultural value, University of Warwick 2015

Hewison, Robert, *Cultural Capital: The Rise and Fall of Creative Britain* London, Verso Books 2014

Isaacs, Jeremy, *Never Mind The Moon*, London, Bantam Books 2000

Jackson, Annabel and Graham Devlin, *The Regional Art Lottery Programme: an evaluation*, ACE Research Report 32, London, Arts Council England 2003

Mortimer, John, *The Summer of a Dormouse*, London, Viking (Penguin) 2000

Organisations in Renewal: A Review of Arts Council England's Stabilisation Programmes 1996–2004, David Pratley Associates 2006

Powell, David, Christopher Gordon and Peter Stark, *Rebalancing our Cultural Capital*, CPS Culture 2013

Smith, Deborah, ed., *The New Art Gallery Walsall*, London, B. T. Batsford 2002

Snoddy, Raymond and Jon Ashworth, *It Could Be You*, London, Faber and Faber 2000

Stetter, Alex, ed., *Pride of Place*, London, The Arts Council of England and August 2002

Ward, David, *Transformation*, Stratford-upon-Avon, Royal Shakespeare Company 2011